Springer Proceedings in Business and Economics

More information about this series at http://www.springer.com/series/11960

Lotfi Tadj • Ajay K. Garg
Editors

Emerging Challenges in Business, Optimization, Technology, and Industry

Proceedings of the Third International Conference on Business Management and Technology, Vancouver, BC, Canada 2017

Springer

Editors
Lotfi Tadj
Information Systems and Decision
Sciences Department
Fairleigh Dickinson University
Vancouver, BC, Canada

Ajay K. Garg
Administrative Sciences Department
Fairleigh Dickinson University
Vancouver, BC, Canada

ISSN 2198-7246 ISSN 2198-7254 (electronic)
Springer Proceedings in Business and Economics
ISBN 978-3-319-58588-8 ISBN 978-3-319-58589-5 (eBook)
DOI 10.1007/978-3-319-58589-5

Library of Congress Control Number: 2017949266

Printed on acid-free paper

This Springer imprint is published by Springer Nature
The registered company is Springer International Publishing AG
The registered company address is: Gewerbestrasse 11, 6330 Cham, Switzerland

Preface

Business and technology are meant to satisfy the needs of humanity in general and consumer in today's global economy and diverse global markets. The management of business, optimization and technology in an objective manner play a key role in both the manufacturing and service sectors and that too in the era of globalization, privatization and liberalization. The worldwide business and technology schools have also accepted the importance of the objective and applied concepts of innovative business styles, advanced technology and optimization in productivity in their curricula at the graduate or undergraduate level. That is why a lot of emphasis has been laid on comparatively newer topics of customer relationship management, supply chain management, optimization along with reliability and redundancy and decision-making in the organizations with the use of latest technology. Similarly, industry has also realized the importance of ever-changing technology to survive and prosper in its business. Keeping pace with the updated technology and innovations in business management for effective decision-making and strategic planning has provided a competitive edge to the organizations.

The present book on the proceedings of the Conference on "Business Management and Technology" organized by Fairleigh Dickinson University, Vancouver, on its 10th-year celebration has four sections, namely, Business, Optimization, Technology and Management. Each section has different but related chapters consisting of various practical, empirical and exploratory studies. These studies and papers thereby discuss in great detail the innovative researches on the respective fields.

The book is the result of amalgamation of vast industrial, research and academic experience of the various authors in their fields. This book is an attempt of bridging the gap between theory and practice. It is an outcome of innovative ideas which emerged out of theoretical studies, real research in the respective fields of the study and practical industrial exposure, which further resulted into latest models to boost the growth and reach to the pinnacle on the performance parameter. We are confident that the results of the various research papers presented in this book would be highly appreciated by international researchers and experts. The organization of the book itself has been made in a unique style. The whole book has been spread into 4 sections and 17 chapters and organized in a flow with a rhythm and continuity.

The main emphasis of the present book is to meet the increasing requirements to keeping abreast on innovations in the respective fields of studies concerning the research papers contributed by professionals and researchers. The planners and decision-makers involved would be benefited by this book to fill the gap between the potential and actual performances in international business with the involvement of latest technology. The main objective of the book is to provide the understanding of latest updates in various related fields which may improve the real and actual performance of business with the concepts of optimization and ever dynamic technology. This book can prove to be a great help and can serve the purpose of a reference book to the researchers, academicians, industrial professionals and students. The results of various research papers presented in this book may act as a big milestone to further practical research, framing new theoretical concepts and bridging the gap between theory and practice in the real professional life. We hope the present book would be able to serve the decision-makers, planners and professional executives for an enhanced performance in global business, if followed in its true spirit.

Vancouver, BC, Canada

Lotfi Tadj
Ajay K. Garg

Contents

Contributors

Willy A. Aroca International School of Hospitality and Tourism Management, Fairleigh Dickinson University, Vancouver, BC, Canada

Satyendra Arya Research Scholar, Department of Management Studies, TMIMT, Teerthanker Mahaveer University, Moradabad, UP, India

Özen Aşik-Dizdar Business Administration Department, Istanbul Altinbaş University, Istanbul, Turkey

Stephen E. Bear Management Department, Fairleigh Dickinson University, Teaneck, NJ, USA

Abdelghani Bouras Industrial Engineering Department, College of Engininineering, King Saud University, Riyadh, Saudi Arabia

Gary Bronson Silberman College of Business, Information Systems and Decision Sciences Department, Fairleigh Dickinson University, Madison, NJ, USA

Daniel Clarke School of Computer Science and Engineering, Fairleigh Dickinson University, Teaneck, NJ, USA

Gerard W. Cleaves Management and Entrepreneurship Department, Fairleigh Dickinson University, Teaneck, NJ, USA

Kent D. Fairfield Management Department, Fairleigh Dickinson University, Teaneck, NJ, USA

Gerard Farias Management Department, Silberman College of Business, Fairleigh Dickinson University, Madison, NJ, USA

Ajay K. Garg Administrative Sciences Department, Fairleigh Dickinson University, Vancouver, BC, Canada

Sonia Gupta Management Department, J.K. Business School, Gurugram, HR, India

Abdelouahed Hamdi Department of Mathematics, Qatar University, Doha, Qatar

Tiffany Keller Hansbrough Management Department, Fairleigh Dickinson University, Madison, NJ, USA

Jeffrey Hsu Silberman College of Business, Information Systems and Decision Sciences Department, Fairleigh Dickinson University, Madison, NJ, USA

Gwen E. Jones Management Department, Fairleigh Dickinson University, Teaneck, NJ, USA

Isabella Krysa Management Department, Fairleigh Dickinson University, Vancouver, BC, Canada

Tushar Mahajan Management Department, Institute of Management Studies, Ghaziabad, UP, India

Sanjiv Mittal School of Management Studies, Guru Gobind Singh Indraprastha University, New Delhi, India

Rakesh K. Mudgal Vice Chancellor, Teerthanker Mahaveer University, Moradabad, Uttar Pradesh, India

Sharmistha Nag Department of Economics, Fairleigh Dickinson University, Vancouver, BC, Canada

A. Ravishankar Rao School of Computer Science and Engineering, Fairleigh Dickinson University, Teaneck, NJ, USA

Mohamed K. Sheriff Administrative Sciences Department, Fairleigh Dickinson University, Vancouver, BC, Canada

S. Stein Smith Lehman College, City University of New York (CUNY), New York, NY, USA

Lotfi Tadj Information Systems and Decision Sciences Department, Fairleigh Dickinson University, Vancouver, BC, Canada

Part I
Business Track

Strategic Management for the Twenty-First Century

Gerard W. Cleaves

Abstract Strategy historically was in the purview of the military. It has come to denote a high-level plan to achieve one or more goals under conditions of uncertainty. Following the industrial revolution and subsequent rise of scientific management in the twentieth century, the use of quantitative tools for optimization (e.g., linear programming) became popular first in the military during World War II and later in industry. While useful for short-term closed problems (e.g., production and distribution planning and process control), they were found inadequate for longer term strategic planning where risk and uncertainty prevail. In the latter half of the twentieth century, various qualitative approaches for analyzing the external environment, the industry, and the firm were introduced including SWOT analysis, scenario planning, five forces model, industrial organization model, resource-based model, contingency theory, stakeholder model, balanced scorecard, blue ocean, and sustainability.

The early years of the twenty-first century have already been full of perils and uncertainty on many fronts including the global economy, terrorism, and environmental concerns. New rigorous quantitative approaches that build on numerous disciplines including economics, optimization, scenario planning and risk management and advancements in science and technology are needed. Risk-Constrained Optimization™ (RCO) is one such approach that warrants further investigation. Rather than seek optimal solutions, RCO seeks to avoid catastrophe and functions more as a filter to locate robust solutions in safe regions by testing them against various kinds of risk.

Keywords Strategy • Quantitative management • Qualitative management • Risk-constrained optimization

G.W. Cleaves (✉)
Management and Entrepreneurship Department, Fairleigh Dickinson University, Teaneck, NJ, USA
e-mail: gcleaves@fdu.edu

L. Tadj, A.K. Garg (eds.), *Emerging Challenges in Business, Optimization, Technology, and Industry*, Springer Proceedings in Business and Economics,
DOI 10.1007/978-3-319-58589-5_1

History of Strategic Management

For more than two millenniums, strategy was the purview of the military. The term strategy, of Greek origin, was meant to describe a high-level plan, usually over a long period of time, to achieve one or more goals under conditions of uncertainty. How many of us have quoted Sun Tzu (circa 500 BC) and the "Art of War" (e.g., "Know the enemy and know yourself.") in teaching strategy?

Modern strategic management started with the likes of Frederick Taylor, Alfred Chandler and Peter Drucker. Taylor, the father of scientific management, advocated discovering the best, most efficient way to perform tasks. Taylor wrote, "The principal object of management should be to secure the maximum prosperity for the employer, coupled with the maximum prosperity for each employee. . . . No one can be found who will deny that in the case of any single individual the greatest prosperity can exist only when that individual has reached his highest state of efficiency; that is, when he is turning out his largest daily output. . . . If the above reasoning is correct, it follows that the most important object of both the workmen and the management should be the training and development of each individual in the establishment, so that he can do (at his fastest pace and with the maximum of efficiency) the highest class of work for which his natural abilities fit him" (Taylor 1911). Chandler emphasized the importance of taking a long-term perspective when looking to the future and that a long-term coordinated strategy was needed to give a company structure, direction, and focus. He succinctly stated "structure follows strategy" in his comprehensive study on DuPont, General Motors, Sears Roebuck, and Standard Oil of New Jersey (Chandler 1962). Peter Drucker conceived management by objectives (MBO) and encouraged a procedure for setting objectives and monitoring progress toward them as a process that should permeate the organization (Drucker 1962). The field of strategy and strategic management became institutionalized following the publication of the Gordon-Howell report on business school curricula published in 1959 (Gordon & Howell, 1959).

Mathematical Optimization

Prior to this milestone event, mathematical approaches to optimization were developed in the 1930–40s, first by Leonid Kantorovich and then George Dantzig who introduced the Simplex algorithm for linear programming (LP). Kantorovich was awarded the Nobel Prize (along with Tjalling Koopmans) "for their contributions to the theory of optimal allocation of resources". His mathematical theories were used for critical calculations on the Road of Life which supplied munitions and food supplies and served as an escape route across frozen Lake Ladoga during the Siege of Leningrad. George Dantzig's approach was used to solve allocation problems circa World War II and later programmed on computers.

During this time, linear programming-based optimization tools were used successfully by companies in the petroleum industry to address many short-term facets of the business including supply and distribution planning, refinery planning, product blending, and process control. These represent closed problems (i.e., those with constraints that exclude any significant deviation from the status quo in important decisions) where the single criteria of profit maximization may be adequate (Cleaves and Masch 1996). During this post-war period of sustained economic growth and a relatively uncomplicated business environment, the payoff from optimization was potentially large, a fact confirmed by the wartime experience (Kirby 2003).

Based on the success of these technologies, the prevailing thinking circa 1970 was that the use of these tools for longer-range strategic planning was imminent. [After all, when the only tool one has is a hammer, every problem begins to look like a nail.] However, conventional LP-based optimization techniques have never proven successful in dealing with open problems that predominate longer-range strategic planning, in which risk and uncertainty are key ingredients. This becomes especially critical as the modern stakeholder view preempts the former shareholder only view. Now the needs of multiple stakeholders need to be factored in. "After 1970, the golden age of western economic growth was swiftly terminated by a combination of cyclical recession and macroeconomic shocks. The business environment became increasingly messy at the same time as the realization dawned on operational researchers that their activities were constrained by a complex of social and political factors operative both within and without the organizations in which they worked. Thus, in a world where there were no clear objectives, little opportunity for quantification, and many stakeholders with different perspectives, the hard mathematical paradigm was subject to mounting challenge" (Kirby 2003).

LP-based models were found to be inadequate since they had three potential major flaws: (1) insufficiency of resulting information, (2) instability and unreliability of solutions, and (3) potential dilution or usurpation of the role of the decision-maker. As a result, LP was abandoned for open, long-range planning problems that involve uncertainty, risk, and complex multiple goals. Circa 1978, the Harvard Business Review stopped publishing articles on optimization, citing a lack of interest among business leaders (Cleaves and Masch 1996).

In 1991, George Dantzig notes in a chapter he wrote for "History of Mathematical Programming: A Collection of Personal Reminiscences",: " ... it is interesting to note that the original problem that started my research is still outstanding—namely the problem of planning or scheduling dynamically over time, particularly planning dynamically under uncertainty. If such a problem could be successfully solved it could eventually through better planning contribute to the well-being and stability of the world" (Freund 1994).

When Dantzig was interviewed in 1999 by OR/MS Today, he was asked what he was currently working on. He replied, "I work on planning under uncertainty. That's the big field as far as I'm concerned; that's the future. . . . all the problems that are solved under deterministic means have that fundamental weakness—they don't properly take uncertainty into account" (Horner 1999).

Qualitative Approaches to Management

Lacking quantitative tools to address longer term strategic management, qualitative approaches for business-level strategy have proliferated over the last 30 years. In his HBR article, "What is Strategy?", HBS Professor Michael Porter first opines that operational effectiveness is not strategy. He argues that the quest for enhanced productivity, quality, and efficiency has spawned philosophies, tools, and techniques including: total quality management, six sigma, benchmarking, time-based competition, outsourcing, reengineering, and change management. However, he further writes, "Constant improvement in operational effectiveness is necessary to achieve superior profitability. However, it is not usually sufficient. Few companies have competed successfully on the basis of operational effectiveness over an extended period, and staying ahead of rivals gets harder every day. The most obvious reason for that is the rapid diffusion of best practices. Competitors can quickly imitate management techniques, new technologies, input improvements, and superior ways of meeting customer's needs" (Porter 1996).

Rather, Porter argues, "strategy involves making choices. Not only doing things differently but also doing different things from competitors. Strategic positioning is key, it involves producing a subset of products or services, servicing most or all needs of a particular group of customers, and segmenting customers who are accessible in different ways. However, even a strategic position can be imitated by a savvy competitor. Trade-offs are essential. The essence of strategy is choosing what not to do. Unnerved by forecasts of hyper competition, managers imitate everything about their competitors. The pursuit of operational effectiveness is seductive because it is concrete and actionable. Many companies are turning their attention to growth. Too often, efforts to grow blur uniqueness, create compromises, reduce fit, and ultimately undermine competitive advantage. The challenge of developing or reestablishing a clear strategy is often primarily an organizational one and depends on leadership. Strong leaders willing to make choices are essential. The leader must provide the discipline to decide which industry changes and customer needs the company will respond to, while avoiding organizational distractions and maintaining the company's distinctiveness" (Porter 1996).

Qualitative Theories of Strategic Management

Three common strategic management theories that have evolved are: the industrial organization (I/O) theory of above average returns, the resource-based theory, and the contingency theory. These largely build on the ideas of Michael Porter and are covered in all the widely used strategic management textbooks from Hitt, Ireland, Hoskisson, Harrison, Lester, and Parnell.

The I/O model of above-average returns emphasizes the dominant external industrial environments influence on the organization's strategic actions. The model stipulates that the industry in which the company chooses to compete has a stronger influence on performance than the decisions made by executives inside the organization. Instead, the firm's performance is largely bounded by the general external macroenvironment (i.e., economic, social, technological, political-legal, global, demographic) and the industry's overall profitability potential (i.e., Porter's "five forces" which include: the threat of new competitors entering the industry; the threat of substitute products or services; the bargaining power of buyers; the bargaining power of suppliers, and the intensity of the rivalry among the incumbent firms). Firms use Porter's five forces model to identify the attractiveness of an industry (as measured by its profitability potential) as well as the most advantageous position for the firm to take in that industry, given the industry's structural characteristics (Porter 1979). Porter further suggests that "firms can earn above-average returns by producing either standardized goods or services at costs below those of competitors (a cost leadership strategy) or by producing differentiated goods or services for which customers are willing to pay a price premium (a differentiation strategy)" (Porter 1980).

The resource-based model assumes that each organization is a collection of resources (tangible or intangible inputs to the production process) and capabilities (capacity for a set of resources to perform an activity) which can be combined in critical and unique ways to create core competencies (Hitt et al. 2013). According to the resource-based model, differences in firms' performances over time are due to their allocation of resources and their ability to uniquely combine them with capabilities that satisfy the criteria of being valuable, rare, costly to imitate, and nonsubstitutable, to identify core competencies which are a source of sustainable competitive advantage (Hitt et al. 2013).

"The contingency theory emphasizes the interaction between the internal organization and its environment. Within this perspective, the fit between an organization and its environment is the central concern. In other words, strategy is most likely to be successful when it is consistent with the organization's mission, its competitive environment, and its resources. In effect, contingency theory represents a middle ground perspective that views organizational performance as the joint outcome of environmental forces and the firm's strategic actions" (Lester and Parnell 2007).

Companies often summarize the strategic landscape using a SWOT analysis that identifies internal strengths and weaknesses and external opportunities and threats. While it presents a concise way to articulate alternatives and emphasizes using one's strengths to overcome weaknesses to take full advantage of opportunities and avoid threats, it will provide little to no guidance in how to do so.

In essence, the I/O model allowed decision-makers to focus on what they "might do" given the constraints surrounding the industry they were in and the different forces acting upon and within the industry. The resource-based model provided some management discretion to focus on those things the firm "can do". The thinking was that the contingency theory would help align and identify the "fit" between the two—identifying which subset of things we "might do" that are within our skills and match our resources. Nowhere do we focus on the things we "should do"—which is a weakness of all of these approaches.

Balanced scorecards were introduced formally toward the end of the twentieth century although many of the underlying concepts had been introduced earlier, with the growth of modern complex organizations. The balanced scorecard is a framework used by business leaders to verify they have addressed both financial and strategic controls, in essence multiple stakeholder interests. Typically, four perspectives are integrated into the balanced scorecard framework: financial (growth, profitability, and risk from the shareholder perspective); customer (perceived value created by the firm's products or services); internal business processes (priorities on the business processes that create customer and shareholder satisfaction, efficiency, productivity); and learning and growth (climate that supports innovation, change, and growth) (Hoskisson et al. 2004).

Sustainability, balancing social, economic, and environment interests, has more recently evolved to become a critical issue for business executives. In a study conducted at Fairleigh Dickinson University entitled "HR's Role in Building a Sustainable Enterprise: Insights from Some of the World's Best Companies", the team identified core qualities of sustainable enterprises including "helping elicit senior management support for making sustainability central to business strategy" (Wirtenberg et al. 2012). While sustainability is certainly a topic that resonates with senior management, the difficulty of making choices and balancing multiple objectives is in the details. As in life, extreme policies in any of the three areas of people, profit, or planet lead to undesirable results. For example, emphasizing profit maximization over people and planet leads to Enron, emphasizing people over profit and planet leads to socialism, and emphasizing planet over profit and people leads to environmental extremism.

Kim and Mauborgne 2004 HBR article "Blue Ocean Strategy" and their subsequent interview with Insead elaborate on the contrasts between red oceans (all the industries in existence today—the known market space) and blue oceans (all the industries not in existence today). "In red oceans companies try to outperform their rivals to grab a greater share of existing demand. As the market space gets crowded, prospects for profits and growth are reduced. Products become commodities and cutthroat competition turns the red ocean bloody. Hence, the term "red" oceans" (Kim and Mauborgne 2005). "In blue oceans, demand is created rather than fought over. There is ample opportunity for growth that is both profitable and rapid. In blue oceans, competition is irrelevant because the rules of the game are waiting to be set. Blue ocean is an analogy to describe the wider, deeper potential of market space that is not yet explored. Like the "blue" ocean, it is vast, deep, powerful, in terms of profitable growth, and infinite" (Kim and Mauborgne 2005). While Kim and Mauborgne argue that blue ocean strategy is equally applicable to well-established companies/industries as well as start-ups, on the surface it appears more of a risk avoidance positioning than strategy. Again, quoting from Sun Tzu, "so in war, the way is to avoid what is strong, and strike at what is weak" [or perhaps Wee Willie Keeler, "hit 'em where they ain't."].

Scenario Planning

A promising approach that has been used in the military and most notably with Shell Oil in the 1970s is scenario planning. "In a scenario process, managers invent and then consider, in depth, several varied stories of equally plausible futures. The stories are carefully researched, full of relevant detail, oriented toward real-life decisions, and designed to bring forward surprises and unexpected leaps of understanding. Together, the scenarios comprise a tool for ordering one's perceptions. The point is not to "pick one preferred future," and hope for it to come to pass (or, even, work to create it . . .). Nor is the point to find the most probable future and adapt to it or "bet the company" on it. Rather, the point is to make strategic decisions that will be sound for all plausible futures. No matter what future takes place, you are much more likely to be ready for it—and influential in it—if you have thought seriously about scenarios" (Schwartz 1991).

In his book, "The Art of the Long View", author Peter Schwartz outlines eight steps to developing scenarios:

1. Identify Focal Issue of Decision—What is of most concern to everyone?
2. Key Forces in the Local Environment—e.g., information about suppliers, customers, and competition
3. Driving Forces—Analyze society, economics, politics, demographics, public opinion.
4. Rank by Importance and Uncertainty—Identify a few trends that are important and most uncertain.
5. Selecting Scenario Logics—The goal is to identify a few scenarios whose differences make a difference to decision-makers.
6. Fleshing Out the Scenarios—Pull everything together in one story.
7. Implications—How does the decision identified in step one play out in each scenario.
8. Selection of Leading Indicators and Signposts—What indicators should be used to monitor each scenario to see if it is actually unfolding (Schwartz 1991).

Scenario planning shows considerable promise. Shell Oil is widely acknowledged for utilizing scenarios starting in the early 1970s. They helped Shell weather the volatility of the 1970s and they continued to produce and use scenarios over the last four decades to anticipate global economic, social and political changes and their likely impact on business. Summaries of these have been shared outside Shell, contributing to important public debates. Schwartz even goes so far as pointing to the use of scenario planning was instrumental in elevating Shell Oil to the largest company in the world (Schwartz 1991). Others question if any significant long-term business advantages could be attributed solely to Shell's use of scenario planning. While they do not criticize the intellectual accomplishments involved in creating the scenarios, they argue the scenarios did not make a significant difference when key decisions were made. Arie de Geus, a former corporate planning director for Royal Dutch/Shell, in charge of business and scenario planning, notes "scenarios are stories. They are works of art, rather than scientific analyses. The reliability of (their content) is less important than the types of conversations and decision they spark. The ability to learn faster than your competitors may be the only sustainable competitive advantage" (de Geus 1997). Given the limitations of the human mind to fully comprehend multiple scenarios, the state of computers in the early 1970s, and the dearth of computational tools—only a few scenarios were used for the Shell analysis.

"Shell's success with scenario planning influenced many other companies to adopt similar systems. By 2000, more than 60% of Fortune 500 companies are using some version of scenario planning." (Jones & George, 2014) However, there are emerging observations from Bain and Co. that while the use of scenario planning peaked at +60% circa 2000, it has dropped precipitously in the last few years to only 20% (Bain & Co., 2015). The author suggests further research is required here to understand the reasons for this curious trend. Perhaps the overwhelming uncertainty in recent years coupled with the proliferation of "fake" information and lack of quantitative tools in downsized organizations makes it hard to develop "likely" scenarios and sustain the process. Alternatively, perhaps the practitioners failed to include "black swan" scenarios, considered highly unlikely.

Bain summarizes on its website best practices as follows. "Strategic Planning is a comprehensive process for determining what a business should become and how it can best achieve that goal. It appraises the full potential of a business and explicitly links the business's objectives to the actions and resources required to achieve them. Strategic Planning offers a systematic process to ask and answer the most critical questions confronting a management team—especially large, irrevocable resource commitment decisions. A successful Strategic Planning process should:

- Describe the organization's mission, vision and fundamental values
- Target potential business arenas and explore each market for emerging threats and opportunities
- Understand the current and future priorities of targeted customer segments
- Analyze the company's strengths and weaknesses relative to competitors and determine which elements of the value chain the company should make versus buy
- Identify and evaluate alternative strategies
- Develop an advantageous business model that will profitably differentiate the company from its competitors
- Define stakeholder expectations and establish clear and compelling objectives for the business
- Prepare programs, policies, and plans to implement the strategy
- Establish supportive organizational structures, decision processes, information and control systems, and hiring and training systems
- Allocate resources to develop critical capabilities
- Plan for and respond to contingencies or environmental changes
- Monitor performance" (Rigby and Bilodeau 2013).

Other than advising, the company to "identify strategies" and "plan for contingencies" the summary offers little or no guidance in how this is accomplished. Nonetheless, a recent study published in the MIT Sloan Management Review in 2016 concludes, "Considering multiple scenarios appeared to have spurred greater appreciation of the benefits provided by flexible implementation strategies that keep more options open. Our results pertain to the effect of a one-time use of scenario planning on long-term decisions. However, we did not examine whether the continual practice of scenario planning would help executives improve when it comes to their long-term decision-making skills" (Phadris et al. 2016).

Twenty-First Century Requirements

The twenty-first century already is full of perils and uncertainty. The goal of business organizations (and perhaps mankind) has changed from rising prosperity for the finite planning period to attaining long-term sustainable survival in an acceptable state. Such change was always necessary, but its unavoidability and urgency have become evident only now, due to constant and intensively growing ecological, geopolitical, and economic threats. Hence, any corporate strategic management problem becomes a risk management problem, and the decision-making criterion should be relevant to survival. As noted by John Maynard Keynes, long-range planning should be focused not on forecasting, which is meaningless, but on taking into account radical uncertainty (Keynes 1937). This can be done only by creating robust and flexible structures that reduce, as protective equipment, the need for knowledge about the future. [When we are in the unknown, we need better space suits] (Masch 2014).

New tools are needed to stretch the planning framework over longer horizons and more complex scenarios. These tools would be used to select strategies that are: (1) optimal, or close to optimal, under favorable conditions; (2) good under a wide range of conditions, and (3) safe or acceptable under the most adverse forecasted conditions (Cleaves and Masch 1996).

Peter Senge observes that breakthrough results can only be achieved by combining efficient component technologies from diverse fields of science and technology. He emphasizes that the power of the whole comes not from the individual parts, but from their combined impact within the process. They form an inseparable ensemble "and are critical for each others' success" (Senge 1990). New rigorous quantitative approaches that build on the disciplines of economics, operations research/management science, decision analysis, scenario planning, financial management, and risk management are needed (Cleaves and Masch 1996).

Risk-Constrained Optimization (RCO)

Risk-Constrained Optimization™ (RCO) is an example of such an approach (Masch 2013; Masch 2010; Masch 2004). RCO analyzes problems under radical uncertainty and presents an enormous set of scenarios. It aims to build a set of strategy candidates that are both robust and flexible in the long-run on large ranges of such scenarios and various kinds of risk. Looking at just the likely scenarios is not sufficient. To prepare for the "unknown unknowns", we must take into account the unlikely scenarios too, even the black swan outlier events. The original version of RCO was applied with good results by Praxair, a large American corporation (Lindner-Dutton et al. 1994) and was granted an American patent in 1999.

"RCO rejects the very possibility of existence of "the best" or "the correct" solution, as well as "the correct" method of finding such a solution. Instead, RCO proposes the concept of a strategy, most acceptable for the decision-makers. RCO screens out the worst and risky strategy candidates; therefore the subjective selection of the final strategy is performed on a reasonably safe subset of remaining candidates." (Masch 2013).

"RCO still optimizes, but on reasonably safe truncated regions of feasible solutions, modifying those regions to select new candidate strategies to be evaluated. Otherwise, optimization models find not optimal but rather extreme solutions, which are risky as is any extreme behavior. They [optimization models] are applied in RCO only for analysis, rather than for construction or selection of the strategy to be implemented." (Masch 2014).

"The decision-maker should participate screening of candidate strategies. That will take into account the knowledge, intuition, opinions, and preferences of the decision-maker, as well as his or her attitudes to various kinds of risk. The analyst probably has no idea how important are those factors and considerations that are not included in the model, while they may be of paramount importance for the decision-maker." (Masch 2014).

Conclusion

Given the drawbacks of existing conventional techniques for strategic management described (i.e., current quantitative approaches are only applicable to closed-systems and qualitative approaches assist with analysis but not decision-making), further investigation of RCO as a framework to support scenario planning is warranted. Perhaps for the first time since creation of both computers and optimization models in the 1940s, RCO unleashes the possibility of combined use at a high level of these two breakthrough advances in modern science and technology. However imperfect, RCO-type models, or their equivalent, may be our best approach for addressing complex problems of strategic management we will continue to face in the twenty-first century.

Acknowledgements The author is grateful to his friend and colleague Dr. Vladimir A. Masch for contributions regarding Risk-Constrained Optimization™ (RCO) which represent his lifelong interests and outstanding accomplishments in the area of decision-making under risk and uncertainty and for his comments and suggestions regarding this article.

References

Bain & Co. (2015) Scenario and Contingency Planning. http://www.bain.com/publications/articles/managementtools-scenario-and-contingency-planning.aspx
Chandler AE (1962) Strategy and structure: chapters in the history of the industrial enterprise. Doubleday, New York
Cleaves GW, Masch V (1996) Strengthening weak links: new opportunities abound for advanced OR technology in managing the supply chain. OR/MS Today
Drucker PF (1962) The practice of management. HarperCollins, New York
Freund R (1994) Professor George Dantzig linear programming founder turns 80. SIAM News, November
de Geus A (1997) The living company. Harvard Business Review, Watertown, MA
Gordon RA & Howell JC (1959) Higher Education for Business. Columbia University Press
Hitt MA et al (2013) Strategic management competitiveness & globalization. South-Western, Cengage Learning, Boston
Horner P (1999) Planning under uncertainty: questions & answers with George Dantzig, OR/MS Today
Hoskisson RE et al (2004) Competing for advantage. Thomson-South-Western, Mason
Jones GR & George JM (2014) Contemporary Management. McGraw-Hill
Keynes JM (1937) The general theory of employment. Q J Econ 51:209–223
Kim WE, Mauborgne R (2004) Blue ocean strategy. Harvard Business Review, Watertown, MA
Kim WE, Mauborgne R (2005) A conversation with W. Chan Kim and Renee Mauborgne. Insead, Fontainebleau, Paris
Kirby MW (2003) Operational research in war and peace: the British experience from the 1930s to 1970. Imperial College Press and The Operational Research Society, London
Lester DL, Parnell J (2007) Organizational theory: a strategic approach. Thomson, Mason
Lindner-Dutton L, Jordan M, Karwan M (1994) Beyond mean time to failure: Praxair's novel reliability modeling techniques keep gas flowing to customers. OR/MS Today
Masch VA (2004) Return to the natural process of decision-making leads to good strategies. J Evol Econ 14(4):431–462
Masch VA (2010) An application of risk-constrained optimization (RCO) to a problem of international trade. Int J Oper Quant Manag 16(4):415–465
Masch VA (2013) Extensions of stochastic multiscenario models for long-range planning under uncertainty. Environ Syst Decis 33(1):43–59
Masch VA (2014) A conversations with Vladimir Masch
Phadris S, Caplice C, Sheffi Y (2016) How scenario planning influences strategic decisions. MIT Sloan Manag Rev 57(4):21–24
Porter ME (1979) How competitive forces shape strategy. Harvard Business Review, Watertown, MA
Porter ME (1980) Competitive strategy: techniques for analyzing industries and competitors. Simon and Schuster, New York
Porter ME (1996) What is strategy? Harvard Business Review, Watertown, MA
Rigby D, Bilodeau B (2013) Management tools and trends 2003. Bain and Company brief, Boston, MA
Schwartz P (1991) The art of the long view: planning for the future in an uncertain world. Doubleday Currency, New York
Senge PM (1990) The fifth discipline. Doubleday Currency, New York
Taylor FW (1911) The principles of scientific management. Harper Bros, New York
Wirtenberg J et al (2012) HR's role in building a sustainable enterprise insights from some of the world's best companies. Fairleigh Dickinson University, New Jersey

Deconstructing the Appeal of Toxic Leaders

Tiffany Keller Hansbrough

Abstract The results of the 2016 United States presidential election continue to puzzle many observers searching for a mechanism to explain the appeal of such an atypical candidate. Indeed, several authors have observed that Donald Trump displays behaviors that are associated with a narcissistic personality disorder (http://www.cnn.com/2016/10/28/opinions/trump-campaign-narcissism-lipman/; McAdams, The mind of Donald Trump, The Atlantic, 2016; https://www.washingtonpost.com/news/the-fix/wp/2016/07/22/is-donald-trump-a-textbook--narcissist/?utm_term=.80214dd189cd). These analyses focus on who the leader is rather than why followers endorse such a leader. Likewise, leadership researchers have begun to explore the "dark side" of leadership (Lipman-Blumen, The allure of toxic leaders: why we follow destructive bosses and politicians and how we can survive them, Oxford University Press, 2005; Kellerman, Bad leadership, Harvard Business School Press, 2004). Here, I argue that a focus on followers provides a better understanding of the appeal of toxic leaders. The appeal of toxic leaders stems from several factors, including implicit leadership theories, parental models of leadership, collusive relationships, as well as denigration out-groups. Taken together, followers play a crucial role in the legitimization of toxic leaders.

Keywords Toxic leaders • Individual differences • Followers

Leadership research has traditionally focused on leaders. The literature is replete with the studies of who the leader is in an effort to determine the traits and behaviors that are associated with leader emergence and effective leadership. However, this approach has been criticized as "leader centric" (Meindl 1990). Given that leadership reflects a dynamic interaction between leaders and followers (Riggio et al. 2008; Shamir et al. 2006), focusing exclusively on the leader does not fully capture the leadership process. Indeed, Shamir (2007) described followers as "co-producers of leadership". Here I contend that a better understanding of follower factors is instrumental to understanding the appeal of toxic leaders.

T.K. Hansbrough (✉)
Management Department, Fairleigh Dickinson University, Madison, NJ, USA
e-mail: thansb@fdu.edu

L. Tadj, A.K. Garg (eds.), *Emerging Challenges in Business, Optimization, Technology, and Industry*, Springer Proceedings in Business and Economics,
DOI 10.1007/978-3-319-58589-5_2

Implicit Leadership Theories

Implicit leadership theories provide a lens through which individuals view, evaluate, and respond to leaders (Lord and Maher 1991; Shondrick et al. 2010). Briefly, observers categorize targets as "leaders" based on how well they match observers' implicit leadership theories, or leadership schemas (Lord et al. 1984). Implicit leadership theories provide structure to cognitions regarding leadership and consist of traits such as sensitivity, dedication, charisma, intelligence, and tyranny that individuals tend to associate with the word "leader" (Lord et al. 1984; Offermann et al. 1994). Although individuals may share a common typical leader schema (e.g., Den Hartog et al. 1999; Lord et al. 1984; Offermann et al. 1994), they differ in terms of what leader characteristics and images they consider ideal (Keller 1999). It should be noted that implicit leadership theories have a clearly defined center but fuzzy boundaries. Therefore, even though there may be wide spread agreement about certain characteristics, such as intelligence, associated with the word "leader" (e.g., Lord et al. 1984; Offermann et al. 1994) there is still variation based on individual differences.

According to the self-concept literature, schemas and prototypes tend to differ in a self-serving manner. Namely, when asked to indicate the characteristics most central to a desirable social category, people will endorse the same characteristics that they believe they possess (Dunning et al. 1991). Likewise, Keller (1999) contends that because being a leader is socially desirable, viewing oneself as a leader, or potential leader, serves as a mechanism to boost self-esteem. Therefore, the ideal leader is analogous to self.

Foti et al. (2012) extended the hypothesis that the ideal leader is similar to self and examined the relationship between ideal leader profiles and self-leader profiles. Importantly, thirty-three percent of sample endorsed either an autocratic or anti-prototypical leader profile that was higher on tyranny and lower on sensitivity than was characteristic of the prototypical, socially desirable leader profile (Foti et al. 2012). The results provide a tangible demonstration that not everyone's implicit theory of leadership is that of an effective leader. Furthermore, Foti et al. (2012) reported that when participants endorsed a more negative view of an ideal leader, they tended to endorse similar characteristics about themselves as leaders.

Parental Leadership Models and Attachment

Variation in implicit leadership theories has also been linked to early childhood experiences. Parents provide children with an initial model of authority and set subsequent expectations for future interactions with leaders (Keller 2003). It should be noted that both social learning and psychoanalytic frameworks suggest that individuals may prefer familiar leadership models regardless of their social desirability. Indeed, Keller (1999) found that idealized leadership images mirrored perceived parental traits. Namely, individuals who perceived their parents as tyrannical were more inclined to consider leader tyranny ideal. These findings may be explained by attachment theory, which suggests that early experiences with caregivers influences expectations, motives, and actions.

Variation in caregiver responsiveness yields three different attachment styles. First, consistent caregiver responsiveness is associated with a secure attachment style. Secure individuals expect partners to be trustworthy and perceive themselves as worthy of love (Shaver and Hazan 1994). Second, inconsistent caregiver responsiveness is associated with an anxious-ambivalent attachment style. Anxious-ambivalent individuals are preoccupied with attachment, have low self-esteem, and worry about rejection from others (Mikulincer and Nachshon 1991). Finally, consistent caregiver unresponsiveness is associated with an avoidant attachment style. Avoidant individuals are defensively self-reliant, may have hostile relationships with peers, and tend to deny their need for connection (Shaver et al. 1996). Attachment styles have been linked to work orientation. For example, secure individuals do not use work to satisfy their unmet needs for love (as do anxious individuals) nor do they use work to avoid social interactions (as do avoidant individuals) (Hazan and Shaver 1990). Keller (2003) contends that attachment may shape expectations of leaders as described by implicit leadership theories. Namely, anxious individuals may project their unmet attachment needs onto leaders, whereas avoidant individuals may harbor negative expectations about leaders. Indeed, leader tyranny may be normalized in the minds of avoidant followers.

Collusive Relationships: The Dangerous Bargain

According to psychoanalytic theory, collusive relationships are characterized by the unconscious interplay of two partners who rely on the complementary reactions of the other to get what each feels is missing from inside him or herself (Willi 1982). Kets de Vries (1999) observes that collusive relationships between leaders and followers will only work if the personality makeup of the two players is complementary. There are two groups of people likely to enter into a collusive narcissistic arrangement; individuals who act as a positive reflective mirror for narcissists and individuals who have unsolved dependency needs (Kets de Vries 1999). In both cases, these individuals lack self-confidence and may identify with a powerful leader in order to bolster a shaky self-image. This need can be so strong that followers may agree to things that they know are wrong; a price they are all too willing to pay. Furthermore, identification with abrasive and aggressive leaders allows followers to vicariously transform themselves from the helpless victim to the powerful actor (Kets de Vries 1999).

Denigration of Out-Groups

Lipman-Blumen (2005) contends that authoritarianism is a hallmark of toxic leaders who often impress followers by exercising power against groups whom followers dislike, fear, or envy. It has long been known that stereotypes about other groups may satisfy a self-esteem motive (e.g., Tajfel and Turner 1979). By viewing out-group members as inferior, one is able to increase one's sense of personal value in a relative sense. Moreover, the creation of out-groups confirms the "correctness" of one's beliefs. By denigrating those who are different, individuals reassert the validity of their own world view (Schimel et al. 1999). Therefore, when toxic leaders attack a low-value group, they rarely encounter significant resistance (Lipman-Blumen 2005). However, leaders rarely stop with one group. Instead, leaders will move on to other targets, but by this time, followers have been "tranquilized into a false sense of security" (Lipman-Blumen 2005, p. 100).

The Appeal of Donald Trump

The above analysis suggests several reasons why toxic leaders, such as Donald Trump, may appeal to followers. First, a significant percentage of individuals endorse either autocratic or anti-prototypical leader profiles that are higher on tyranny and lower on sensitivity than prototypical leader profiles (Foti et al. 2012). Therefore, these individuals are more inclined to endorse leader characteristics such as tyrannical, domineering, and manipulative. Foti et al.'s (2012) results also suggest that this group of followers may view such behaviors as within the latitude of acceptance. Therefore, followers who endorse autocratic or anti-prototypical leader profiles would not view tyrannical behavior as aberrant. Instead, tyrannical behavior may have solidified support for Donald Trump from some followers because it was consistent with their mental models of ideal leadership.

Second, some followers may be drawn to toxic leadership models simply because they are familiar. Parental models of tyranny may provide the foundation whereby leader tyranny is not only expected but is also considered ideal (Keller 1999, 2003). Therefore, Trump's leadership style may have unwittingly resonated with some individuals because his leadership style mirrored that of their parents.

Individuals may also be drawn to toxic leaders because of self-esteem motives. Self-esteem needs can be met by (1) endorsing a leader who perceived as similar to self, (2) identifying with a powerful leader, and (3) endorsing a leader who denigrates out-groups. First, some individuals may have been drawn to Trump's leadership style because they perceive themselves to possess similar characteristics. Therefore, endorsing Trump provided a mechanism to validate some followers' sense of self as well as provided followers with an opportunity to view themselves as "leader-like". Conversely, some individuals may have been drawn to Trump's narcissistic behavior because it enabled them to identify with a powerful leader as a means to bolster their shaky sense of worth. Finally, Trump's derogation of outgroups may have strongly appealed to individuals who failed to benefit from the fruits of globalization. For example, Trump had widespread support among blue-collar workers and individuals living in rural areas. By promising to secure the boarder and build a wall to keep out the terrorists and "bad hombres" (Castañeda 2017), Trump may have bolstered some followers' comparative sense of worth.

In conclusion, a focus on who the leader is fails to fully explain the appeal of toxic leaders. Instead, the appeal of toxic leaders stems from a variety of follower factors and helps explain why followers may grant toxic leaders power. Followers may gravitate toward toxic leaders because their behavior is consistent with followers' leader images, followers may use leaders as a vessel onto which they project their unmet needs, or the messages articulated by toxic leaders may seize upon cultural biases and stereotypes. Taken together, the appeal of toxic leaders is much less about the leader than it is about the followers.

References

Castañeda J (2017) Mexico's forceful resistance. Retrieved from New York Times. https://mobile.nytimes.com/2017/01/27/opinion/mexicos-forceful-resistance.html

Den Hartog DN, House RJ, Hanges PJ, Ruiz-Quintanilla SA (1999) Culture specific and cross-culturally generalizable implicit leadership theories: are attributes of charismatic/transformational leadership universally endorsed? Leadersh Q 10:219–256

Dunning D, Perie M, Story AL (1991) Self-serving prototypes of social categories. J Pers Soc Psychol 61:957–968

Foti RJ, Bray BC, Thompson NJ, Allgood SF (2012) Know thy self, know thy leader: contributions of a pattern-oriented approach to examining leader perceptions. Leadersh Q 23:702–717

Hazan C, Shaver PR (1990) Love and work: an attachment –theoretical perspective. J Pers Soc Psychol 59:270–280

Keller T (1999) Images of the familiar: individual differences and implicit leadership theories. Leadersh Q 10:589–607

Keller T (2003) Parental images as a guide to leadership sensemaking: an attachment perspective on implicit leadership theories. Leadersh Q 14:141–160

Kellerman B (2004) Bad leadership. Harvard Business School Press, Boston

Kets de Vries MFR (1999) What's playing in organizational theater? Collusive relationships in management. Hum Relat 52:745–773

Lipman AJ (2016) The narcissism of Donald Trumps' candidacy. Retrieved from CNN opinion. http://www.cnn.com/2016/10/28/opinions/trump-campaign-narcissism-lipman/

Lipman-Blumen J (2005) The allure of toxic leaders: why we follow destructive bosses and politicians- and how we can survive them. Oxford University Press, New York

Lord RG, Maher KJ (1991) Leadership and information processing: linking perceptions and performance. Routledge, Boston

Lord RG, Foti RJ, De Vader CL (1984) A test of leadership categorization theory: internal structure, information processing, and leadership perceptions. Organ Behav Hum Perform 34:343–378

McAdams DP (2016) The mind of Donald Trump. The Atlantic

Meindl JR (1990) On leadership: an alternative to the conventional wisdom. Res Organ Behav 12:159–203

Mikulincer M, Nachshon O (1991) Attachment styles and patterns of self-disclosure. J Pers Soc Psychol 61:321–331

Offermann LR, Kennedy JK, Wirtz PW (1994) Implicit leadership theories: content, structure and generalizability. Leadersh Q 5:43–58
Riggio RE, Chaleff I, Lipman-Blumen J (2008) The art of followership: how great followers create great leaders and organizations. Jossey-Bass, San Francisco
Schimel J, Simon L, Greenberg J, Pyszczynski T, Solomon S, Arndt J (1999) Stereotypes and terror management: evidence that mortality salience enhances stereotypic thinking and preferences. J Pers Soc Psychol 77:905–926
Shamir B (2007) Introduction: from passive recipients to active co-producers—the roles of followers in the leadership process. In: Shamir B, Pillai R, Bligh M, Uhl-Bien M (eds) Follower-centered perspectives on leadership: a tribute to James R Meindl. Information Age Publishing, Greenwich
Shamir B, Pillai R, Bligh MC, Uhl-Bien M (eds) (2006) Follower-centered perspectives on leadership: a tribute to the memory of James R Meindl. Information Age Publishing, Greenwich
Shaver PR, Hazan C (1994) Attachment. In: Weber AL, Harvey JH (eds) Perspectives on close relationships. Allyn and Bacon, Boston, pp 110–130
Shaver PR, Collins N, Clark CL (1996) Attachment styles and internal working models. In: Fletcher G, Fitness J (eds) Knowledge structures in close relationships: A social psychological approach. Erlbaum, Hillsdale, pp 25–61
Shondrick SJ, Dinh JE, Lord RG (2010) Developments in implicit leadership theory and cognitive science: applications to improving measurement and understanding alternatives to hierarchical leadership. Leadersh Q 21(6):959–978
Tajfel H, Turner JC (1979) An integrative theory of intergroup conflict. In: Austin WG, Worchel S (eds) The social psychology of intergroup relations. Brooks-Cole, Monterey
Willi J (1982) Couples in collusion: the unconscious dimension in partnerships. Hunter House, Claremont

Corporate Venturing: Implications in a Globalized Environment

S. Stein Smith

Abstract Strategy and business management continue to evolve and change in the face of rapidly evolving business environment, but there appears to be a need for improved management techniques. Disruptive innovation, fast follower strategies, and blue ocean techniques have been discussed at length within both the academic and market-oriented publications, but there are alternative options available to innovative and creative management professionals. Adhocracy, and the concept underpinning this idea—the requirement of businesses and management teams to respond dynamically to changes in the business environment, is a reality in the globalized competitive landscape. That said, in order to develop coherent and logical strategies to achieve sustainable advantages it is necessary that the organization have reliable information from which to base decisions. Accounting professionals, specifically management accountants embedded within various aspects of the organization, are uniquely positioned to take advantage of these requirements. Organizations and management professionals need quality information to make quality business decisions, and this where accounting professionals who are able to effectively leverage technology can add significant value to the organization. Innovative thinking, creativity, and the ability to effectively use technology to make better business decisions are very possibly the competitive advantage of the twenty-first century. Management professionals must take note, and be sure to utilize the information available to better navigate the business landscape in a globally competitive and dynamic business environment.

Keywords Adhocracy • Accounting • Finance • Management • Business management • Corporate venturing

---

S.S. Smith (✉)
Lehman College, City University of New York (CUNY), New York, NY, USA
e-mail: ss2864@camden.rutgers.edu

L. Tadj, A.K. Garg (eds.), *Emerging Challenges in Business, Optimization, Technology, and Industry*, Springer Proceedings in Business and Economics,
DOI 10.1007/978-3-319-58589-5_3

Introduction

In a business environment, increasingly governed and driven forward by technology, globalization, and a rapidly changing consumer landscape, it is important that organizations evolve. It is important to note, and recognize, that simply selecting a management theory to utilize at the organization is not enough to spark innovation within the organization. Reviewing the academic research, market examples of failed strategies, and financially lagging organizations provides ample evidence to support this assertion. With that acknowledged, it is important for organizations to be able to embrace strategic thinking, strategy, and an increasingly holistic method of management to succeed in a diverse and rapidly challenging environment moving forward. Specifically, the concept of corporate strategy and strategic planning must evolve and along with the changes in stakeholder and consumer requirements. While the term disruptive innovation is possibly overused in the media and literature, the essence of what disruptive innovation represents provides a valuable framework for management professionals. Particularly within the context of international business, competing with international organizations—and collaborating with colleagues across national boundaries—flexibility, and dynamic thinking are essential. Strategy, from an organizational perspective, must be able to respond to changes in the market, efficiently leverage internal resources, and integrate changes necessary to successfully compete. Simultaneously, it is imperative that, while innovative ideas and concepts are developed and implemented, the financial ramifications of such decisions are realistically evaluated. Accounting and financial professionals must take advantage of these changes in the business environment, and management thinking, to develop strategically oriented concepts that can be implemented to improve organizational competitiveness. Faced with a number of competing organizational frameworks, matrices, and concepts, one appears to be taking hold in various types of markets.

The Problem with Incumbents

Corporate venturing, in essence, represents the fact that many established organizations may, in reality, be ill-equipped to fend off new entrants into the marketplace. Many of the same policies and procedures that drive efficiency and the structured organizational allocation of resources may slow down decision-making. Entrenched incumbent organizations, including current market leaders such as Exxon, Amazon, Uber, Facebook, and Microsoft, continually face threats of disruption and dethronement in the form of new competitors and changing business requirements. Companies such as Kodak, Blackberry, Palm, and MySpace are just a handful of the high-profile organizations that have been unable to effectively fend off new entrants and market changes. Leveraging academic research and innovations is, in and of itself, insufficient to achieve innovation—it must be applied to commercial challenges and market opportunities (Vertès 2012). The research conducted by academics offers an opportunity to analyze information and data applicable to market-based challenges and opportunities. It is important to acknowledge that many incumbent organizations do, indeed, establish and defend market positions over extended periods of time, including household names General Electric and IBM. This is true, but management professionals must also be alert to concepts implemented by startup organizations that may be of benefit to large institutions. Prior to integrating such ideas, an overview of what is perceived as the strengths of startups is required.

Strategic Differences

Depending on the type of management philosophy embraced by the senior leadership of the organization, the tactics and strategies utilized by an incumbent organization may be unwillingly sowing the seeds of future disruption. Management teams, by placing shareholders first and foremost among stakeholder groups, may very well sacrifice long-term investments in research, capital assets, and employee training to satisfy quarterly earnings goals. Investing in venture capital initiatives, however, does not appear to be a suitable substitute for either organic innovation or corporate venturing (Ford and Nelsen 2014). Such tactics and strategies will, when coupled with financial engineering concepts including stock repurchases, inevitably increase earnings per share, and most likely result in a higher stock price. Short financial benefits, however, corrodes the long-term strategic thinking, planning, and investments that are necessary to develop and sustain a competitive advantage over the longer term.

That said, it is also important to recognize that organizations managed purely with a customer perspective, which does include firms such as Amazon, might not be able to survive the financial rigors of the market long enough to benefit from the longer view embraced by management. Threading this proverbial needle is a challenge, but it is a challenge faced by management at every organization, and is addressed more or less effectively by different combinations of management philosophies and leadership techniques. Drilling specifically into theory of innovation, and disruptive innovation, it is easy for organizations and management personnel to simply assign the word innovation to product line innovations. Merely assigning the work innovation to various products and services does not make the idea innovative—it simply weakens the association between innovation and the organization in question.

Opportunities to Develop

Startup organizations, or even established organizations that are new entrants to a specific market, are often characterized and defined by the fluid and free-form way in which decisions are made and resources are allocated. A voluminous collection of literature and market-based discussion exists that extols the virtues of flexible decision-making, but drilling down, several key themes emerge. First, decisions related to personnel and financial resources are made rapidly and in a fluid fashion; this enables new entrants to react dynamically to market demands. Second, a focused mission or organizational drive usually exists, and this is almost universally linked to upsetting the incumbent firm or market leader. Versus a mature organization whose management team might have numerous demands, the management professionals at startup organizations will be able to pivot more rapidly as situations evolve. Third, management teams at new entrants can take advantage of products, services, and technology already introduced and adopted by the marketplace without incurring the expenses associated with research and development. Lastly, and perhaps most importantly, it is the motivational aspect employed at startup organizations, specifically the potential for equity-based compensation, which can result in significant payouts upon successful introduction of new products and services.

Clearly, management entrenched at incumbent organizations, organizations that are global in nature, or companies that have to fulfill the expectations of shareholders might not be able to fully embrace the uniqueness of a startup organization. Meeting the needs of shareholders, sometimes shareholders that have controlling interests in the organization, requires that management of publicly traded organizations operate differently than those of privately controlled enterprises (Goshen and Hamdani 2016). That said, it is important to recognize the benefits and opportunities to learn from organizations disrupting the market, creating new markets, or making new products that are attracting new customers. Flexibility; the focus on customer engagement, retention, and development; and the ability to judge decisions framed in the long-term context can certainly benefit any organization. Incumbent organizations have the resources, personnel, industry presence, and connections to make the necessary investments in these areas. The aspect that is lacking, most likely, is the reality that resources, in and of itself, are insufficient to achieve success in the marketplace. Management personnel must be able to recognize the changing marketplace; identify new customers and the opportunities such customers bring to the organization; and react appropriately to new developments in the business landscape.

Corporate Venturing

The tensions and differences between organizations and management teams in place at different types of institutions can appear to be insurmountable. Even organizations and management teams associated with innovation and dynamic product development, such as Apple, Inc., have been recently accused of running out of new ideas and tactics. Especially in large and successful organizations, it can be difficult to embark upon new, and risky, concepts traditionally associated with innovation and innovative thinking. Drilling specifically into the field of biotechnology, it is readily apparent that true innovation and breakthrough discoveries must be a joint effort between financial and intellectual capital. Corporate venturing, virtually by definition and structure, provides a hierarchy and structure linking together management strengths of incumbent teams and dynamic thinking associated with startup companies. Specifically, the fact that the resources, both financial and personnel wise, necessary to successfully implement such a change to organizational structure, are already at the disposal of larger organizations is especially pertinent to such organizations. The most important step, however, is to identify the appropriate opportunities for the organizations in question. The underlying concept behind corporate venturing is that the parent company, usually a large incumbent company, will set up an independent arm of the firm. While the specific approach of corporate venturing might vary slightly, with some organizations setting up a venture capital arm, such as Google Capital, which focuses purely on financial investments and management expertise to assist smaller ventures, this research will focus on the incubator-like approach associated with corporate venturing.

Opportunities

Merely identifying that corporate venturing might be applicable to the organization is only the first step in the process of successfully developing a corporate venture strategy, and implementing this strategy among management personnel. Corporate venturing and the possibilities embedded in the idea have the potential to unlock innovation, creativity, and new ideas among the individuals tasked with developing and operating this branch of the company. Establishing, in essence, a spin-off entity that also has the benefits of broader organizational resources and information provides an almost ideal environment to test, tinker, and develop new ideas. Whereas in the marketplace a product failure, stumble, or service issue can result in a tumbling stock price, loss of market share, and attraction of customers by competitors, a failure within the corporate venture remains within the organizational family.

Internal failures, either in products or services, are less costly in the short term and long term than external failures that reach the marketplace. While costly to a certain extent, clearly, and requiring internal time and resources to address, internal failures do not have the effects on reputations, profits, and customer engagement that external failures generate. External failures involve costs to the organization, in the present and moving forward, damage the brand equity of the company, and inevitably make future product or service rollouts take place under increased levels of scrutiny. A primary benefit of establishing a corporate venture model, and a benefit that can be explained and demonstrated in quantitative terminology to management personnel, is the reduction in costs and potential damage to brand equity that external failures cause. This is not the only opportunity embedded in the corporate venture construct, but it provides a basis for management to quantitatively explain the concept to peers and colleagues.

An additional opportunity provided to management willing to use and embrace the idea of corporate venturing is that it provides a testing environment and proving ground for management training, developing, and innovative concepts. Implementing new management ideas, whether it be holocracy, various different types of innovation, or simply trying out new concepts, can be difficult when done within the constraints of existing operations. Having a testing ground, and this be expanded upon later, provides numerous opportunities for management personnel to develop and experiment with new concepts. This opportunity, presented to the organization at virtually no additional cost, is simply one that cannot be ignored by organizations seeking to further expand and develop. Seizing this opportunity, even if only by establishing a small program, or experimenting with a telecommuting policy, is something that should be embraced by management personnel. An isolated, cost-effective, and internal opportunity to build out, experiment, and develop new management theories, ideas, and construct product and service items is something no management team can afford to ignore. That said, however, the benefits of corporate venturing are also prevalent in the marketplace, which provide opportunities for study and refinement.

Benefits of Corporate Venturing

Under this more integrated model, which for the purposes of this research will be associated with the phrase corporate venturing, the startup organization is fully owned and managed by the management team of the incumbent. Sponsoring and funding early-stage developments and research provides a unique opportunity for established corporations to develop new ideas and opportunities (Mitchell 2009). Although the venture operates as an arm of the incumbent firm, the day-to-day operational decisions are made separate from the processes utilized at the parent organization. Structured as a startup organization, and ideally located in a separate physical location from the parent organization, the corporate venture organization can add value to both the spin-off entity and parent organization (McCammon et al. 2014). The goal of the spin-off is similar to that of any new entrant—to disrupt and upset the incumbent.

Corporate venturing and corporate capital holds potential for both private industry, public practice, and academia (McCammon et al. 2014). This separate management structure, distinct physical location, and removal from traditional organizational decision-making lines allow for a flexible and fluid decision-making process that resembles those present at dynamic organizations. Such a structure is currently in use by many high-profile organizations in the marketplace, but even in the face of success at entities like General Electric, Amazon, and Alphabet, several areas remain in need of further research and analysis. Perhaps the most pointed example of the possible failure of such a decentralized model is the Indian conglomerate Tata. Currently embroiled in a governance, and operational, upheaval linked closely to the disparate nature of management and operations, this entity serves as a warning to management not to undertake corporate venturing without understanding the managerial implications first.

That said, there are benefits to the organization that are directly derived from the fact that management, by nature of adopting corporate venturing, will undergo changes. Training, additional materials, resources, and information are inevitably necessary to prepare management to successfully maximize the benefits and opportunities of corporate venturing. Since the very concept of corporate venturing is, in essence, a new concept not traditionally embraced by management personnel, the implications for managers can be profound. In addition to understanding the basics of corporate venturing, however, management personnel must also link these ideas to broader business goals. Linking back to the benefits and opportunities of corporate venturing, implications associated with corporate venturing encompass business strategy, innovation at large within the organization, and developing new lines of business.

Management Implications

Management professionals tasked with implementing a corporate venturing framework must understand several key aspects of strategy and strategic decision-making. Unless the leadership of an organization desires to hire a large number of external consultants, in addition to the necessary external resources to launch a new venture, the spin-off entity will be staffed almost entirely by existing personnel. An important decision that must be made before the corporate venture organization begins operations in earnest is the education and training of management professionals. Specifically, the training and education should focus on the two following areas. First, an examination of strategic thinking and planning, including disruptive innovation and corporate venturing, must be analyzed both in general terms and as they applied to the organization. Second, and a step that is often overlooked, is that the management team that will be leading, at least initially, the corporate venture spin-off, must be properly incentivized to apply these concepts to business plans. In essence, merging and combining the various perspectives of operations, management, and external stakeholders can create positive benefits to the organization (Guenther and Hoppe 2014). Without incentive and motivation to apply the concepts being introduced via education and training, the likelihood of success will decline. One possible approach to this possibly difficult problem would be to link initiatives, in lieu of traditional bonuses, to non-salary compensation. In other words, provide the employees tasked with leading this challenging idea with a tangible financial incentive to work and pursue these goals aggressively. Even more beneficial, since the ideas, resources, products, and services produced by the spin-off entity are contained within the parent company, any and all insights that market competitors might use will instead become intellectual property of the organization. Drilling down specifically, there are two distinct areas on which management professionals should focus when trying to implement a corporate venturing strategy at their organization.

Strategy and Business Development

When attempting to link together the specific product and service offerings to the strategic underpinnings, namely, disruption, employed at the corporate venture, it is important to not only assess the specific strengths of the organization, but also the larger areas influenced by broader business trends. Sustainability, improvements in corporate governance, and increasing the engagement between organizations, customers, and other stakeholders are emerging in importance for organizations, regardless of industry focus. Building connections between the different concepts of business strategy and innovation is something that must be undertaken by management and operational personnel throughout the organization (Chungyalpa and Bora 2015). Linking together these growing areas of business importance to the business development tactics developed and employed by the corporate venture should be the driving force behind this idea. Once these broader connections have been analyzed, examined, and established, the development of strategic initiatives and ideas will become more realistic.

It is important that, while management examines the connections between broader business areas and the specific market objectives of the organization, technology and other opinions are also sought out. Technology, specifically the opportunity for initiatives and ideas to go viral via social media, provides a very cost-effective way for management to bootstrap ideas, opportunities, and to evaluate market sentiment. Gaining a better understanding of the market reaction to the ideas and concepts developed via the corporate venture model is important. Viewed within the context of new and innovative ideas, it is critical that good and bad ideas alike are vetted prior to major capital investments in these ideas. This is an important step as management professionals seek to move from merely outlining strategy at the corporate venture to action-oriented business steps and operational decision-making.

Operations at the Corporate Venture

Subsequent to an understanding of what exactly the goals and objectives of the corporate venture are, and should be, moving forward, management is faced with implementing these initiatives and ideas. From the perspective of management, this requires a holistic mindset, analyzing the business from a high level, but also differentiating the goals of the corporate venture into two separate buckets. First, the financial returns of the corporate venture must be tracked, analyzed, and reported so that effective and efficient evaluation can take place. Second, and arguably more important than the dollar-for-dollar initial return on the investments on behalf of the corporate venture, is the linkage to overall stated goals of this idea. Circling back, the core prerogative and goal of this spin-off entity is to foster an environment, with proper incentives, of creativity, fluid decision-making, and a goal to disrupt and upend the incumbent organization. This approach can take several forms and will clearly differ depending on the organization, but should connect with the strategic imperatives and themes outlined previously.

Transitioning from strategic thinking and outlines to operational actions, management should ask the following questions:

1. What do our competitors perform more effectively than our organization?
2. Is this differentiation generating beneficial returns, and are these differences able to be replicated?
3. What would we change about our organization if we could, and what are the top pain points internally?
4. Do our customers have common complaints and pain points that we can improve?
5. Are the resources available within the organization to let us manage these goals and objectives?

After gathering the answers to these questions, a logical next step is to construct a process and roadmap that will enable the management and staff within the corporate venture to address deficiencies. As management assembles this plan, requests resources from the parent organization, and coordinates with personnel tasked within the corporate venture, there are two key points that must be integrated into the decision-making process. Expanded upon below, both of these broad areas are important, but cannot be implemented simply by management experts alone. It is critical, and a point that must be emphasized throughout the process, that financial experts and expertise must be leveraged and brought to bear to understand the requirements of the corporate venture. As the corporate venture begins and accelerates operations, it is imperative that the financial goals and objectives of the corporate venture remain linked together.

Accelerating Strategy

As management professionals seek to implement the tactical goals, namely, to disrupt the parent organization, they must also remember to utilize the connections and information available in a global business environment. Supply chains, personnel, and financial capital are global in nature, and will flow to the areas in which they are best treated. With this global emphasis at the forefront of conversations regarding corporate venture capital, there are several factors that should be taken into account. Put simply, while the goals and objectives will vary from organization to organization, the underlying goals of corporate venture capital should be to improve either the performance of the organization, or to provide sources of information for future development.

Strategy is, regardless of the specific organization or management team in question, at the forefront of management decision-making and analysis in the marketplace. Examining market research, scholarly research, and mainstream media coverage, it is apparent that strategy and strategic thinking are of critical importance for management professionals across the board. Perhaps most important is the required blending of shareholder, stakeholder, and customer needs in the development of strategy (Hawker and Edmonds 2014). Traditional strategy, involving an extensive process of planning, review, and building out new ideas and tactics for the organization, is often a time-consuming and costly endeavor. Such a structure simply is not ideal for the current environment, which demands increased agility and nimbleness from even the largest organizations. Anecdotal evidence gathered from the dramatic structural changes underway at General Electric demonstrates that even market-leading, global, and brand-name organizations must reinvent themselves periodically. This market-driven need for virtually continuous innovation and improvement also provides both a justification and need for corporate venture adoption.

An important aspect of building innovation into the corporate venture pipeline is to make sure that specific management personnel are charged with implementation. The essence of the sprint model of management and leadership development is to emphasize the importance of getting a product or service ready for testing, rather than spending time developing a product that might have fewer errors, but be slow to market. Drilling down specifically into the sprint management model, it appears that the corporate venture model provides an almost ideal platform for utilizing such a management model. In essence, the sprint methodology requires that management personnel set aside all routine or non-mission critical work to focus on the specific tasks and project at hand. Comparing these requirements with the purposes and structure of a corporate venture model, it would appear that the focused environment and singular objectives built into the corporate venture structure provide an ideal platform for this method to develop. The steps involved in the venture require an almost pressure cooker-like environment and mindset for successful implementation. Since the corporate venture model is built around redefining the strategy and strategic thinking of the parent company, this represents an opportunity for management to experiment with a sprint management model without risking an unnecessarily large amount of capital.

Building the Sprint with a Global Team

The purpose of the sprint is to develop and produce within 1 business week (5 days) a product or service ready for customer testing and review. Embedded within the corporate venture mindset, the sprint methodology of innovation management becomes something that is both logical and necessary. Putting this concept into practice, however, necessitates the management team form a so-called war room from which they can lead the sprint process to completion. First, the management team is assembled, and the various ideas forming the focus of the corporate venture entity are outlined. Brainstorming should occur on the first day of the sprint model, complete with a vigorous debate on the merits of ideas proposed during the brainstorming. Led by a moderator, respected by the remainder of the management team, this debate should result, through iterations, in one idea that is realistic to achieve and customer focused. A customer-centric framework through which to evaluate the proposed ideas and concepts is especially important for the sprint model when used in a corporate venture framework. Since the product or service will be subject to (either internal or external) customer testing and review at the conclusion of the week, it is imperative that the entire process gear around this fact.

Second, after the proposed idea is selected, development must begin on what the ultimate users will receive and evaluate. At this stage in the process, and embedded within the benefits of the sprint technique, is a sense of urgency that must be integrated throughout this process. The demo product or service does not have to be perfect—it does not even have to exist beyond an approximate prototype or online presence. The purpose of developing such a rapid prototype and model is to gauge initial customer feedback and sentiment. Globalization can be especially helpful in this regard. As the core sprint team cannot work 24 h a day, specific technical or development aspects of the project can certainly be outsourced to global compatriots around the world. For example, if the objective of the sprint is to develop a prototype website for customer engagement with the latest interaction of customer service chatbots, why not initially debut the program with an overseas audience. This allows for additional testing, iterative feedback, and improvements while remaining within the proposed 1-week timeframe for development and testing.

Third, and linking together the importance of strategic testing within a sprint model, is that, even if the concept is not a success, it has not absorbed either the time or personnel linked with the parent organization. In essence, by creating the corporate venture entity, the organization provides employees and management professionals the necessary freedom to experiment and fail without fear of loss of budgetary authority or other departmental consequences. The underlying goal worth reiterating is that by setting up a corporate venture unit that has the flexibility to implement the sprint platform, anything discovered or proved by the spin-off entity is of worth to the parent. Expanding this conversation, the idea of corporate venturing and the sprint methodology are readily applicable to a global organization.

One of the key benefits of globalization, free trade, and global sourcing agreements is the ability of management to source human talent, products, and services from across the globe to fulfill the needs of stakeholders. With the ability of any business, regardless of where they are headquartered or located, to leverage and attract talent on a global basis, the ability to manage said resources only increases in importance. This reality represents one of the most pertinent reasons why corporate venturing is especially applicable to globally operating organizations. These specific benefits and opportunities, however, require more in-depth analysis before full implementation, and associated benefits can be derived from adopting such a strategic framework.

Global Corporate Venturing

Management professionals, regardless of industry or specific market niche, face similar issues when seeking to expand and further develop the business. Increasing competition, global supply chain issues, social media, activist shareholders, and consumers around the globe require a management style and philosophy that is much more dynamic and flexible than those previously utilized. At the same time, however, it is difficult to escape or offset the pressure to meet and/or exceed the quarterly revenue and profit targets set by analysts, and expected by the marketplace. Experimenting with new ideas and concepts, including the sprint development platform and corporate venturing, can be costly endeavors if undertaken in a home market, or within the view of market analysts unaccustomed to such ideas. Akin to the aptly named conglomerate discount, where organizations with disparate operations and interests are discounted in price compared to more focused peers, management professionals focusing on longer-term development may be undercut by short-term financial pressure.

Global operations, particularly as they pertain to leveraging the corporate venture model to develop customer-centric products and services, provide management the following opportunity. Prior to full-fledged testing, product development, or even entering a new market or product area, the parent company can and should leverage the capabilities of the spin-off entity. Effectively taking advantage of the insights and information generated as a result of operating the spin-off in either case, the parent entity can effectively focus on innovative and creative R&D that would otherwise be untenable at the corporate level. Specifically, even if all the corporate venture organization can reasonable accomplish, at least at first, is to help management avoid costly market blunders, this alone justifies the continued operation of the spin-off entity.

Accounting and Financial Ramifications

Every business decision must be undertaken with a reasonable understanding of the risk profile of the decision along with the projected payoff for the project. Drilling down specifically, it is clear that, although corporate venturing will focus on strategy and innovative thinking, the financial implications of establishing a corporate venture must play an important role in evaluating proposed initiatives. That said, traditional metrics such a return on investment (ROI), earnings per share (EPS), and return on assets (ROA) might not be entirely adequate for evaluating corporate venture projects and concepts (Lei and Jun 2016). Understanding that, while the goals of corporate venturing are eventually financially oriented in nature, traditional financial metrics and measures might not be applicable is a critical part of ensuring a successful implementation of the corporate venturing model.

Since the goal of a corporate venture spin-off, ultimately, is to create new ideas and concepts that can be utilized in the marketplace, it may very well require investments and cash flows that do not initially generate positive returns. However, while the financial returns of a corporate venture might not be initially apparent, the intellectual property and ideas derived from these initiatives are quantifiable. It is important to remember that financial returns are a result of operational performance and excellence, and do not exist in a vacuum. Ideas; concepts; and management professionals tasked with leading the corporate venture entity must have both the aptitude and ability to evaluate longer-term projects and initiatives. When presenting the projects, ideas, and concepts proposed by the corporate venture, there are several factors that must be taken into account.

Strategy and Financial Literacy

First, the linkage between organizational goals and the financial investment required by the corporate venture must be established both in strategic and financial terms. Management must only be able to draw a linkage between organizational strategy and the required financial resources and tools. This focuses on the importance of financial literacy as it pertains to business decision-making, and not simply the importance of financial literacy for individual decision-making. Put simply, if the management team cannot effectively communicate the importance and connection between corporate venturing goals and the financial resources needed for these objectives, it will remain increasingly difficult to achieve the stated objectives and goals of the corporate venture entity. Understanding the sources of financing available to the corporate venture entity, both internal and external in nature, is an area in which management can present and fully develop perspectives and tools that can benefit both the separate entity and the organization as a whole.

Second, and since every initiative, product, or service requires financial resources and support, it is especially important for corporate venture management to bridge the gap between concept and cash flow realities. Even if the individual project or idea will not, in and of itself, generate significant profits or positive cash flows, providing a framework and map forward will assist the management in conveying the importance of specific goals. Articulating the differentiation between net income and cash flow, as well as illustrating the tools and technology available to help evaluate proposals put forward for consideration, will assist the management at the parent organization to efficiently evaluate the performance of the corporate venture entity.

Lastly, but perhaps most importantly, an objective rationale and evaluation of corporate venture projects create an organizational environment more likely to support these ideas. Especially when collaborating with colleagues around the globe, it is especially important to present arguments and concepts in a format that is universally understood and can be synthesized across cultural lines. Forming a foundation for concepts and ideas grounded in the reality of the business at large presents a unified objective that can be evaluated in an equitable format.

Corporate Venturing and Management Decision-Making

Framed within the context of global business and decision-making, the value and potential that corporate venturing provides to management professionals can be summarized as follows. First, it isolates risk and reward of creative and innovative concepts from the parent organization while allowing the spin-off entity the necessary latitude to experiment and create new offerings for the organization. Second, channeling the innovative and disruptive theories and ideas in the marketplace, including disruptive innovations, provides the incumbent organizations with the ability to test, develop, and implement products and services ahead of offerings from competing organizations. Particularly in a global business environment, with operations, customers, and supply chains located on global levels, the ability of an organization to experiment and develop products on a market-to-market basis provides numerous benefits to management professionals.

Management is, of course, a blend of strategic thinking and financial analysis to accomplish the goals of the organization, and corporate venturing provides a venue for proactive management teams to leverage this reality. Corporate venturing provides a platform and venue for management to present, develop, and analyze both new ideas, and the real-world effects of these ideas on the business. Presenting new ideas and concepts, either at an organizational level or on a market by market basis, requires that management theory must also be meshed within a logical financial framework with innovative concepts. Innovation, distilled to core concepts, represents the reality that organizations must be able to both react, and proactively plan for future opportunities and challenges. Financial restraints, however, often constrain the ability of incumbent organizations to proactively engage in innovative thinking. Management teams tasked with developing the corporate venture models and projects are presented within an opportunity to, perhaps, have the best of both larger organizational resources and the flexibility of a smaller organization. Corporate venturing, the implications and opportunities it provides for management professionals at both a strategic and financial level, and the real-world utilization of such a model present a compelling case for increased implementation. Technology, customer requirements and expectations, and the realities of competition in a global marketplace require a rethinking of strategy and strategy implementation. Corporate venturing, clearly, is a disruptive concept, but provides the tools necessary for organizations and management professionals to successfully develop concepts for the market, and organizational development.

References

Chungyalpa W, Bora B (2015) Towards conceptualizing business strategies. Int J Multidiscip Approach Stud 2(1):73–83

Ford D, Nelsen B (2014) The view beyond venture capital. Nat Biotechnol 32(1):15–23. doi:10.1038/nbt.2780

Hawker NW, Edmonds TN (2014) Strategic management concepts for antitrust: cooperation, stakeholders and sustainability. Antitrust Bull 59(4):769–788. doi:10.1177/0003603X1405900404

Goshen Z, Hamdani A (2016) Corporate control and idiosyncratic vision. Yale Law J 125(3):560–617

Guenther EM, Hoppe H (2014) Merging limited perspectives. J Ind Ecol 18(5):689–707. doi:10.1111/jiec.12125

Lei W, Jun P (2016) Research on the investment performance evaluation of corporate venture capital with intuitionistic fuzzy information. J Intell Fuzzy Syst 30(3):1783–1790. doi:10.3233/IFS-151890

McCammon MG, Pio E, Barakat S, Vyakarnam S (2014) Corporate venture capital and Cambridge. Nat Biotechnol 32(10):975–978. doi:10.1038/nbt.3029

Mitchell P (2009) Corporate venture funds chase early-stage deals. Nat Biotechnol 27(5):403–404. doi:10.1038/nbt0509-403

Vertès AA (2012) Syndicate innovation venturing: translating academic innovations into commercial successes. *Challenges* 3(2):70–83. doi:10.3390/challe3020070

Creating and Developing a Sustainable Resort Development in a World Heritage Site: A Case Study of Cusco, Peru

Willy A. Aroca

Abstract This is a perception study of the impact that sustainable resort development has, and will have, on the resident population of the Cusco region of Peru. The increase in development in the area is a result of the city's recent designation as a World Heritage Site and the resulting impact on the income, quality of life and environment of residents of Cusco and the surrounding has been assessed. Participant stakeholders responded to questions concerning how the development and launch of sustainable resorts in the Cusco region will affect their community. The research reflects the varying concerns and perceptions of each sector interviewed. Despite the differences in social and financial status, residents seem united in their overall concerns about how the new designation and resulting development will affect the local environment.

Keywords Resort development • World heritage site • Sustainability • Environment

Introduction

The following paper will outline the research strategies and methodology used to examine sustainable resort expansion in Cusco, Peru. Resort developers have seen an increase in the demand for sustainable initiatives from investors because of the region's historic value and ecological environment. Cusco is as an international World Heritage Destination because of its unique culture and the desire to protect this site. The Peruvian government, through the Department of the Environment, also recognizes the need to address the impact of resort development in the area while encouraging investment by national and international companies to invest in tourism-related activities.

W.A. Aroca (✉)
International School of Hospitality and Tourism Management, Fairleigh Dickinson University, Vancouver, BC, Canada
e-mail: waroca@fdu.edu

L. Tadj, A.K. Garg (eds.), *Emerging Challenges in Business, Optimization, Technology, and Industry*, Springer Proceedings in Business and Economics,
DOI 10.1007/978-3-319-58589-5_4

Evidence of the environmental impact in Peru is seen in the increased erosion of usable land, the pollution to the water supply, the increase demand for potable water and the need for waste management services. In addition, there is evidence of vegetation loss, threat to habitat diversity, safety and the damage to the Inca artefacts found in the region. The Peruvian government recognizes that tourism is one of the world's largest industries, creating revenues approaching $5490 billion annually. The industry directly employed an estimated 73 million people worldwide in 2004 and experienced significant growth in Latin America. A sustainable enterprise in a world heritage site, regardless of size, must meet the requirements of a wide variety of influential stakeholders, including Eco tourists and community groups. The focus of the research is on sustainable resort developments in the Cusco region of Peru in order to determine the impact of this type of building practice. There is an opportunity for the building and development industry to entice investors to provide financing for sustainable developments and specifically, green resort developments. The key benefits of such green resort development can be measured in economic, social, environmental and institutional terms. Cusco, Peru was chosen as the focus of this research due to its location in a country where many of the world's standards of sustainable development are being studied and strategies tested.

Since the adoption in 1972 of the Convention Concerning the Protection of World Natural and Cultural Heritage, some 450 sites throughout the world have been formally designated as World Heritage Sites. These sites, by reason of their special historic, scientific, or aesthetic qualities, have universal value (Drost 1996, p. 479). It is not surprising, therefore, that many of these sites are favourite tourist attractions (Ibid). By generating revenue and drawing attention to their importance, tourism can be a positive force for the preservation of World Heritage treasures (Ibid). There has been an increasing interest in the impact of tourism on World Heritage Sites over the past 20 years. This has been motivated in part by the commonly held view that World Heritage Listing increases visitor numbers (Landorf 2009, p. 53). The commitments which countries undertake in signing the convention include a general recognition of the duty to ensure the identification, promotion, conservation, and transmission to future generations of the cultural and natural heritage described in the convention (Drost 1996, p. 480). The privilege to promote World Heritage Sites is accompanied by an obligation to protect these sites (Drost 1996, p. 481).

Peru

Since the time of the sun worshipping Incas, the land of gold as Peru is known has fuelled the imagination of many travellers. This vast country still holds tremendous fascination as Peru has spectacular landscapes across three distinct and contrasting environments: an immense desert coastline, a tropical Amazonian rainforest and the majestic Andes Mountains. There are also three main ethnic groups in Peru. The first are indigenous Peruvians, living primarily near the high mountains, but also found in the deepest parts of the Amazon region. The second group is the mestizo population, a mix of the native Peruvians and the Europeans who came to Peru from Spain. The mestizo population are found mainly in urban centres but are also scattered throughout Peru. The third main ethnic group is the black population, which is mainly found in the coastal areas of the country. There is also a very small white population as well as Chinese and Japanese immigrants. This ethnic diversity contributes to the human heritage and the local population's perception of tourism development in all regions of Peru.

History and Tourism in Peru and Cusco

In 1970, Peru received 133,546 international visitors. Because of economic and political turmoil, there were significant slumps in the 1980s and 1990s, but over the past 15 years, there has been a steady increase in arrivals (McGrath 2004, p. 427). In 1994, a sharp increase to 386,120 was recorded and was largely attributed to the improved economic conditions brought about by the capture of Abimael Guzman, the leader of the Maoist terrorist group, The Shining Path (Ibid). By the year 2000, the goal of one million visitors was achieved 2 years ahead of schedule (Ibid). Visitor arrivals came mainly from Europe and North America, but there has been a substantial increase in the past 5 years from Latin America; in particular Brazil, Chile and Argentina. The economic confidence has impelled an increase in tourism from the local national market.

Tourism organizations in Peru exist at the national, regional and local level. At the national level, tourism activity in Peru is under the jurisdiction of Ministry of Industry, Tourism, Integration and International Trade (MITINCI), and international promotion of Peru is undertaken by the Commission for the Promotion of Peru (PROMPERU) (Ladkin and Bertramini 2002, p. 78). In 2003 in order to denote the new importance now afforded to tourism in Peru, the Ministry of Foreign Trade and Tourism (MINCETUR) was formed, enabling greater attention to be given to tourism (McGrath 2004, p. 427).

The City of Cusco, known to the Incas as the 'navel of the world' was their imperial capital and the most important place of pilgrimage in pre-Columbian South America. This remains the case for present-day tourists, and the overwhelming majority of visitors to Peru go to Cusco because it is the most accessible gateway to Machu Picchu, the Inca trail, and the sacred valley of the Incas that encompasses the Urubamba valley.

Background

The tourism industry is a major contributor to the gross national product of many nations and is one of the fastest growing industries in the world (Gilmore et al. 2007, p 253). The growth in tourism has created new challenges to tourism sites in terms of increase numbers of visitors, and their potential detrimental impact on the environment. This is becoming evident in popular tourist locations that include the unique and fragile environments of World Heritage sites (Ibid). Sustainable development is important to Cusco and Peru as the consumer demand for products of high environmental integrity will increase, including an emphasis on products that are recyclable or minimize the impact on land and water. Developers are well aware that consumers will dictate the market and its demand. Peru has the potential to develop a sector of the economy that is largely based on sustainable products and services. This strategy can give the country a market advantage if properly designed. Whereas comparative advantages involve the resources available to a destination, competitive advantages relate to a destination's ability to use these resources effectively over the long term (Ritchie and Crouch 2003, p. 23). Developers that base their projects on sustainable building practices will also have a clear competitive advantage and will be able to distinguish themselves in the market place.

A sustainable resort development makes economic sense and can lead to sizable returns on investment. Sustainable developments and practices are increasing in Peru across all building sectors as developers are learning that it can be profitable to engage in green building projects. Developers who utilize sustainable practices can internationally compete with the world's best practices through certification, environmental impact reporting, and triple bottom-line performance. Some of the challenges that Cusco faces in its path to sustainability include managing the transition to sustainable energy and protecting the natural assets of its tourism industry.

The government of Peru, in conjunction with the developers, will need to evaluate a life-cycle cost method to assess total building costs over time. This includes the initial cost from the design and construction, operating costs related to waste, water, energy, maintenance and repairs as well as other environmental costs such as the impact on transportation, water and infrastructure. The ecological footprint or carrying capacity of Cusco will need to be evaluated with regard to maintaining its productivity, adaptability and renewal. Tourism carrying-capacity refers to the carrying-capacity of the biophysical environment with respect to tourism activity and development (Ceballos-Lascurain 1992).

The Green Globe certification program, which is a component of the Tourism Sustainability Council (TSC), includes a series of benchmarks in conjunction with international standards for the sustainable operation and management of travel and tourism businesses (Green Globe 2010). Cusco will need to focus on land use planning and management to ensure that the development projects: avoid visual intrusiveness, minimize negative impacts, and are coordinated with other sectors to promote complimentary and balanced development blueprints.

Inkaterra hotels, a luxury resort company with properties located in Cusco, Machu Picchu and the Amazon rainforest, has pioneered and promoted sustainable tourism in Peru since 1975. Each year the company hosts more than 65,000 travellers, providing authentic sustainable experiences with respect and support for the region's diversity and culture (Inkaterra 2010). The company and its developers have designed their lodges specifically to reduce the impact of new construction. Their commitment to sustainable development incorporates conservation and scientific research that includes the respect for cultural, social and environmental values. Inkaterra helps protect more than 17,000 hectares of original forest through an agreement with the Peruvian government, helping to reduce directly 3,315,000 tons of carbon. Inkaterra has become a truly Carbon-Neutral organization and every guest has a 100% Carbon Neutral hotel stay experience (Inkaterra 2010).

Literature Review

A review of available literature on the topic of the World Heritage program and its effectiveness in helping preserve cultural and natural treasures was conducted as part of the research for this study. The articles address the advantages and disadvantages that World Heritage designation brings to a destination, depending on how the site is managed. The literature researched was focused on the rapid rise in popularity of World Heritage destinations and the subsequent impact on hotel development and other changes to the local environment. The literature identifies current trends in sustainable resort development in heritage sites, one of which focuses on the need to preserve the remaining ecosystems, as so much has already been lost. Scientific models have overestimated the resilience of ecosystems, owing to an inadequate understanding of their complexity (Magee 2005, p. 6). Australia is one of the places in the world where building projects are based on a systems-thinking approach and where individuals and leaders have had the motivation and desire to find innovative solutions (Ibid). Some of Australia's greatest natural features are protected in World Heritage Areas and these protected areas are actually a cost-effective solution for Australia (Ibid). For example, the Great Barrier Reef alone contributes nearly $1 billion (AU) directly to the economy per year, with over $600 million (AU) from tourism alone (Ibid).

Another example is the attention to sustainable infrastructure as an issue in the hospitality-design industry today (Wang and Wang 2009, p. 53). A group of pioneers of the green hospitality movement has been sharing their views, challenges and triumphs in working toward a carbon-constrained future. The basis of sustainable hospitality operation is a three-part balance, expressed as "profits, people and planet" (Ibid).

Research Objectives

The objective of this research study is to assess sustainable resort developments in the region of Cusco, Peru in order to determine the impact of this type of building practice. Peru's most important and valuable asset is its natural environment and currently holds ten World Heritage site designations. UNESCO, which launched its World Heritage program in 1972 to help preserve cultural and natural treasures, has more than 900 sites around the world. With a variety of diverse ecosystems to protect, Peru has taken the world lead in measures to ensure that these precious resources are protected while also devising strategies that allow visitors to enjoy these unique treasures.

Peru also recognizes that the built environment as its largest man-made asset. The technologies available for the built environment's design, planning, construction and operation will always be fundamental to the productivity and competitiveness of Peru's economy, the quality of life of its people, and the ecological sustainability of the country. By recognizing that the demand for nature-tourism experiences is increasing worldwide, Peru is positioned to take advantage of an emerging market that demands large and small-scale sustainable resorts that limit damage to the natural environment.

A survey of existing literature that debates and addresses the issues was used to establish a basis for this research. Most models of sustainable development can be traced back to two key publications: the 1987 World Commission on Environment and Development's Brundtland Commission Report, Our Common Future and Agenda 21, the international agreement on sustainable development framed at the United Nations Conference on Environment and Development (Landorf 2009, p. 54). The Brundtland report defined sustainable development as "the advancement that meets the needs of the present without compromising the ability of future generations to meet their own needs" (Ibid). During the latter half of the 1980s, many Third World countries turned to ecotourism as a foreign exchange earner that was potentially less destructive than alternatives such as logging, oil extraction, cattle ranching and banana farming, commercial fishing, or conventional mass tourism (Honey 2008, p. 23). These countries viewed sustainable tourism as minimizing negative effects through as a force for minimizing emphasis on low impact construction, controlled visitor numbers, and care in visitor interaction with the local flora, fauna, and human population (Ibid). Further, such practices could, in some instances, be more profitable. Studies in various countries have found sustainable tourism and related economic activities may be a better form of land use than cattle ranching or agriculture (Ibid).

The variability of sustainable tourism success may be partly due to different methods for evaluating conservation. Some researchers have measured conservation as an ethic, discernible through people's attitudes or values. Others have evaluated conservation as a set of behaviours, either observed or reported, including how much people hunt or harvest timber, or how they dispose of waste, or whether they have established a reserved or protected area (Stronza and Pegas 2008, p. 264). McKercher and Du Cros note that the best way to manage on-site impacts and maintain the popularity of an attraction is to manage actively the tourists' experience of it. Accordingly, Goulding has identified three factors that are important for managing tourist on-site experiences (Du Cros 2007, p. 227). First, as applied to Cusco, scene setting would welcome visitors to the city and assist them in becoming well oriented and adjusted to the new setting. Second, routing and mapping would provide clear signage or pointers essential to the management of visitor flow. Third, crowd density control would maximize the visitor experience in Cusco and the surrounding destinations such as Machu Picchu and the Sacred Valley of the Incas (Ibid).

Primary Research Design

This study was able to examine investors, consumers and operators in a transforming community located in Cusco, Peru. Also included are studies of other resort developments from both internal and external perspectives as well as their implementation of best practices in resort operation. One of these operators is the Lanfranco Group, a Peruvian hotel company focusing on sustainability in its ownership and operations of eco-lodges throughout Peru. Lanfranco Hotels is currently considering designing and planning a sustainable infrastructure carrying capacity that will maintain and sustain communities within the region. The current government of Peru, under the Department of Environmental Services, is also investigating the nucleus of the community, and sustainable amenity migration in reviewing resort development activities.

The multi-faceted research was focused on the concept of sustainability as it pertains to the hotel and tourism industry in Peru. Primary research from consumers, investors and operators was assessed. On-site investigations and interviews with professionals involved in the projects was the basis for the case studies. The chosen sites varied in their approach, location and financial success but each was located within a particular ecologically sensitive environment requiring sensitivity to the impact of new development. Research recommendations were made by Lanfranco Hotels founder Alejandro Gonzales Prada Lanfranco. The input from the varied sources provided insight into the quantitative and qualitative role of the operators, consumers and investors. According to Pansiri, the linkage between mixing methods and strategic alliances, collaboration and networking in tourism is fundamental because not one single method can capture everything. The study included current, independent resort owners; tour operators; and ecologists as well as prospective investors. The research provided key data to support best practices and identify critical factors needed to build a sustainable community that is also a heavily visited tourist destination.

Methodology: Qualitative Data

This study used qualitative personal interviews that were able to reveal the individual perceptions of a resort development concept. Qualitative data has a quality of irrefutability if it is established as trustworthy (Robson 2002, p. 93). A semi-structured interview was proposed where the individuals involved in the interviewing process were able to adjust the questions on the basis of what was deemed appropriate. As more visitors are attracted to the region of Cusco as a World Heritage destination, a site development is created that goes beyond sustainable engineering and financing (Magee 2005). The methodology question was able to explore additional issues affecting the environment in the area as well as providing an understanding of other issues such as erosion, polluted water supply, vegetation loss, threats to habitat diversity, safety risks, and damage to Inca and other indigenous artefacts.

Sampling Frame

The travel service professionals in Peru are employed by a wide range of organizations including El Ministerio de Turismo del Peru (Tourism Ministry of Peru), El Ministerio del Medio Ambiente (Environment Ministry), international hotel management companies, international travel related agencies; national hotel management companies; destination management organizations for Peru, tour operating companies and independent hotels. Data collected for the qualitative research used a semi-structured telephone interviews with ten subject experts. Additional experts in related fields were also interviewed and subsequently increased the sample size. Organizations and organizational leaders interviewed included Alejandro Gonzales Prada Lanfranco, owner of the Lanfranco Group and the Hotel Munrique; and Mario Sotillo Vizcarra, general manager of the Sonesta Hotel Cusco. Additional interviews were conducted with the managing director of one of the leading destination management organizations in the region as well as front line staff at the Sonesta Hotel Cusco and Inkaterra Hotel Cusco. The study was able to take into consideration the homogeneity of the group (Robson 2002, p. 158). A minimum of 12 participants were included in the research supported by Robson (2002).

Instrument Design

The study took place in April of 2011; the data collected for the qualitative research used a semi-structured telephone interview with the participants. The list of questions was submitted in advance to give the interviewees an opportunity to prepare a portion of the answers prior to the call. The participants were asked to commit to an interview period of between 30 min and 1 h. The interview carefully followed the announced order of the questions and maintained the agreed time schedule as a courtesy to the interviewees. There was a follow-up email message to each participant and included the information that the final draft of answers would be submitted to confirm that the answers given had been properly recorded.

Methodology: Quantitative Research

Quantitative research is carried out in real world settings, and requires a developed conceptual framework or theory so that it is known in advance, what to look for as well as what may be feasible (Robson 2002, p. 4). This quantitative research project was seeking to determine: whether there is potential for growth of the sustainable resort concept in the Cusco region, the effects of the government interaction in its development, and the impact this growth will have on the local community and other key stakeholders.

This quantitative research project used a multi-stakeholder approach in which leaders and key members from different sectors of the community who have a strong interest in sustainability issues were surveyed. Typically, these stakeholders led teams of people who address particular issues such as land-use and transportation, economic and social issues (Sustainable Cities 2010). The quantitative research approach included public participation by using the "Imagine" methodology (Imagine Calgary 2010) and surveys. The Imagine methodology was first used in Chicago, Illinois in 1992 as a framework for engaging the public and multiple stakeholders in the development of a long-term sustainability plan for the city. Subsequently, Calgary adopted the methodology for its long-term planning process in 2005 and it has been used in other cities around the world. Cusco could benefit from this type of methodology as it engages stakeholders in the growth of sustainable resort development in a designated world heritage site.

Research Design

A non-experimental, fixed design quantitative research method was to be utilized to collect the data with the involvement from students in the hospitality and tourism department at the National University San Antonio Abad in Cusco, Peru. Due to circumstances surrounding the 2011 Peruvian national elections, colleges and universities were not available for the research as previously planned. Further research in this area will be explored at a later date.

Survey Analysis

The following findings and conclusion of the research indicate that the creation and development of a sustainable resort development in a World Heritage site will continue to experience challenges in its fruition. The research encompassed a number of issues affecting the tourism industry and samples varied from stakeholder responses from hotel operators, tour providers, industry leaders and tourists who had seen the development of the destination prior to its inclusion as world heritage site. The tourism industry in Peru is controlled by a handful of tour operators who command price distribution and relationship building. The majority of the large operators are promoting sustainable tourism practices and development in order to meet the demand of tourists. Furthermore, the development of the Internet and Internet-related travel has created a higher demand for sustainable tourism and transparency amongst industry stakeholders. The research indicated that sustainable tourism in Peru is in the early adoption stages and its development has increased in the past 15 years coinciding with the decline of activity from the Shining Path terrorist group. According to the research, sustainable tourism education has increased at the university level. University programs in hotel operation, tourism development, and sustainable tourism have increased. There is a higher demand and greater interest from individuals eager to enter the tourism industry as practitioners, educators and investors. There is also evidence from the research that career development in the industry and opportunities to establish business opportunities for local and foreign investors have increased recently, not only in the Cusco region but also in other developing regions of Peru. Based on the research, the findings indicate that sustainable practices are being implemented throughout Peru. More hotel companies are implementing sustainable practices in solar energy use, water usage and reusable products. However, the return on investment for sustainable practices is a major concern to the industry operators and developers. Currently, there are no incentives from the government of Peru to promote sustainable development, and there are limited regulatory practices being implemented by local and federal governments.

Market Study

World Heritage sites have the potential to: increase local economic development, enable distribution of visitors from well-known sites to those with fewer visitations, raise awareness of the World Heritage program, and enrich the visitor experience (Hawkins 2004, p. 293). The economies of developing countries with World Heritage sites, particularly in Latin America, are highly vulnerable and are affected by the processes of globalization and increasing dominance and control by multinational corporations (Akama and Kieti 2007, p. 743). Some preliminary suggestions include sharing benefits from interpretation, preparation of promotional materials, management practices, and branding based upon the World Heritage label (Ibid). The most commonly accepted definition of eco-tourism in a world heritage site incorporates the concept of experiencing the natural environment and protecting the environment from the impact of visitors. Ideally, tourism development and ecological sustainability should be complementary and mutually reinforced (Nzama 2008, p. 166). World Heritage sites often encourage unsustainable population growth combined with an increase in natural resource consumption. The economic systems in a destination like Peru often fail to value the environment and its resources and also allow inequity in ownership, management and use of natural resources. In addition, deficiencies in knowledge and its application and legal institutional systems that promote unsustainable practices can also be a barrier (Ibid).

Eco-tourism in Peru is in its infancy. It is a new trend but is becoming a major contributor to the country's economic growth. According to the research, most eco-resorts have been developed within the last 10–15 years as the demand for environmentally sustainable holidays has expanded. Eco resorts typically offer the tourist a holistic ecological experience that includes sightseeing, accommodations, and enjoyment of the natural environment.

Most international tourist destinations have been developed by national governments and international hotel investors with little consideration for the population (Ernoul 2009, p. 229). According to the research, the perceptions and concerns of the local population are rarely considered but results also indicated that tourism has had a very positive impact on the residents' quality of life. However, such studies were based on a single event rather than the development of an institutionalized eco-tourist resort program.

Results

Thirty per cent of the survey population were residents of Cusco, Peru and 50% of the population had worked in the tourism industry in the city. All of the population surveyed had visited the Cusco region; 90% of those surveyed had lived in Peru and had travelled throughout the Cusco region. Of those surveyed 50% were professionals who had worked in the hospitality and tourism industry. Ninety per cent of the total population surveyed claimed to have been affected, either positively or negatively, by the growth in the construction of eco-resorts in the region.

When the participants were asked about how educated the tourism industry in Peru was about sustainable practices, the response was overwhelmingly positive. All participants acknowledged that, since the eradication of the Shining Path terrorist group and the influx of tourism dollars infusing the economy, the growth and development of the tourism industry has rapidly evolved. During the 1980s and 1990s, Peru experienced almost 20 years of one of the bloodiest civil wars in contemporary South American history (Caruso 2007, p. 572). During that period, the Peruvian state contended legitimacy and rule with the insurgent Partido Comunista del Peru – Sendero Luminoso (PCP-SL), commonly known as Sendero Luminoso ('Shining Path'). The conflict resulted in 70,000 deaths and a significant drop in tourism (Ibid). The arrest and imprisonment of the group's leader in 1992 opened the door to a new era for Peru and a resurgence of international travel to and within the country.

Seventy per cent of those surveyed acknowledged that there is increasing evidence of sustainable practices throughout the region. Recycling bins have been installed throughout the Cusco airport as well as on residential streets and town squares. Community groups have been formed to promote recycling, waste management and protection of the local environment. Additionally, sustainable tour operators, such as KISWAR based in Cusco, support the principles of sustainable and responsible travel (Kiswar 2011). There has also been an additional investment by hotels in areas such as energy conservation. According to Mario Sotillo Vizcarra, general manager of the Sonesta Posada del Inca in Cusco, hotel owners and investors are improving efficiency by reducing operating hours and maximizing their use of energy. Hotel owner and developer Alejandro Gonzales Prada Lanfranco from the Lanfranco Hotel Group acknowledges that the education programs in sustainable practices have had a substantial growth throughout Peru. However, best practices need to be reinforced and extended in the development of educational services in the tourism and hospitality industry.

Concerning the perception that the industry works in a collaborative effort and are taking the lead on sustainable tourism practices; 50% of the population responded favourably and 50% of those surveyed felt that the major airlines, hotel and tour operators were the groups taking the lead in best practices. The survey indicated that there is a need for more collaborative effort and development; however, the survey indicated that 70% of the population felt that the government is the primary stakeholder who needs to take the initiative and lead in directing collaborative efforts of the tourism and hospitality industry. When the participants were asked to identify the benefits of sustainable practices in the Cusco region and to determine potential barriers to these practices, 100% of the respondents felt that preserving the environment, practicing sustainability, and maintaining the authentic experience were of most importance. The primary obstacle noted by 50% of those surveyed was a lack of education combined with corruption; while 50% felt that the main barrier was the overall cost to the consumer.

The results from the small business interviews regarding incentives from the government, private investors or international government organizations to promote sustainable developments showed that the government of Peru has not created an incentive for local small businesses to develop more sustainable resorts. Twenty per cent of the respondents felt that the government had levied additional taxes on the tourism industry but felt that tax revenue had not been invested back into the sector. There was an acknowledgement from the small business owner that the government is investing heavily in promoting Peru as a destination. The small business interviews showed that 80% of those surveyed felt that there is an effort to continue to promote Peru as a destination and there are efforts by the government to increase awareness of those sustainable developments being implemented throughout the country.

The Colca region of Peru, an area forty miles west of Cusco, known for deep canyons inhabited by the Peruvian condor, is experiencing a surge in sustainable eco-resort developments. A new luxury resort development owned by the Orient Express Company was recently built in the area. The property, Las Casitas de Colca, received mixed reviews from those surveyed. Thirty per cent of those surveyed felt that it was created to cater to the luxury international market and that the concerns of the local community had not been addressed. The positive impact on the agricultural professional group was perceived as mainly negative with only a small group benefiting from direct work opportunities. Most of the local community expressed negative feelings about the resort's impact in terms of a loss of land and the strain on fresh water supplies. Small family farmers make up the majority of the population in the valley, but their concerns regarding the impact on their livelihoods during construction and the undesirable affects they have already felt from the new site were not addressed. This resort could potentially lead to a shift in population demographics and local social structure by pushing out the local farmers.

When participants were asked about government involvement and incentives in the implementation of sustainable systems such as water use, utilization of solar and other sustainable sources, as well as drainage and energy, 50% of those surveyed acknowledged that companies are implementing solar energy practices but the government has not created an incentive system or regulatory process to protect the impact of new resort developments. Seventy per cent of those surveyed acknowledged that concern continues to grow about the impact of hospitality operations on the natural environment. While the impact may not be as significant as that of other industries in the region such as mining, the size and growth of the hospitality industry, especially in the Cusco region, could lead to a greater impact on the environment. The Cusco region has learned through its operations that its top three demand issues are the difficulty in diversifying demand from local domestic leisure consumers, the high seasonality of demand, and the high cost of meeting the needs of its range of target markets. Environmental issues often are limited to the natural environment and tend to focus on issues of global climate change, pollution, habitat and ecosystem degradation and resource consumption. The results from the interviews regarding the demand from tourists for more sustainable resort concepts resulted in 90% of those surveyed agreeing that international tourists are concerned about the impact on the environment while 50% of the respondents felt that the local tourist is slowly recognizing the impact and starting to demand more sustainable practices from developers in the region.

Although the hospitality industry has addressed environmental sustainability concerns in Peru, economic sustainability continues to be a key concern and a major challenge of all hospitality businesses. Addressing some of the environmental concerns in a transparent and proactive manner may promote investment recovery for hospitality firms within a realistic time frame. Of the small businesses surveyed regarding investment on sustainable resorts developments, one hundred per cent of those surveyed recognize that sustainable resort concepts is not only a consideration, but also a potential long-term financial incentive. Gonzales Prada of the Lanfranco Hotel Group is currently working on adding a sixty-bungalow ecological resort development in the northern part of Peru and has implemented a water and sewerage treatment centre to prevent beach contamination. Gonzales Prada notes, "I live on the beach and I am not only going to preserve the beach but I must have a commitment to the environmental stewardship of the region" (personal interview, April 20, 2011).

When participants were asked about the rewards of building a sustainable resort development in a World Heritage site, one hundred per cent of the respondents agreed that respecting and protecting the natural environment as well as giving back to the community in all components including economic, social and environmental are the main priority. When participants were asked about the economic benefits of a sustainable resort, out of one hundred per cent of those surveyed agreed that there are market segments that place a high value on the environment and will seek to support the environment in their purchases. One hundred per cent of the survey respondents also recognized that the ecotourism market that emerged in the late 1990s in Peru reflects environmental concerns, particularly in areas such as air and water quality and food safety which are pertinent to global tour operators in World Heritage sites like the region of Cusco, 80% of those surveyed reported that there are social benefits to the population but 20% agreed that they do not expect to see any social benefits from the government in the near future as a result of sustainable resort development.

Despite the influx of new job opportunities in the region due to the establishment and construction of resort developments, only a minority of the local population are benefiting from direct work opportunities. However, according to Mario Sotillo, general manager of the Sonesta Cusco, there are signs that new developments are changing their hiring practices. The new Marriott Cusco has established a set of guidelines to train residents from the local community and to protect the jobs designated for management for locally trained and educated staff. The perceived future impact on the incomes for the resident population as a whole is questionable, with 40% of the population surveyed unsure of how the new developments will affect their incomes. However, when broken down by professional group, the results varied. Ninety per cent of tourism professionals interviewed believed that their income would continue to increase with the opening of new resorts.

Concerning the impact on the community and stakeholders benefits from infrastructure upgrades and development, 90% of those surveyed believed that the community would benefit and the impact would be positive for local development. However, according to Aldo Serrano from wholesaler Viajes Union, the infrastructure developments could benefit the local community with the construction of a new international airport in the Urubamba region that had been previously approved and consequently delayed due to political issues. According to Serrano, one of the concerns from the government was the fact that the international visitors would fly directly to the Cusco region and bypass Lima and other regions.

According to Gonzales Prada and the Lanfranco group, there are a number of other factors which have been queried in regard to the development of the Cusco region. First, the Peruvian government has practiced centralized, exclusionary decision-making in awarding tourism contracts, planning for tourism development and utilizing the sites for personal financial gain. Second, according to Gonzales Prada there has been controversial granting of concessions for access to the sanctuary of Machu Picchu for the filming of commercials at the site with damage to the ruins resulted from the activity. Third, there is an inconsistency in wages that has been a frequent, on-going cause of contention with the World Heritage Committee and the Peruvian National Institute of Culture.

When the participants were asked if they felt that the community residents should control and maintain a role in the decision-making process of the hiring, training and locating of new resort developments; 20% felt that the community needs to be involved in the decision-making process; 30% felt that their input is of great importance but the decision should be ultimately that of the government; 50% felt that the decision lies with the developer since the project is primarily their investment. Concerning economic benefits for stakeholders in the community, 50% felt that there should be a certain amount of revenue designated for community improvements and sustainable practices determined by the community; 50% felt that a portion of the revenue generated needed to be controlled by the local municipal offices and government officials assigned for this specific task. Ten per cent of those surveyed recommended the implementation of el "Canon de Turismo" similar to the "Canon Minero" which is a harmonized special tax placed on mining companies and used only for the development of the region where mines are depreciating the environment. When the participants were asked about collaborative efforts in the implementation of sustainable and ethical resorts in bringing knowledge to the local community, 70% of the respondents felt that there are countries around the world that are implementing best practices in sustainable development but are willing to share their knowledge in the development of the Cusco region; but 20% felt that it would probably take time for best practices to be implemented.

Mario Sotillo of Sonesta Hotel Cusco contended that local companies are implementing Corporate Social Responsibility practices in their core development of the region. All of those surveyed acknowledged that there is concern for the development, preservation and protection of the region as a World Heritage destination. The city and the region depend on revenue from tourism; consequently, the incentive to maximize this will have an effect on the long-term impact on the region.

Discussion

Despite the expansion of new job opportunities in the region, the rate at which the Cusco area shifts to a sustainable economy will depend on whether the decision makers adopt integrated, holistic approaches to the preservation and management of a World Heritage destination. The challenge is complex and requires a systematic approach, which, if effectively adopted by committed stakeholders in the region, can achieve a real change in the operation of the Cusco region tourism project. The barriers to a sustainable society are complicated by both local and global interests. The Peruvian society must achieve the right mix and balance between the local, state and global market, between competitive and cooperative action at the local, national and global stages, and between government and non-government organizations. Most members of society think that environmentalists and developers do not agree on much (Magee 2005, p. 57). However, the concerns of developers and ecologists can achieve balance through a better re-proportioning of short and long-term needs as well as government leadership (Ibid).

There was no statistical data regarding the number of jobs being produced by new resort developments in the Cusco region. However, according to Sotillo, the regional government of Cusco has implemented a program where job priority will be given to the residents of the region. Opposition to sustainable development exists because of a lack of access to resources and information (Magee 2005, p. 57). Similarly, ethnic prejudice continues to be a contributor to the disaffection of indigenous people in tourism development in the Machu Picchu and the Cusco region of Peru (Adams 2010, p. 112). According to Aldo Serrano, top down activities such as mining are given higher priority by the government of Peru than the considered development of tourism service opportunities. Government control often yields short sighted, overly centralized and insensitive tourism development as seen in other regions of Peru (Adams 2010, p. 112). The results also indicate that support for resort development in a World Heritage destination has the residents' endorsement based on their evaluation of the benefits and costs. The supported path relationship between the community of Cusco's satisfaction, perceived benefits and costs suggest that community satisfaction is an important concept for understanding a community's perception of tourism development impact (Nunkoo and Ramkissoon 2010, p. 269).

What is unclear for the local community of Cusco is the part that their own culture plays in cultural tourism and heritage preservation in the area. The fear is that the community can become increasingly excluded from the tourism and heritage management process of the area (Tucker and Emge 2010, p. 51). Designation as a World Heritage destination can create building regulations and the necessity to obtain permission for any alteration work on many of the historical districts of Cusco (Ibid). The process of obtaining work permits is costly and can take a number of years as the official protection board responsible for giving permits does not hold regular meetings (Ibid). Furthermore, working groups in the Cusco region do not cooperate with each other or interact within the work environment in order to create effective professional management teams. According to Sotillo, to date there have been no formal public meetings explaining the needs and strategies for the region to the local population. Identifying value in a potential resort operation is dependent on evaluating the environment as well as social and economic factors central to its success. Hotel developers and owners will place the most emphasis on ensuring the operation will offer a return on investment that is commensurate with the risk to the investment capital. This can be a dangerous viewpoint for evaluating the market for a sustainable resort development (Parker and Khare 2005, p. 36). An initial cost benefit analysis may prove attractive and motivate an entrepreneur to undertake project development based only on the financial rewards of building a sustainable resort in a World Heritage destination, assuming that these rewards will provide the money to support community projects and provide protection for the environment (Ibid). Understanding complex success factors will take time and require first hand investigation of proposed sites and some level of initial community discussion in the Cusco region over the project potential. It is at this early stage that most entrepreneurs, interested in investing in Peru, will have the best opportunity to mitigate risks to the investment by understanding the project's challenges and potentials (Ibid).

Competitive Cluster Approach: Cusco

Resort development in a World Heritage Site will continue to see growth. The hospitality industry is thus at the very core of the globalization of international business (Wang and Wang 2009, p. 57). Hospitality companies, therefore, need to consider the implications of the global context in which they operate and must be prepared to address the questions that arise from this changing environment. Tourism activity within the World Heritage designation creates a commercial sector, or market in which goods and services are produced for sale (Prideaux 2000, p. 227). In essence, the economic factor of demand is the process that alerts potential tourists to the existence of a particular destination such as a resort and leads to travel to that destination

(Ibid). In essence, the resort market is the location where goods and services are produced and sold (Ibid). World Heritage designation and resort development formulation can be illustrated by the effect of a range of demand and supply forces on a resort development located in the region of Cusco. Some assumptions include:

1. The price system operates in a manner that matches the demand for resorts in the Cusco region with the quantity which suppliers and investors are willing to produce.
2. Supply forces create the conditions necessary to stimulate further development in the Cusco region
3. Demand factors can be manipulated by factors such as advertising and marketing the Peru brand and the World Heritage designation to create demand for the services provided by the resort development
4. Demand conditions relate to the reaction of tourists faced with a choice of a holiday destination.
5. Resort developments are assumed to include the private sector as well as relevant public sector interests. Privately own resort developments are assumed to be profit maximizers.
6. Equilibrium point occurs where demand for sustainable resort development equals supply of resorts at a given price.
7. Access cost refers to the cost of transport from tourism-generated regions to the resort (Prideaux 2000, p. 228).

Clearly, the strategic issues surrounding resort development will require collaborative action. Porter's Diamond Model affirms that the competitive advantage of a hotel developer at the destination level will be determined by four fundamental elements, which, when combined, form the four points of the competitive diamond (Hawkins 2004, p. 296). These elements and their interaction with one another explain how the resort development industry remains innovative and competitive within a World Heritage Destination (Ibid). The four points are factor conditions; demand conditions; related support sectors; and strategy, structure and rivalry among firms (Ibid).

Factor Conditions

Economic theory suggests that successful destination's basic resources, which include land, human resources and capital, determine the competitive advantage (Hawkins 2004). The Cusco region has been able to sustain its cultural heritage while advancing in other competitive areas such as educational systems, technology and currently developing specialized infrastructure that will be able to sustain a capacity increase to the destination. Of particular attention is the addition of culinary offerings that are attracting a wide array of visitors to the region. Peruvian cuisine is being branded and marketed globally and the government is currently financing and marketing the Peru brand through social media outlets.

Demand Conditions

It appears that, as globalization advances, the local market will become insignificant. However, current research and discussions with Mario Sotillo, Vladimir Gamarra and Aldo Serrano suggest that there are high expectations by local consumers which are driving firms to a more competitive and innovative position. A number of these resorts are taking into consideration a code of practice that is being certified by a national eco-rating program as part of the sustainable innovation practices in a competitive destination. Resorts are becoming more competitive in the local market and promoting optional dates and commercial discounts for regional customers and off-season packages to attract the local market.

Related Support Sectors

The existence of specialized and efficient support industries helps foster competition in destinations by allowing the cluster to have lower costs, superior quality and rapid product turnover rates. This has been the case of additional resorts, restaurants, transportation systems and destination management organizations that are contributing to the success of the region.

Firm Strategy, Structure and Rivalry

Competition is dependent upon an environment that promotes innovation and efficiency. The current regional airport in the Cusco region, Velasco Astete, is being upgraded to receive additional national and international visitors to the region. Consequently, the number of flights and airlines traveling to Cusco from other regions of Peru has dramatically increased. According to Vladimir Gamarra, the number of flights has doubled in the past 3 years. The effectiveness of the cluster is forcing firms to reduce costs in order to stay competitive while improving quality, and developing new markets.

Additional Factors

More important than each individual sector or element of the diamond is the interaction between each linked group. According to Sotillo, Gamarra and Serrano, the stakeholders in the region are currently informally working together to increase the quality of the services being provided and are continuing to improve sustainable practices that are important to the preservation and maintenance of the region.

The Peruvian government is also playing a significant role in the cluster development by maintaining order, facilitating technology advances, and eradicating terrorism.

Conclusion

The protection, enhancement and improvement of the various components of man's environment are the fundamental conditions for the harmonious development of tourism. Similarly, rational management of tourism may contribute, to a large extent, to protecting and developing the physical environment and cultural heritage, as well as improving the quality of life (Drost 1996, p. 481). Tourism is often seen as a tool for increasing economic activity in developing countries. New tourist complexes and services are rapidly being constructed in the region of Cusco, which includes the Urubamba valley and goes as far as the Colca valley region, with the given justification being an increase in demand and economic opportunities for the local population. Since UNESCO listed the area of Cusco as a cultural World Heritage Site, the area has become one of Peru's major cultural destinations. However, the relationship between the Cusco region, the local community and cultural tourism has become one of contradiction and confusion. Furthermore, a general landscape of inappropriate architectural change has occurred which is inconsistent with World Heritage Site status in the area.

Most opposition to sustainable development exists because of a lack of access to resources and information. The working models and successful frameworks needed to achieve sustainable development are available, and this is no longer considered a risky endeavour into unknown territory. Businesses in a World Heritage destination can, in fact, be both competitive and sustainably developed in an increasingly hierarchically flattening and competitive world. The concept of sustainable development is malleable; it should be shaped to fit a range of world views and location-specific factors. Stakeholder collaboration, such as the Imagine Calgary model previously mentioned, has been offered as one way of achieving this in Peru. Furthermore, the importance of collaboration as a process of joint decision making among key stakeholders of the Cusco region with regard to the future of the Cusco region has been accepted by many studying inter-organizational relationships in tourism settings, and community participation in decision making in particular.

However, defining World Heritage site stakeholder groups in locations such as Cusco is exceptionally problematic. There are stakeholders whose right to participation is based on economic, social, spatial or temporal qualities, and deciding on equitable decision-making that affects the community of Cusco is of considerations rather than on personal or financial investment. Consequently, assigning equitable decision-making power as these choices effect the community of Cusco becomes a complex and contentious process. Simpson has noted that specific examples of community involvement in the planning process are rare. If it does occur in the region of Cusco, input will likely be restricted to consultation in relation to strategies developed by formal planning bodies, rather than active participation in strategy development. On occasions where genuine community participation has been sought, the difficulty of achieving any form of equitable consensus has resulted in unsatisfactory outcomes.

Comprehensive, long-term planning can help cities foresee and overcome problems of rapid urbanization and resort overdevelopment. Cities that emphasize walking, cycling and public transportation are healthier financially and spend less of their wealth on transport costs. Sustainable development is still far from accomplished, and there is significant room for innovation to achieve genuine sustainability. The World Heritage Sites and the government of Peru are increasing budgets for research and development regarding eco-innovation and eco-technologies, but more needs to be done. In addition, resort development companies are still inexperienced in handling environmental issues. However, companies which are able to soonest identify opportunities and embrace innovation-based solutions will garner major competitive advantages. Regardless of the new resort developments in the region, the World Heritage brand will be pivotal to the marketing effort for the region. The World Heritage brand has the potential to increase Cusco's global exposure and distinction and will encourage support and preservation of the destination. Based on the research, it is recommended that the World Heritage organization continues to collaborate with hotel and resort operators, tour operators, and destination development organizations. It is further recommended that there be on-going support from museums, historical sites, religious sites and culinary destinations in sustaining the Cusco brand.

Despite the progress made in Cusco, it is clear that additional support, workshops and pilot projects will be needed in order for industry stakeholders in the Cusco region to exchange information regarding on-going research and practices relating to World Heritage Site developments. The findings of this study have indicated that local communities within the Cusco region have a positive attitude towards sustainable tourism development, and this response engenders the following:

- Provide education and learning programs for the local community to enhance their understanding of sustainable resort development, and the role of such projects in the protection of the Cusco region so that it retains its World Heritage Status.
- Assist small business owners such as small hotel operators; bed and breakfast operations, and hostels by equipping them with the skills and knowledge to develop products that lead to sustainable use of resources.
- Develop clear strategies that will bring a balance between the sustainable use of the natural resources in the Cusco region and the aim of meeting the intended long-term goals of the local and national government and the survival of small businesses.

As a follow-up to these findings, further research is necessary to discern whether local community members have adapted to sustainable practices and product development. It will also be of interest to see the evolving impact on the destination's economy as a result of Cusco's World Heritage designation.

References

(1992) Tourists for conservation. Interview: Hector Ceballos-Lascurain. People Planet 1(3): 28–30. Accessed from MEDLINE with Full Text database

Adams J (2010) Interrogating the equity principle: the rhetoric and reality of management planning for sustainable archaeological heritage tourism. J Herit Tourism 5(2):103–123

Akama JS, Kieti D (2007) Tourism and socio-economic development in developing countries: a case study of Mombasa Resort in Kenya. J Sustain Tourism 15(6):735–748

Caruso G (2007) Shining path: Guerrilla war in Peru's Northern Highlands, 1980–1997 - by Lewis Taylor. J Agrar Change 7(4):572–576

Drost A (1996) Developing sustainable tourism for world heritage sites. Ann Tourism Res 23(2):479–492

Du Cros H (2007) Too much of a good thing? Visitor congestion management issues for popular world heritage tourist attractions. J Herit Tourism 2(3):225–238

Ernoul L (2009) Residents' perception of tourist development and the environment: a study from Morocco. Int J Sustain Dev World Ecol 16(4):228–233

Gilmore A, Carson D, Ascencao M (2007) Sustainable tourism marketing at a world heritage site. J Strat Market 15:253–264

Green Globe (2010) Green Globe: the premier global certification for sustainability. http://www.greenglobe.com/. Accessed 18 Oct 2010

Hawkins D (2004) Sustainable tourism competitiveness cluster: application to world heritage sites network development in Indonesia. Asia Pac J Tourism Res 9(3):294–307

Honey M (2008) Ecotourism and sustainable development: who owns paradise? 2nd edn. Island Press, Washington, DC

Imagine Calgary (2010) Imagine Calgary: plan for long-range urban sustainability. http://www.imaginecalgary.ca/imagineCALGARY_plan.php. Accessed 17 Oct 2010

Inkaterra (2010) Inkaterra hotels sustainable program. http://www.inkaterra.com/en/carbon-neutral/sti-partnership. Accessed 18 Oct 2010

International Center for Sustainable Cities (2010) Sustainable cities: five approaches to long-term planning. http://sustainablecities.net/. Accessed 17 Oct 2010

Kiswar (2011) Sustainable tourism. http://www.kiswar.com/. Accessed 15 May 2011

Ladkin A, Bertramini A (2002) Collaborative tourism planning: a case study of Cusco, Peru. Curr Issue Tourism 5(2):71

Landorf C (2009) Managing for sustainable tourism: a review of six cultural world heritage sites. J Sustain Tourism 17(1):53–70

McGrath G (2004) Including the outsiders: the contribution of guides to integrated heritage tourism management in Cusco, Southern Peru. Curr Issue Tourism 7(4/5):426–432

Magee J (2005) Sustainable resort development: case study from Australia that make business sense. Columbia University, New York, NY

Nunkoo R, Ramkissoon H (2010) Modeling community support for a proposed integrated resort project. J Sustain Tourism 18(2):257–277

Nzama AT (2008) The promotion of sustainable tourism within the world heritage sites: lessons from iSimangaliso world heritage park in South Africa. J Tourism 9(2):161–177

Parker S, Khare A (2005) Understanding success factors for ensuring sustainability in ecotourism development in Southern Africa. J Ecotourism 4(1):32–46

Prideaux B (2000) The resort development spectrum - a new approach to modeling resort development. Tourism Manag 21(3):225

Ritchie JB, Crouch G (2003) The competitive destination: a sustainable tourism perspective. CABI Publishing, Cambridge, MA

Robson C (2002) Real world research: a resource for social scientists and practitioner-researchers, 2nd edn. John Wiley & Sons, Etobicoke, ON

Stronza A, Pegas F (2008) Ecotourism and conservation: two cases from Brazil and Peru. Hum Dimens Wildl 13:263–279

Tucker H, Emge A (2010) Managing a world heritage site: the case of Cappadocia. Anatolia 21(1):41–54

Wang J, Wang J (2009) Issues, challenges, and trends, that are facing hospitality industry. Manag Sci Eng 3(4)

Part II
Information Technology Track

E-Voting Technologies Usability: A Critical Element for Enabling Successful Elections

Jeffrey Hsu and Gary Bronson

Abstract The focus of this paper is to examine electronic voting technologies from the perspective of usability in controlled environments. Voting has been an accepted means for electing candidates, receiving public approval for referendums and budgets, and for many other tasks where the will of the people, whether a broad population or a select group, can be recorded and measured in a tangible way. Because of advances in technology, together with problems inherent in manual forms of voting, the concepts and issues relating to electronic voting (e-voting) and various other technology-based forms, are been proposed, discussed, and examined. The goal of all such systems is the casting and recording of the votes from eligible voters as they intended to be cast, with adequate security. This security requires that there be no identifiable connection between the voter and the vote that is cast, while providing an audit trail that can be used to validate that every vote was counted and tallied, as cast. Current research has shown that such systems form the majority of the nascent e-voting technologies, primarily because they have come closest to solving the usability and security issues inherent in technology-based voting systems.

Keywords Direct Recording Electronic Machine (DREs) • Electronic voting • Internet voting • Optical mark recognition • Usability • Voter-Verified Paper Audit Trail (VVPAT)

Background

One of the most critical elements of democracy is to enable voting and elections for candidates, referendum issues, and other matters of critical importance. As a result, the technologies used to support and ensure accurate recording, storing, and reporting of voting results need to be reliable, and resistant to fraud and tampering. In

J. Hsu (✉) • G. Bronson
Silberman College of Business, Information Systems and Decision Sciences Department, Fairleigh Dickinson University, Madison, NJ 07940, USA
e-mail: jeff@fdu.edu; grbronso@fdu.edu

L. Tadj, A.K. Garg (eds.), *Emerging Challenges in Business, Optimization, Technology, and Industry*, Springer Proceedings in Business and Economics, DOI 10.1007/978-3-319-58589-5_5

Table 1 Major categories of electronic voting technologies

Electronic voting technology	Methodology
Direct Recording Electronic (DRE) machines	Votes are cast on a computer touch screen and counted as they are cast
Electronic Ballot Printers (EBPs)	A touch screen produces a machine-readable paper ballot, which is subsequently read by a vote-counting scanner
Optical Mark Recognition (OMR) systems	Specially marked ballots are scanned and counted
Internet Voting	Votes are cast using the Internet to a central vote-counting computer

Table 2 Major associated advantages and disadvantages of e-voting

Anticipated advantage	Associated disadvantage
Speed of tabulation	Security
Accuracy of tabulation	Lack of standards
Convenience	Lack of transparency and openness
Increased participation	Lack of verifiable audits
Increased fraud prevention	Increased fraud
Long-term labor cost savings	Increased maintenance costs
Increased user accessibility	Legal conflicts

addition, they need to be clearly understandable, be designed to reduce user mistakes and errors, and also allow for the accessibility for users with disabilities.

In an age where the Internet, advanced computer technologies, and other advances have taken hold, there is a sense that voting has been left behind somewhat in the technological revolution. Many elections are still being conducted using paper ballots, mechanical lever devices, and punch cards. At the same time, there are readily available electronic devices that are much more sophisticated and can replace the manual means currently being used (Everett 2007; Jones 2003). Table 1 lists the four major categories of e-voting technologies:

Table 2 lists the major anticipated advantages expected from electronic voting, regardless of the technology used, along with current concerns and their associated disadvantages.

Voting technologies have been given less attention than other kinds of information systems, especially in relation to usability and user interface aspects, so a careful examination of the research and findings in this area would be useful and valuable. Much of the voting done today is still conducted using paper ballots and manual counting, or machines whose technology dates back to the late nineteenth century (Jones 2003, 2006).

The objective of this paper is to provide a comprehensive look at e-voting technologies, from the perspective of usability and security, within a controlled environment. A controlled environment is one where voting is conducted in centralized polling places. A key feature of this type of environment is that it provides a clear mechanism separating voter identification and authentication from the vote casting process. Although this particular mechanism is not a necessary condition for e-voting, as other separation mechanisms are possible and presented, by separating the authentication process from the actual voting and tallying process, it places the emphasis on the e-voting system's ability to correctly record and tally all of the votes while providing a reliable audit trail.

That a controlled environment is not a pre-requisite for e-voting has been demonstrated in Estonia, which has advanced the furthest in using a non-controlled environment by implementing Internet voting (Alvarez et al. 2009). In this type of an uncontrolled environment, there is no supervision of either the voter or voting machine. Thus, voting can take place at home, on a personal computer, on a mobile device, or a publically available computer location. Therefore, concerns about secrecy, authentication, and voter-intimidation all come into play. Currently, despite the Estonian experience, there is currently no form of Internet voting that has been able to provide definitive solution to all of these concerns (IDEA Policy paper 2011). As such, this paper will be concerned with e-voting within a controlled voting environment. In this paper, the problems, shortcomings, and risks involved with specific kinds of voting technologies, in relation to usability and accessibility, within a controlled environment are explored and a conceptual framework for evaluating e-voting usability is presented. Finally, the future of voting technologies usability and opportunities for future research are presented.

History and Evolution of Voting Technologies

Voting itself has had a long history, and has taken many forms, but has for the most part, been a task accomplished without much in the way of advanced technologies. It could be said that voting technologies have lagged behind information technologies used in many other areas.

To start, the term "ballot" is derived from the Italian word for "ball," and comes from an ancient technique where balls were put into a box to represent votes cast. Later manual forms included pieces of paper, political party tickets, and even ballots printed as newspaper advertisements (Everett 2007; Jones 2003).

Even today, paper ballots are still used in many U.S. rural communities, in many municipalities of developed nations, and for many elections of smaller scale (Everett 2007; Jones 2003).

The "mechanical lever system," invented in 1892, was used as early 1900, and was the predominant type of voting technology in the United States through the 1960s. While this device recorded and tabulated final total votes for each of the candidates, it did not keep a record of each individual voter's choices. The only connection between the individual vote and the vote cast was the machine number and ticket for that voter, which was primarily recorded on paper (Everett 2007; Zaino and Zaino 2004; Jones 2006).

Of more recent emergence, even though it may appear to be less advanced, is the punched card system. Because it was less expensive than mechanical lever systems, punched card voting systems came upon the scene in the 1960s and became the most popular voting device for some 30 years. It almost entirely replaced mechanical lever machines, which were largely discontinued in terms of manufacture in the early 1980s. The operation of a punched-card system is relatively simple: there is a paper ballot card, and using a clipboard-sized device, holes are punched for the candidate of choice. The holes are then used to tally the votes for a candidate, which can either be processed manually or fed into a reader to a computer for processing (Everett 2007; Jones 2003; Jones 2006).

Problems associated with punched card ballots are votes not counted due to multiple selections, unreadable cards, cards where holes are not fully punched out (known as "hanging chads"), and blank cards. In a comparison of various methods, punch cards were shown to be one of the least reliable methods.

In the United States, one of the outcomes of the 2000 presidential election crisis was the passing of the Help America Vote Act (HAVA) by Congress in the Fall of 2002. The purpose of this legislation was to provide both funding and implementation assistance to states to improve their voting systems and procedures. This was the first major federal investment toward improving the election system in the history of the nation, and the first election-oriented legislation enacted since the voting rights act of 1965. Some of the key goals of this act, aside from funding the improvement in technologies used for elections (in particular, from paper and more manual methods to DRE systems) was the focus on several important needs and goals for the machines. These included vote verification, notification and correction of errors, providing ballots in languages aside from English, and managing the needs of persons with disabilities (Everett 2007; Zaino and Zaino 2004).

Optical scanning machines are another form of technology, which have been used for voting. Much like the technology used for standardized tests of various kinds (ScanTron is a commonly used device), it involves the use of specialized forms on which there are specialized circles, bubbles or rectangles printed. A voter would select a candidate or response, and indicate by filling in the corresponding item on the form. One of the issues with this kind of technology arises in the case of improperly recorded selections. If someone was to erase a previously made choice, makes stray marks, or the like, errors may occur and the vote be recorded improperly or not at all. Optical scanning systems represent a lower cost option compared with more costly DRE systems. There are optical scan devices that count the votes at each precinct (allowing voters to correct errors), and in other cases are collected and then scanned at a central location (Everett 2007; Norden et al. 2006; Zaino and Zaino 2004).

The most technologically advanced voting devices currently in use are DRE touch screen systems (see Table 1). The term DRE stands for Direct Recording Electronic, and typically conducts the voting process using a touch-screen display or other display unit. In the simplest form of this machine, a voter walks up to the device booth, is either pre-authenticated by polling personnel or authenticates oneself with either a smart card or a token, and then indicates his/her choices by touching selections on the screen. There are "full-face DRE" systems where all of the races, candidates, and amendments are displayed on the screen and the voter needs to indicate his/her choices using buttons on the screen. This is in contrast to "scrolling DRE" systems (Conrad et al. 2009; Everett 2007; Norden et al. 2006).

In terms of usage, DRE technology progress was slow prior to the 2000 United States presidential election, after which calls for improvements to voting systems received increased attention and gained momentum. Many states have moved from other types of voting to using DRE technology. However, it is reported that as of 2004, less than 30% of the total votes were cast using DRE machines. In 2006, roughly 34% of all counties in the United States were using DREs, with votes cast by more than 60 million people.

Security

One of the major initial concerns of e-voting is security. Not only should the tally of finalized votes, but also the confidentiality of individual votes, should be safeguarded. This includes initial authentication that the voter is who he/she identifies themselves as, and an audit trail that can be used to verify that the vote tallied accurately matches the vote cast, without specifically identifying the voter.

In a controlled environment, the authentication process is separated from the voting process by individual voter verification prior to any voting. This can also be accomplished by an identity card and a corresponding PIN verification or thumb scan. At present, only Estonia provides this later type of verification system using a national identity card and PIN verification (Alvarez et al. 2009).

The second step in the security procedure relies on a viable audit-trail. At present, the concept of a Voter Verified Paper Trail (VVPAT) system, a concept introduced by Rebecca Mercuri (Mercuri 2002), has taken center stage for providing a viable audit trail. In practice, a paper trail can only fully verify e-voting results if all the paper verifying ballots are counted, which is impractical due to time considerations. An alternative is to define a sampling procedure that can be used to randomly and quickly provide a confidence level for the e-voting results. Although the emphasis of this paper is on the usability of e-voting technologies, the necessity of being aware of the verification process underlies this usability factor, as the audit trail is always a paramount consideration in the final implemented and adopted e-voting systems. As will be seen, only those systems that both meet the usability factors to be presented and provide audit trails (almost all of which are of the VVPAT types) have been successfully adopted.

However, prior to focusing on issues related to the use of DREs, it is worthwhile considering e-voting in a non-controlled environment, which is typified by using the Internet. Because of the widespread use and availability of the Internet, it has been argued that this is an ideal medium from which to conduct elections. In practice, the Internet reduces or eliminates the need for persons to travel to election locations, and can remove barriers for people with mobility and accessibility limitations.

It would also offer wider availability in terms of access times, and avoid the problems inherent in other voting methods and means. However, the use of the Internet for e-voting brings up a host of issues and concerns that are yet to be solved (Everett 2007; Norden et al. 2006). Many of these issues have plagued the security of the Internet in general and include the impact of viruses, denial of service attacks, and other security risks. Thus, despite its apparent convenience and seeming appropriateness, Internet voting could have a large-scale catastrophic effect, especially in the case of service interruption or disruption, and contested outcomes (Mercuri 2002). Currently, only Estonia, which has a verifiable national identity system, a unique political, legal, and cultural framework, and a highly integrated internet infrastructure, has implemented this type of voting (Alvarez et al. 2009).

In addition to the vulnerability of the Internet infrastructure itself, individual computers attached to the system form a highly vulnerable voting platform. This includes the installation of malicious software designed to manipulate the operation. Additionally, many computers are not kept in secure locations, and can easily be compromised. Attacks of this nature can also occur from the Internet as well, in the form of worms and viruses (Rubin 2002). The domain name system (DNS) is also a vulnerable point of weakness, in that by using what is called a cache poisoning attack, it is possible to change the information relating to domain names and IP addresses. In effect, a voter could type into a browser the correct URL, only to be directed to a different web server, which is controlled not by the election authority but by an adversary intending to manipulate the process, or prevent votes from being cast. This could be circumvented by knowledgeable users, but it is uncertain how many end users are familiar with the arcane process of certifying the authenticity of server certificates (Rubin 2002).

Further Security Considerations

There are several different available DRE units, with all of the major manufacturers offering proprietary software to be used in conjunction with the DRE devices. Three of the major firms include Dominion Voting, Sequoia Systems (acquired by Dominion), Hart Intercivic, and Election Systems and Software. This introduces the problem of proprietary software.

Because the software code for voting machines is currently proprietary, whether it is vulnerable to security problems is a guarded secret. As a result, the ability to capitalize on and manipulate elections through flaws and security weaknesses in the software can be exploited for political gain. As a result, there have been calls to implement widely the voluntary voting system guidelines and a voter-verified paper audit trail (VVPAT), described above. These provide some stated and specific guidelines for voting system certification (equipment, documentation, testing), and guidelines for providing voters with a receipt of their vote(s) for verification purposes, respectively. Both of these are discussed in greater detail later in this paper.

Regardless of the DRE being used, however, there are major problems inherent and associated with the current technology. DRE touch-screen machines have been associated with the terms "vote scam" and "black box voting," and are regarded as being unreliable by opponents. The reasons for these negative reactions include the lack of vote verification, as the voter does not really know what the system is registering as their vote. The manipulation of the votes cast once inside the system, is also of concern, because, aside from viewing what is showing up on the screen, there is no guarantee that the software is actually recording the vote being displayed. In effect, someone is trusting the system to do what it says it would (Norden et al. 2006).

Usability

A system designed for a task as important as voting needs to be easily understood and be simple and easy to use, especially because it is intended to be used by a broad and diverse set of users, with varying educational, comprehension, and physical abilities.

In the previous sections, a number of different voting methods and technologies were introduced and discussed. These ranged from manual methods, to voting machines and equipment, to electronic technologies spanning from DREs to the Internet. While there is a great deal of diversity in terms of what methods are being used, the focus in this paper is on electronic technologies with a primary attention given to DRE systems (both full face and scrolling), because they are the primary types of systems in use. Although there are a number of issues related to electronic voting technologies, from the technical to the applied, the issue that is the focus of this paper is on the usability of a DRE e-voting machine.

The usability of an electronic voting machine is a measure of how well the system enables a voter to correctly cast a vote that is the voter's intended choice, if the system allows voting to be completed in a reasonably quick and efficient manner, and also if it can instill in the voter both confidence in the results, and satisfaction with the process (Everett 2007; Roseman and Stephenson 2005).

Usability implies that the voting system is clear, unambiguous, easy to use, and allow its users to have a sense of confidence and trust that their voting choices are being recorded accurately, and that their votes will be handled in a confidential and secure manner. Thus, a usable system must be "user-friendly" and be able to be easily understood by voters of different educational, cultural, and literacy backgrounds, but also in making accommodations for persons with disabilities. It would also pose a problem if a person cannot understand the operation of the machine, and as a result either cannot cast a vote, or inadvertently votes for a different candidate than the one originally desired.

This is especially important for e-voting, because little or no training is usually provided for the people doing the voting. Attempting to understand how to use the system is usually accomplished, quickly, during the few moments spent at the voting booth or location. Voters also come from different socioeconomic and educational levels, but they all need to accomplish the same task.

Table 3 Major identification of required DRE usability features

Type and size of display
Variable display elements
Activation method
Interaction devices
Audio, Braille, Languages
Write in mechanism
Review screen

In addition, because voting in many democratic countries and societies is considered a right and privilege, there must be a strong sense of trust in the voting methods and/or technologies used. Moreover, because of the fact that users generally see the e-voting machine screens and user interface for the first time when actually voting, there is a need to make any displayed vote to be as clear and unambiguous as possible. Of particular concern is whether it is clear which selection box or button corresponds to which candidate, how many choices are allowed, and whether the selected choice can be easily identified by the voter.

Although many states and districts now use DREs, there has not been a clear consensus on whether the use of DRE voting machines has resulted in greater satisfaction, faster completion times, or in reduced error rates, and while some work has been done in this area, the number of empirical studies appears to be fewer than for other kinds of specialized information systems (Norden et al. 2006).

Table 3 presents the key options and features required of a DRE, from a usability perspective, and the options required to meet these features are enumerated below.

Type and size of display. This relates to the size of the screen or panel, and other related factors including resolution, font size, and color versus monochrome displays. These can play an important part in terms of how usable a system is and also the level of accessibility to a wide range of voters. Can the display clearly present information to persons with less than perfect vision or other types of handicaps?

Variable display elements. This is concerned with the flexibility in which screen display can be changed, in terms of font size, resolution, colors, etc. and other factors. This would be helpful in the case of promoting accessibility for a wider variety of users. Greater flexibility is good, in that the information can be presented in different ways depending on the needs of users, including those with handicaps and visual deficiencies.

Activation Method. This means by which a voter session can be set up, or "reset" for receiving the next user's votes. This may involve the use of a card, controls operated by a poll worker, or the entry of an ID number. This is critical not only from a security and authentication perspective, and safeguards needs to be in place to prevent the same person from voting multiple times, for example.

Interaction devices. How does a voter interact with the system? It could involve the use of a touch screen, mouse, or other kinds of input. In addition, how does a user actually select a choice, through a button to be pressed, a selection area on the screen, or some other approach? The use of sound and tactile elements, window pop-ups, and signals to indicate if something has been or needs to be done, are all things that can influence how well a user interacts with the system.

Audio, Braille, Languages. This is intended for assuring accessibility, including the ability to announce the choices using speech, display of the races and choices in Braille, and other features designed to assist blind and visually impaired voters. The option to display options and other information in other languages can also be a design option.

Write in mechanism. How can write in votes be recorded? The most common form is to have a keyboard available that can allow someone to indicate his or her write-in choice. There also may be ways to write in a candidate using some kind of handwriting mechanism. An error to prevent is where a person submits both a listed candidate choice, and also enters a write-in choice.

Review Screen. This concerns the ability to review ones' choices before final entry into the system for tallying. This is important since there are concerns about whether the choices made have been entered correctly, and so this can help to alleviate concerns. One approach to a review screen is to provide the information on the screen for the voter to verify. This can be extended further to include a paper copy of the voter's choices that can be produced by the system, allowing for manual recounts and verification of the electronic votes. This later approach VVPAT (Voter Verified Paper Audit Trail) has an additional advantage, providing the voter with a way of verifying that his/her vote has been cast properly. Opponents believe that approach is flawed in that it may introduce privacy concerns, and being a set of paper votes, can be prone to tampering and manipulation.

Verification

As with many other kinds of transactions involving mechanical and electronic technologies (order, delivery, making a reservation, etc.), there should be some form of verification of the amount paid, choices made, or action performed, given to the user. This may be in the form of a message on-screen, a receipt, or an auditory confirmation, for example.

For e-voting systems, the issue centers on verification of a voter's selections. On many systems, including many mechanical lever devices and DREs, there is a lack of verification given to the user about the choices made. A person can of course scan and review the selections highlighted on the screen, however it would be ideal to allow for the formal review of a person's choices prior to the formal submission of votes. This is an important step, even given the fact that some studies have shown that often a user will not pay much attention to the selection after the choices have been made, and in the extreme case candidate names can be changed, races can be added or deleted, and the votes can be switched to other candidates, and in many cases the user will not notice the change (Everett 2007; Norden et al. 2006).

Because of this situation, there have been recommendations made to display a review screen at the end of every voting session, so that users can carefully review and verify their choices. Aside from displaying the races that the voter has participated in, together with the choices made, the system should advise the user of undervotes or overvotes or other errors, and also allow users to modify their choices and correct any errors that have been made. Undervotes occur when a voter does not select any choice in a single choice race, or does not select the maximum allowable choices on a multi-selection slate of candidates. Overvotes occur when there are too many choices made, such as when a voter is asked to select one candidate, but selects two or more instead (Everett 2007; Norden et al. 2006). The manner in handling undervotes and overvotes should also be addressed, since there is an easy means of notifying users of these potential problems on an electronic system.

Error Reduction

A key measure of a highly usable electronic voting system is one that helps to reduce user errors, and also allows for the user to correct errors in the case of mistakes. The minimization and management of errors is important, so that a user can be more effective in completing a voting task. The likelihood of errors can also be increased because of the voting environment, in that noise, distractions, and the many people present in the same room may be cause for focus and concentration to be more difficult. However, it is interesting to note that while performance can degrade under situations of high stress, the presence of moderate levels of stress may actually improve performance over similar situations with little stress (Wickens and Hollands 2000). The different kinds of voting errors are first listed in Table 4, and described in more detail below.

Errors of omission and errors of commission. Errors of omission refer to those errors that are made when something is not done. This could be in the form of not selecting a candidate on the ballot when it was intended to do so. An undervote could be considered an error of omission. An error of commission is an error that is

Table 4 Primary voting errors

Omission and Commission
Planning and Execution
Post-completion errors
Hits, Misses, False Alarms

made, such as voting for the wrong candidate or votes for more than the number intended, such as for two when one was the maximum (also known as overvotes) (Wickens and Hollands 2000).

Planning failures and execution failures. The classification of errors can also be done using the planning and execution failure categories, where the former is concerned with intentions and whether they are sufficient to bring about the expected result. The latter is focused on the situation where the intention is correct, but the user makes an error in the execution of the task. In terms of voting, slips and lapses fall into the category of execution errors, where the intention is correct but there is an error in the execution (Wickens and Hollands 2000; Reason 1990).

Postcompletion errors. This is another common error that occurs during voting, in that while a user completes most of the process, an error of omission occurs at the very end. A typical example of this might occur when someone is done selecting choices, and may even have reviewed them on the screen, but does not press a button or click a link to send the choices to the system (Wickens and Hollands 2000; Byrne and Bovair 1997).

Hits, Misses, False Alarms. The purpose of a DRE review screen is to allow a user to reviews one's choices and to confirm if all the selections made are correct. In more theoretical terms, this is a form of signal detection problem (Green and Swets 1966) where the user needs to distinguish a signal (error) from noise (correct choices). The possible outcomes from this review task would include hits, misses, and false alarms. In the first case, an error made is detected during the review. In the next, a person reviews all of the choices, but fails to uncover an error that has been made. The third possibility is where a problem (mistake or error) is reported however no error was actually made. This third outcome is more common when concerns about the accuracy and security of DREs are raised, and this heightened awareness also tends to reduce the number of misses. It is also interesting to note that satisfaction on an e-voting system does not necessarily correlate with performance. A system on which a user has optimal performance may not bring about the highest levels of satisfaction (Andre and Wickens 1995; Bailey 1993).

As mentioned previously, residual votes are a measure of the difference between the total valid votes cast and the number of ballot cast in total. In essence, it is a measure of the degree or proportion of error when compared with all the total votes cast. This has been used in previous studies to look at the error rates of voters, however there are complicating factors in the sense that it is difficult to tell whether an error was due to an abstention, or actually a result of an error by the voter. Since studies have shown that the rate of votes intending not to make a certain voting selection is less than 1%, higher rates tend to indicate that the design of the system or the ballot may be causing these errors (Herrnson et al. 2008). Kimball (2005) found that among the different kinds of DRE systems, the ones with a full panel of choices tended to have the highest residual vote rates, compared with those with a scrolling display or optical scan devices.

Finally, some general suggestions and observations can be made about using electronic voting systems and usability.

In general, because of the wide variety of users, it would be important not to assume that users have a certain level of technological ability, and to assume the minimum. In accordance with this, it would be a good idea to use as little technical jargon as possible, express instructions in simple and clear language, and to place relevant instructions in places where they can be readily observed and followed. Using consistent terms, symbols, icons, and others ways of directing the user would also help. Ballot design, a potential cause for voter problems, should be carefully considered, avoiding approaches which place the same candidate for the same office in different columns, or on different pages on a scrolling DRE system. These can bring about confusion and result in errors during the voting process. When designing a new ballot, it would be a good idea to do some usability testing on it before being using in a live election.

Offering voters the ability to both cast, and then review, votes, would also be helpful, since this will help to ensure satisfaction and confidence in the electronic voting system and process. Provide feedback on where a voter is in the process would also be helpful, together with providing feedback in the case of errors, and also allowing a user to easily correct any errors, if necessary.

Assessment of Usability

The three key measures of usability are correctness/effectiveness, efficiency, and satisfaction/confidence inherent in the voting process.

Correctness can be measured by the residual vote rate, efficiency is generally associated with the time needed to complete the task, and satisfaction or confidence are more subjective measures that can be assessed by surveys, questionnaires, or more qualitative measurements (Norden et al. 2006). This is related to a framework proposed by the National Institute of Standards and Technology, to use the ISO metrics detailed in ISO 9241–11. This breaks down the assessment of usability into three main metrics, which are satisfaction, effectiveness, and efficiency (Laskowski et al. 2004).

Satisfaction measures the subjective satisfaction of a voter using the system, and includes not only satisfaction in general, but also how confident users are that their votes were recorded accurately. In general, a survey or questionnaire using the system usability scale or SUS is used for this (Brooke 1996).

Efficiency measures generally relate to the amount of time needed to complete a task, and a higher level of efficiency generally relates to assuring that only an acceptable amount of time is needed to complete the voting task. A long length of time needed to complete a voting task, or a long wait associated with doing so, increases frustration and reduces the interest and willingness to vote. Additionally, it has been noted that there is a speed/accuracy tradeoff that must be taken into account.

Speed/Accuracy Trade Off. The speed/accuracy tradeoff is always present when voting, because while there is no specific time limit, the general expectation is that someone should not take a long time to vote in several races, and perhaps a public question or two. In general, while users tended to take the time to complete a task optimally, the pressure and stress of the voting task may result in a voter sacrificing accuracy for speed (Wickens and Hollands 2000; Fitts 1966).

Another issue that has emerged in terms of elections and balloting concerns the ordering of candidates on ballots. In many kinds of elections, previous studies have shown that a candidate's position on the ballot can have an impact on how many votes select that particular candidate. As would be expected, candidates that are listed first tend to be favored (Alvarez et al. 2006). In order to reduce the effect of ballot order, some ballots, whether paper or electronic, would alternate the candidates so that the different candidates would take turns being listed in various orders.

For instance, in Australia, there is a requirement for randomization of the candidate names, to avoid the bias of a fixed ballot order. This is one aspect which technology can play a positive role, in that a computer can easily randomize the order of the candidates and come up with an accurate tabulation of the results. If the order was changes on paper ballots, there would be a potential for error since election officials may get confused and start tallying based on the votes for a certain location on the ballot (King and Leigh 2009).

Ballot design, an issue brought to the forefront by the infamous butterfly ballot of the 2000 presidential election, showed that confusing arrangements of ballots can cause erroneous voting, and can often result in the election being decided in favor of the candidate who in fact had actually lost, if the votes were accurately cast. If a ballot has unnecessary complexity and/or inconsistencies, as in the case of the butterfly ballot, for example, then the possibilities of errors are increased. Other sources of problems include symbols used to indicate political parties, which can vary from using symbols to various animals. Instructions which are vague or misleading (such as asking the voter to vote for one, when there are multiple candidates together), can lead to confusion, with the resulting errors and problems (Alvarez et al. 2006).

Voting should also be a relatively quick process, especially if there are not an excessive number of races requiring votes at the same time. If there is a long wait and an unreasonable amount of time needed for persons to cast their votes, then frustration and dissatisfaction can result. From a longer term perspective, the experiences of a user during a certain election may also affect his or her interest or intention to vote in future elections (Roseman and Stephenson 2005).

Research Framework for E-Voting Usability (Table 5)

Table 5 E-voting usability research framework

Category	Issue/Factor	Manual voting implementation	e-voting implementation	e-voting research issues
Voting venue issues	Voter authentication and activation	By approved personnel at polling stations	Same as manual in a controlled environment or by national identity cards and PINs or fingerprint scans	Authentication in non-controlled environments
	Voter privacy	Shielded voter kiosks	Separation of paper voter audit trail from accepted e-vote	Connection between actual vote and e-vote that provides an audit trail without revealing voter identity
Voting system	Display size	Not applicable	Depends on the range of users and system implementation options	Determination of an optimal size and accessibility
	Display elements (font, color, braille, sound, foreign languages)	Visual elements set at time of printing. Sound elements not available	Variable and can easily be modified to accommodate sight requirements of users, foreign language needs	Determine ranges for fonts, and availability of sound for sight impaired
	Display interaction	Mechanical levers or pencil marks or punch-outs	Typically touch screen; sometimes mouse or stylus	Consideration of options such as buttons or mouse
Verification	Vote review	Visual	Availability of changing votes on the screen	Determination of effective methods of providing review and changes Errors during voting
	Vote tally	Mechanical or optical	Software	Open source vs. proprietary software issues
	Audit trail	Paper recounts	Voter-verified paper audit trail (VVPAT)	Usefulness of VVPAT Confidentiality
	Audit speed	Limited by recount time	Random sampling of the paper trail	Optimum and time efficient sampling algorithms

(continued)

Table 5 (continued)

Category	Issue/Factor	Manual voting implementation	e-voting implementation	e-voting research issues
Error management	Error of omission	Votes may or may not be reviewed prior to submission	System may warn of missing votes	How common are these errors? How can these be avoided or reduced?
	Errors of commission	Votes may or may not be reviewed prior to submission	System may warn or prompt for confirmation. Error reported to voter	How common are these errors? How can these be avoided or reduced?
	Planning failures	May not be observable	May be observable in an experimental setting	How common are these errors? How can these be avoided or reduced?
	Execution failures	May not be observable	May be observable in an experimental setting	How common are these errors? How can these be avoided or reduced?
	Post completion errors	May not be observable	System may warn that process is not completed	How common are these errors? How can these be avoided or reduced?
Ballot and candidate order	Ballot design/ format	Depends on fixed design that is chosen and printed	Variable and can be set with different options	What is the optimal design for a certain voter type? Accessibility issues
	Candidate order	Depends on chosen order in printed ballot	Variable and can be set with different options	Influence of order in voter selection
Voter background	Individual differences	All voters receive the same ballot	Ballot may be variable based on system and options	Does a variable ballot format affect the coting process? In what ways?
	Accessibility	Polling place accommodations	Display and ballot may be variable based on voter needs	Which accessibility issues are most critical?

Summary/Conclusion

The realm of e-voting is complex, as it evolved first from manual and then mechanical means, to the present day, where at least a good portion of the voting is being done using an electronically supported, computer-based device. This paper looks at e-voting, first from the perspective of history and evolution, and then in terms of what kinds of technologies are prevalent and in use today. From there, the objective was to look at e-voting technologies from the perspective of usability, first by defining usability as it relates to e-voting, and then to look at various aspects of usability (and to its related aspect, accessibility) that are relevant to the examination of e-voting systems.

The development of a research framework allows for the categorization and structuring of the aspects, which are most critical to examining the usability of e-voting systems. The main categories examined include voting venue issues, voting system elements, verification, error management, ballot and candidate order, and voter background.

In examining these issues, there are several conclusions that can be drawn. While e-voting systems such as DREs are in wide use and probably will be the dominant e-voting technology in use for some time, there are other considerations that go beyond the ability to ensure that the systems are easily understandable and easy to use, and that persons with handicaps and disabilities can properly understand the choices and cast a vote.

One issue is trust in the system. A votes need to feel assured, that a system developed by a commercial firm, using proprietary hardware and software, is actually recording and reporting the votes cast. A concern is the "black box" concept where the information (vote selection) goes in, but the voter is not sure what happens to their vote once it enters the system. Are there any review, controls, or auditing of the results? What about the possibility of vote rigging and vote fraud being done by the software?

Another is the security of the votes being cast. While the voter indeed knows what votes he/she had cast, how will the security and confidentiality of the votes be protected? At polling places, the booths and kiosks are shielded so that there is privacy when the votes are cast. In the case where VVPT is being used, it can provide for the confirmation by the voter, and also an opportunity for a manual recount, however having paper printouts can be a problem in terms of storage, security, and ensuring the privacy of each vote.

Finally, there is the concept of Internet-based voting, where there is no longer the necessity to travel to a polling place to cast a vote. This appears to be a viable option for the future of voting; however, it is extremely problematic in terms of security, authentication, and network issues, which render it not a viable possibility for the foreseeable future. However, this is an area that will attract, and deserves further attention, since the potential is great if these problems can be solved. This is a definite area for further research, since voting is a right and a privilege, and requiring that someone travel (especially someone with disabilities) to vote, may in some ways be disenfranchising that person from his/her right to vote.

Despite many advances in terms of better understanding user interface, usability, and security, there is comparatively less research being done on electronic voting technologies and how they can be made more usable and accessible, compared with other kinds of information systems.

In terms of technologies, further investigation into various usability features and designs of effective interfaces, especially in meeting the needs of persons with physical or learning disabilities, or language problems, is an area worth further investigation. Examining the current options available, and coming up with more innovative options would be one useful avenue for research. From there, research into an adaptive and accessible e-voting system could also be investigated. Instead of designing specific stations to meet a specific "special need," modifying the interface to meet the needs of the users, in an adaptive fashion, would be a useful area for investigation.

Additionally, there is a need for further investigation in terms of user interface design analyses for current e-voting systems, with the goal of seeing how usability might be improved with different combinations of screen designs, ballot arrangements, and supportive technology (audio, voice recognition) to allow for a better experience and to reduce errors.

Another area of investigation might be to see what kind of satisfaction levels and assessments can be attributed to a system that goes beyond the task of accepting and recording votes; instead this would involve enhancing the system to become a kind of voter "decision support" or "voter support" system, suitable for someone who has not kept up with the candidates, platforms, and issues. Aside from merely doing the task of collecting notes, the system could provide the necessary information to voters who have yet to make a choice on a candidate or issue, and would like to obtain further information before making a decision.

Finally, given the emphasis on wireless mobile devices, a logical area to explore would be the possibility and promise of mobile voting technologies and applications. While challenges do exist in this, much like Internet-based voting, the area does seem to hold promise if certain concerns and risks are able to be addressed.

The entire spectrum of considerations and issues for e-voting are vast and infinite, and the entire area is ripe with opportunities for further research and investigation.

References

107th U.S. Congress (2002) Help America vote act of 2002. U.S. Government Printing Office, Washington, D.C., pp 107–252. Retrieved 10 Oct 2008

Alvarez RM, Hall E, Trechel H (2009) Internet voting in Estonia. Political Science and Politics 42(3):497–505

Alvarez RM, Sinclair B, Hasen RL (2006) How much is enough? The "ballot order effect" and the use of social science research in election law disputes. Election Law Journal: Rules, Politics, and Policy 5(1):40–56

Andre AD, Wickens CD (1995) When users want what's not best for them. Ergon Des 3:10–14

Bailey RW (1993) Performance vs. preference. In: Proceedings of the human factors and ergonomics Society 37th annual meeting. Human Factors and Ergonomics Society, Santa Monica, CA, pp 282–286

Byrne MD, Bovair S (1997) A working memory model of a common procedural error. Cogn Sci 21:31–61
Brooke J (1996) SUS: a "quick and dirty" usability scale. In: Jordan PW, Thomas B, Weerdmeester BA, McClelland AL (eds) Usability evaluation in industry. Taylor and Francis, London, pp 189–194
Conrad FG et al (2009) Electronic voting eliminates hanging chads but introduces new usability challenges. International Journal of Human-Computer Studies 67:111–124
Conrad FG, Lewis B, Peytcheva E, Traugott M, Hanmer MJ, Herrnson PS (2006) The usability of electronic voting systems: results from a laboratory study. Paper presented at the Midwest Political Science Association, Chicago, IL. April 2006
Everett SP (2007) The usability of electronic voting machines and how votes can be changed without detection. Doctoral Dissertation, Rice University
Fitts PM (1966) Cognitive aspects of information processing III: set for speed versus accuracy. J Exp Psychol 71:849–857
Green DM, Swets JA (1966) Signal detection theory and psychophysics. John Wiley and Sons, New York
Gonzales CV (2012). The new Belgian e-voting system, EVOL2/e Voting Lab, unpublished paper
Herron MC, Sekhon JS (2003) Overvoting and representation: an examination of overvoted presidential ballots in Broward and Miami-Dade counties. Elect Stud 22:21–47
Herrnson PS et al (2008) Voters' evaluation of electronic voting systems. Am Polit Res 36(4):580–611.
IDEA (International Institute for Democracy and Electoral Assistance) (2011), Policy Paper
Jones DW (2003) A brief illustrated history of voting. http://www.Cs.Uiowa.Edu/~jones/voting/pictures/#ballota. Retrieved 23 Sept 2005
Jones DW (2006) Technologists as political reformers: lessons from the early history of voting machines. Presented at the Society for the History of Technology Annual Meeting, Las Vegas, 13 Oct 2006
Kimball DC (2005) Summary tables on voting technology and residual vote. http://www.umsl.edu/~kimballd/dk_vote.htm. Retrieved 5 Mar 2007
King A, Leigh A (2009) Are ballot order effects heterogeneous? Soc Sci Q 90(1):71–87
Laskowski SJ, Autry M, Cugini J, Killam W, Yen J (2004) Improving the usability and accessibility of voting systems and products. NIST Special Publication:500–256
McCrae RR, Costa PT Jr (2003) Personality in adulthood: a five-factor theory perspective, 2nd edn. The Guilford Press, New York
Mercuri R (2002) A better Ballot box? IEEE Spectr 39:46–50. October 2002
New York Times (2004) Gambling on voting. Opinion. 13 June 13 2004
Niemi RG, Herrnson PS (2003) Beyond the butterfly: the complexity of U.S. ballots. Perspect Polit 1(2):317–326
Norden L et al (2006) The machinery of democracy: voting system security, accessibility, usability, and cost. Brennan Center for Justice, New York
Reason J (1990) Human error. Cambridge University Press, Cambridge, UK
Roseman GH Jr, Stephenson EF (2005) The effect of voting technology on voter turnout: do computers scare the elderly? Public Choice 123:39–47
Rubin A (2002) Security considerations for remote electronic voting. Commun ACM 45(12):39–44
Traugott MW, Hanmer MJ, Park W-H, Herrnson PS, Niemi RG, Bederson BB, Conrad FG (2005) The impact of voting systems on residual votes, incomplete ballots, and other measures of voting behavior. Paper presented at the annual conference of the Midwest Political Science Association, Chicago, IL, 7–10 April
Trewin S (2006) Physical usability and the mobile web. In: Proceedings of the 2006 International cross-disciplinary workshop on web accessibility (W4a). ACM Press, New York, pp 109–112
Wickens CD, Hollands JG (2000) Engineering psychology and human performance, 3rd edn. Prentice Hall, Upper Saddle River, NJ
Zaino J, Zaino J (2004) A new era in voting technologies. Dispute Resolution Journal 59(3):10–21

Big Data Revolution: Is It a Business Disruption?

Mohamed K. Sheriff

Abstract This paper examines big data revolution and whether big data intertwined with analytics would disrupt the culture, data architecture, data structure, management and security of business, which in turn could fundamentally transform the way business compete, operate, develop product and product profitability. The variety, velocity, veracity, and volume of a typical twentieth-century business data and traditional technology are contrasted against the twenty-first-century business data and innovative technology. The final hypothesis is that big data revolution intertwined with analytics is an innovation that is transforming business. Therefore, there is a need for more businesses to adopt and benefit from big data technology. After close and critical review of big data technology intertwined with analytics, it is argued that a fruitful approach would be the development of a suitable Information Technology and Computer Science academic courses that would reflect big data technology.

Keywords Big data • Information technology • Traditional technology • Business

Introduction

Even though there was burgeoning World Trade Organization, prior to the turn of the twentieth century, marketing and business concepts and principles for consumers were still limited to a large extent to a brick and mortar business which was primarily local. Or at best subjected to catalogue shopping from a brick and mortar business that was primarily local or not far away. Why is that? In addition to the traditional technologies that were used in the twentieth century and other reasons, the promises that ecommerce brought with it in the mid and late 1990s did not seem to materialize as expected because at the end of the twentieth century the ecommerce bubble busted raising many questions and doubts on the minds of business

---

M.K. Sheriff (✉)
Administrative Sciences Department, Fairleigh Dickinson University,
Vancouver, BC, Canada, V6B 2P6
e-mail: msheriff@fdu.edu

L. Tadj, A.K. Garg (eds.), *Emerging Challenges in Business, Optimization, Technology, and Industry*, Springer Proceedings in Business and Economics,
DOI 10.1007/978-3-319-58589-5_6

leaders on whether the ecommerce business was a hype. That said IT investment and innovations in previous waves of IT enabled innovations, and in the area of productivity, transformed businesses. To what extent, that is debateable.

Furthermore, although there were personal computers on every desk in business organizations by the end of the twentieth century, the Enterprise Resource Planning (ERP) Information Systems (IS) in every business organization at the time was the only source of data collection. As such the veracity and variety of data was limited to one source thereby making the data in the said IS historical, incomplete and inaccurate when contrasted to twenty-first-century business data. In addition, the variety of data that was collected was primarily structured and limited to one source. Furthermore, there were few thousand petabytes of information (Lesk 1996) by the turn of the twentieth century, which can be extrapolated as the average volume and velocity of data collected annually for significant number of organizations was mostly around the gigabytes range or at best less than eight tetra bytes annually for significant amount of businesses.

In contrast, today (twenty-first century), in terms of variety, the technique of collecting data from many different sources and storing it in a common storage systems in which the data collected can be structured, semi-structured and unstructured was unheard of in the twentieth century or at best was not ubiquitous in business organizations by the end of the twentieth century. Equally important in terms of velocity, collecting tetra bytes or peta bytes of streaming data per day or in a week was also not ubiquitous in business organizations by the end of the twentieth century. In contrast, today, 2.5 Quintillion bytes of data are created every day, which exceeds by far the data that was around the turn of the twentieth century (Walker 2015).

As such, in the advent of big data technology, peta bytes of streaming data are now collected per day by businesses from smart phones, other mobile devices, and social media sites. The data that is collected is largely unstructured, which raises the question of how important the amount of data is for businesses? As such, what is the role and influences of big data on businesses? Is it in turn disrupting and transforming businesses, which in turn are influencing economic activities that in turn are impacting the development of societies? This paper is attempting to answer the said key questions. In answering the said questions, this paper will first define big data, followed by how we got to where we are about big data and its transformation on business.

What Is Big Data?

From the work done by John Mashey, Gartner, Open Data Center Alliance and others, big data is described as large, complex, and disparate volumes of data being created by people, tools, and machines. Hence, the traditional data processing methods and software of the twentieth century are inadequate to deal with big data in an effective and efficient way. In short, big data refers to massive amounts of data, the size and variety of which are beyond the processing capabilities of traditional data management tools to capture, manage, and analyze in a timely manner. As a result it requires new, innovative, and scalable technology to collect, host, and analytically process the vast amount of data gathered in order to derive real-time business insights and value that relate to culture, consumers, risk, profit, performance, and productivity management which in turn will enhance shareholder value hence transform business.

In a nut shell, because of big data business moving away from the twentieth-century traditional method of database and Information Technology (IT) of collecting and processing data to the twenty-first century, there is a need for a new innovative method of collecting and processing of huge amount data. Hence, the question becomes how did we get here and how has big data transform business institutions?

Twenty-First Century Business Data and Technology—Where Are We and Why?

Firstly, the typical tools, methods, and techniques used in the twentieth century could not extract tetra or peta bytes of data per day from different sources, neither can it collect them, nor can it store structure, semi-structure and unstructured data in the same infrastructure and also analyze the said data without a huge cost attached with it. Furthermore, the tools, methods, and techniques of the twentieth century could not manage the said data per day without a huge unsustainable cost or at least huge licenses cost, let alone manage the huge annual cumulative data. Equally important and in contrast to the twenty-first century, business data differ in volume, variety, veracity, and velocity (the four "Vs"). As a result there was no point in the twentieth century, in which data was a sole product of business or businesses, were developed that solely relies on streaming data as its primary product. Hence, there was no way companies like Twitter, Reddit, Facebook, YouTube, etc. would have thrived in the twentieth century. In short, the intangible was not a product (e.g., Twitter) rather the tangible was and examples of such tangible companies are manufacturing and physical producing asset companies. Therefore, the twentieth-century data technology had minimal influence on transforming businesses from developing intangible products, which was largely absent prior to the turning of the twenty-first century.

Consequently, by the end of the twentieth century, the collecting of streaming data in the tetra or peta bytes range by day and the use of it on businesses was largely absent which in turn had little impact on businesses and economic activities of countries primarily based on post-industrial and asset-based economics. Consequently, market size was small and limited hence a global market rather than a local one was a dream. The said dream in turn led to the need and creation of World Trade Organization with the expectation that the world will become a global village united together in business and network of businesses, which in turn will benefit the citizens of the world.

Given the prevalence of local markets and the challenges small and medium size businesses were facing in the areas of expansion and competing globally led to business being in the hands of handful of elite business people that were largely supported by governments. For example in the United Kingdom in the 1950s, 1960s, and 1970s, a citizen could spend his or her entire day moving from one organization to another or from taking a bus to work or to shopping, by moving from one joint venture owned by business elite and government to another owned by the same partners or owned by companies that are too big to fail. The same can be said for most countries at the time.

Furthermore, in the absence of big data technology, the fundamental principles of supply and demand before the turn of the twentieth century was fueled by the economics of scarcity. As such, supply and demand was in a state of perpetual reversible equilibrium. Hence, depending on the directional shift from demand to supply or vice versa, the price of products per service function changes for the worst. In effect, the influence of "people data" and "identity data" was either absent or largely minimal in significance, which in turn affected the impact of "smart data" which was minimal or non-existence in businesses.

That said, within the first decade of the twenty-first century, over two billion people have embraced the Internet. Currently, there are over 3.6 billion people who have access and are connected to the Internet (Miniwatts 2016). As a result of the rapid embracement of the Internet (with the extensive range of information and services such as the World Wide Web, etc.) in the first decade of the twenty-first century, a new business model called e-business/e-commerce reaches a crescendo of no return. The new business model deviated from the traditional brick and mortar model of doing business and marketing. What was the result? A virtual business and marketing model which is a major driver that created a new distributing channel. This channel has helped businesses gained access to a wider global market thereby making a global village ever nearer; this has resulted into attracting consumers all over the world hence fostering a sustained growth of national economies and also started the march toward a single global market place which is continuing at an accelerated pace.

In addition, it has led to the transformation of the previous domestic supply chain to the current global supply chain and value chain. Hence, a global value chain of procurement, manufacturing, and logistical activities performed by suppliers, companies, and logistics providers that provide the specific values that customers look for in the products and services they buy was born as a new model of doing business. It is preferred over a domestic supply chain because there are many opportunities in today's global economy to obtain higher valued goods and services from companies in foreign countries than might be available from domestic companies. Such a business model has given rise to online companies; examples of such companies are eBay, Amazon, etc.

Furthermore, online businesses provide easy access to information about opportunities as well as ways to transact them. This has led to the creation of many online businesses all over the place such as Reddit, Instagram, Twitter, and Facebook in the USA to similar online businesses in South East Asia, Middle East, and Africa.

Efficient use of e-business allows companies to increase their profits by reducing the cost of doing business. In many ways, e-business is the most significant catalyst to making global business more efficient and within the scope of more businesses. In a nutshell, if a business adds a significant "internet/Social Media" component to its marketing and sourcing, its global opportunities expand greatly. The interconnectivity provides and stores information, as a result shortens the supply chains because companies direct purchasing strategies, logistics, and supply management to the Internet.

Also, because business-to-business (B2B) relationships and business-to-consumer (B2C) interaction and communication have evolved around the Internet, it is relatively easier and cheaper, when compared to brick and mortal type of business, to create a very low operational cost for online business that is cost-effective, efficient, and highly profitable. This relative easiness, very low operational cost, and very high profit margin have inspired and given rise to new breed of young entrepreneurs that created companies such as Google, Facebook, etc. Such successful businesses by young entrepreneurs have transformed business and our behavior in that everyone and anyone with the drive and motivation can form their own companies and become millionaires or billionaires, which is different from the old establishment business elite model in which only the few with huge capital can do global business.

At the nucleus of the online businesses are the collection of huge amount of unstructured streaming data not only from websites but also from various Internet connecting sources such as smart phones, mobile devices, machine data, video, audio, corporate and technical documentation ranging from best practices, research reports, medical abstracts, problem reports, customer communications and contracts to emails and voice mails, etc. Many of these data collected are either structured, semi-structured, or unstructured data. The unstructured data are one of the largest and fastest growing of data available to businesses globally. In these stacks of streaming unstructured data often lies gob of information critical for realizing important trends and relationships for businesses thereby creating new opportunities, which in turn will lead to analyzing and solving problems thereby transforming business culture.

In contrast to the twentieth century, businesses can now leverage leading tools and techniques to harvest tetra or peta bytes of data per day. For example, in 2012 Wal-Mart was generating more than 2.5 petabytes (250 bytes) of data relating to more than 1 million customer transactions every hour (Open Data Center Alliance 2012) and on August 22, 2012 Facebook reported that its system processes 2.5 billion pieces of content (links, comments, etc.), and 500+ terabytes of data each day. Furthermore, it is pulling in 2.7 billion like actions and 300 million photos per day, and it scans roughly 105 terabytes of data each half hour (Constine 2012). Handling and analyzing such big data in the twenty-first century is very different from what was handled and analyzed by businesses in the twentieth century.

As such, big data has brought with it a paradigm shift of how we store and process data. Hence understanding the key features of this paradigm shift is essential for business transformation, which in turn has led to competitive advantage thereby bringing success. In effect, the transformation has occurred on the twentieth-century data architecture and structure because of the paradigm shifts caused by big data. How? Because of the following:

- More data is being captured and leveraged in a continuous process
  - With the traditional technique of the twentieth century, only a small subset of the available data that was captured was analyzed or is being analyzed whilst with using the big data technique all available data is analyzed.
  - Also, using the traditional technique of the twentieth century, data is analyzed after it is been processed and stored in a warehouse or mart whilst the big data technique analyzes streaming data as it is generated and in real time.
- Reduce effort required to leverage data
  - With the traditional technique of the twentieth century, data is carefully cleansed before any analysis whilst big data technique analyze information as is and cleanse as needed
- Data leads the way and sometimes correlations are good enough
  - Traditional technique starts with hypothesis and test against selected data while big data approach explore all data and identify correlations

Why the Paradigm Shift?

Firstly, the cost of storing and processing of huge amount of tetra or peta bytes of streaming data per day was very expensive and still remain so if the traditional structural database technique put forward by Edgar Codd (which was the technique used in the twentieth century) and later adopted by Oracle is used in the process. Consequently when it comes to big data, the traditional database method is called into question or has reached it limits or has run out of course as such traditional database methods need revision. Why? In continuing with the tradition database methods means businesses will pay huge amount of dollars on licenses fees and that will not be efficient for sustainable business operations that rely primarily on technology given that real-time scalability was also a serious issue in the twentieth century.

Furthermore, the technique to process structured, semi-structure, and unstructure data that are stored together particular unstructured data was mostly in research laboratory if existed at all by the end of the twentieth century. In short, the structural database technique and rules developed by Edgar Codd that was used in the twentieth century and was also the bedrock for database technology developed by major technology companies such as Oracle, Microsoft, IBM, etc., are inadequate to deal with the processing and storage of peta bytes of streaming data per day in a cost-effective manner, let alone the data that can be accumulated annually from such peta bytes of data per day.

Secondly and equally important, the twentieth-century traditional database methods, techniques, and structures developed by Edgar Codd and others for data systems were built with a predetermined set of data requirements. As a result, analytics results on twentieth-century business data were primarily historical reporting therefore the paradigm shift was inevitable. Why? Business was bent on harvesting and harnessing large volume and variety of data in an effective and efficient technique hence the shift to innovative technology of the twenty-first century.

Because of the limitations of the twentieth century, traditional technology businesses of the twenty-first century were not and are not thinking in the direction of using traditional database especially where big data is involved. As a result businesses such as Google, Amazon, Instagram, etc., developed an innovative way to collect, store, and process data that is different from the twentieth-century traditional Relational Database method of Edgar Codd, thereby transforming business operations. Hence, the twenty-first-century big data technology in which data storage platforms are not restricted to a predefined rigid data model, as such data systems are capable of handling structured, semi-structured and unstructured data, was born. As a result many companies such as MongoDB, Hardoop, and Cassandra, which focuses on document-oriented database, semi-structured, unstructured files were created and developed.

Consequently, the integration of structured, semi-structured, and unstructured data has led to the improvement of analytics reporting. As such, for businesses such as Facebook, Google, Amazon, Reddit, etc., big data intertwine with analytics in the twenty-first century has led to real-time reporting which has also led to a real-time decision. The said insight generated by the analytics has transformed businesses in a way that was not seen in the twentieth century. One such example is in the area of customer profiling in which businesses are now able to profile and predict their customer behavior, etc. Another example of the impact of big data and how it has transformed businesses is to look at how YouTube, Online Movie Channels, Google, eBay, and Amazon experience has changed.

By analyzing the vast array of data points that has been collected by the said businesses from different sources specifically in terms of what the customer did, these said businesses can now generate real-time generic and specific recommendations that are tailored for their tens of millions of customers. For these said businesses and more big data, revolution has improved their performance and creates a competitive advantage for them. As such, through big data analytics, insight decisions for customer satisfaction strategies are now made in a structural approach, which in turn has lead to marketing segmentation strategy, more customer acquisition and retention, which in turn has transformed business in the twenty-first century.

In contrast to the twentieth century, these capabilities, familiarities, and confidence were not found even though they were needed. Why is that? Despite the technological innovations and progress that was made in information technology in the twentieth century, traditional businesses struggled to federate customer information from variety of multiple systems and file formats (Word, PDFs, and Excel documents, pod cast, charts, images, scans, videos, etc.). For example, according to

International Data Corporation (IDC), unstructured data accounts for more than 90 percent of the data in today's organizations and unfit for traditional processing. Furthermore, according to the McKinsey Global Institute 15 out of 17 U.S. business sectors have more data stored per company than the U.S. Library of Congress. An example of one of these companies is Twitter which receives 200 million tweets per day—that is 46 megabytes per second (Open Data Center Alliance 2012). In addition. in 2010 Forrester reported that 62 percent of organizations use between 100 terabytes (TB) and 9 petabytes (PB) of data.

However, given all these statistics and in contrast to the traditional technique, which was the technique in the twentieth century, big data revolution intertwines with analytics has overcome the said traditional limitations in a cost-effective manner. In the process, big data technologies intertwine with analytics have made the federation and analysis of data from large variety of systems across an organization an ongoing business activity. Consequently, it has opened up opportunities to ingest, store, and process data from a variety of new sources such as mobile devices, external social media data (e.g., websites, blogs, etc.), emails, and marketing data, etc.; also it has led to the consolidation of customers, products, and sales data from various separate business departments.

The housing and intertwining of semi-structured, unstructured, and structured data in a single infrastructure have led to a federated vision of looking at customers, products, and sales in an effective and efficient manner. Furthermore, big data revolution intertwine with analytics has enabled the processing of unstructured data and have also increases system intelligence which has resulted in improve performance in sales, increase understanding of customer needs, support marketing initiatives, and enhance fraud monitoring. In short big data revolution has allowed businesses to integrate volume, variety, and veracity of data sources with relatively low effort in a short timeframe. Examples of businesses that have successfully transformed themselves by adopting the twenty-first-century big data revolution intertwine with analytics are Google, Facebook, Amazon, etc.

In the area of security, businesses such as Apple, Amazon, Google, etc., have used big data analytics to profile their customers so that they could sell or suggest products to their customer that they are likely to be interested in or will buy; or even advertise products or services to their customers. One method the said businesses have used to capture more data on their customers so that they could profile them is through the use of apps that are found on various mobile devices be it iPads, smart phones, or wearable technologies. The said businesses have developed apps or third parties have developed apps that are found in mobile devices for customer use. These apps could range from a shopping app to a fitness app, to apps use for finding business location, etc. When customers use these apps be it shopping apps or fitness app, enormous amount of data is collected which in turn is used to profile customers for potential sales or advertisement. How does the profiling works? The data collected is linked to an entity, which can be a unique identifier such as a user credentials, user account or user payment method such as a credit card number or unique meta-data, etc., from which a profile is built. For the process of profiling to continue unabatedly, businesses must earn the trust of their customers by making sure that their customers' data are not only safe but also privacy is also upheld. As a result, security is now transforming businesses in the twenty-first century in a way that it never did in the twentieth century.

Companies such as Reddit, Time Inc., News corporation Australia, Domain Group, infor, Gumi, SpaceApe, etc., which cannot handle the huge amount of streaming data per day, were forced to outsource their IT data operations hence the development of Utility Computing companies such as Google, Amazon, Drop Box, etc., which in turn has led to the transformation of IT business operations. During the twentieth century, utility computing companies were unheard because the prevailing culture at the time was for companies to have its own IT department handle all IT-related jobs and tasks. Today, because of big data some companies cannot keep pace with the amount of data that they should be storing, processing, and simultaneously do other IT-related tasks and jobs, as such companies are transforming their culture from in-house IT department to letting utility computing companies such as Amazon, Google, Drop Box do their IT-related tasks and jobs for them which in turn has led to a new business opportunity in IT utility. As electricity utility was to the twentieth century so also is utility computing is to be in the twenty-first century which in itself is a transformation.

Equally important, the development of innovative big data databases and software tools that has the infinite capacity to store, manipulate, and present information has also led to financial engineering paradigm that has helped transform derivatives pricing, portfolio management, risk management, trading, corporate financing, etc. At the core of financial engineering paradigm is big data revolution, as a result big data revolution has helped create a service-based digital economy that western hemisphere countries and South East Asian countries greatly relying on as a source of economic engine growth, which has inevitably necessitates changes not only in finance but also necessitates changes in the financial institutions and systems that were designed for a different era particularly for the twentieth century. Hence, resulting in an entirely new economy called the digital economy, which is a component of the knowledge and service economy.

Moreover, as a result of the digital economy which is fuel by big data technology which in turn is transforming online businesses, database mining, software to name a few, the measure of GDP has been transformed from measuring only tangible assets and finite resources (such as oil extraction) to now measuring tangible assets, intangible assets (such as databases, software, online businesses, etc.), finite resources and infinite resources (such as databases, software, online businesses, etc.). Using new estimates of employment and investment in Big Data as set out in Chebli, Goodridge et al. (2015) and Goodridge and Haskel (Goodridge and Haske 2015) and treating transformed data and data-based knowledge as capital assets, Goodridge and Haskel estimate that for the UK: (a) in 2012, "Big Data" assets added £1.6bn to market sector GVA; (b) in 2005–2012, account for 0.02% of growth in market sector value-added; (c) much Big Data activity is already captured in the official data on software – 76% of investment in Big Data is already included in official software investment, and 76% of the contribution of Big Data to GDP growth is also already in the software contribution; and (d) in the coming decade, data-based assets may contribute around 0.07–0.23% pa of annual growth on average. Information and Communications Technology Council (ICTC) estimates that Canada's big data service market generates approximately $1.1 billion annually in revenues. This market is expected to nearly double by 2020 as investments in big data services and infrastructure increase.

As the digital economics statistics information indicates, advances in big data technology have not only led to the globalization of businesses but have also led to the transformation of businesses, markets, and economics principles. As such, this has led to a new profiling and predictive global ecosystem for commerce. Consequently calling for the institutions and systems that were conceived for a different era as a result of cultural and political economic hegemonies to be reform, if they are to survive or continue to function effective and efficiently in the twenty-first century. The transformative and cultural power of big data has inevitably not only necessitates changes in the economy and business but has also necessitates changes in the institutions and systems that were designed for a different era. Thereby, creating a new economic paradigm called global digital economy, which is a component of the knowledge economy. For example, estimates of the existing global big data market vary from a low of $23.76 billion to $125 billion. The global big data market outlook for 2020 varies from a low of $76 billion to a high of $190 billion annually (ICTC 2015).

According to statista.com, as of the fourth-quarter of 2016, the microblogging service averaged at 319 million monthly active users (MAU). At the beginning of 2016, Twitter had reached 310 MAU per quarter. Therefore, through big data revolution, news media such as blogs, twitter, and other social media, have transformed our culture and created a venue for public discourse, increase production and distribution of knowledge, which has resulted in collective voice, collective intelligence, and collective responsibility. Hence, national and local issues of grave consequences and mayhem are transitioning to global issues because people from different parts of the world are now having their say in real time. Partly because of new media, the 2017 executive order on immigration signed by USA president Trump is an example of a local issue that became a global issue through collective voice and collective responsibility. Hence, more and more people from different parts of the world are engaging in real-time public discourse than ever before regarding a particular issue. Therefore, our national identity is transitioning to global identity of collective voice, collective intelligence, and collective responsibility. By judging against the current standards through new media such as blogs, twitter, and other social media, we can now see compared to the past (i.e., before the turn of the twenty-first century) how limited the opportunities were for consumers, citizens, companies, and other organizations to communicate openly and broadly to a wider audience and how our society has been transformed from a relative close society to an open one. Hence big data technology impacts on e-commerce, online marketing, online supply chain, and new media are transforming business, economic, social responsibility, foot print, and society.

Conclusion

Micro work such as Brynjolfsson, Hitt et al. (Brynjolfsson et al. 2011), Bakhshi, Bravo-Biosca et al. (Bakhshi et al. 2014) and Tambe (2013) suggests a correlation between knowledge gleaned from data analytics to productivity. Macro estimates have estimated the possible gains to GDP: for example, CEBR (2012) estimate that in 2011 the aggregate economic benefits derived from data and data-based knowledge were £25.1bn. Therefore, there is no doubt that big data revolution intertwines with analytics has enabled big data value chain for business. How? Through new ways of consolidating variety of data and also analyzing the said data led to big data value chain which in turn led to transformation of businesses. Consequently, through big data revolution intertwines with analytics we can ask and answer questions in new ways regardless of the variety and volume of data. Therefore, big data has provided the counter measure of handling and analyzing enormous, dynamic, and varied datasets hence the traditional method limitation in handling variety of data and its different sources has been solved in an effective and efficient innovative way. For example, Google, Amazon, Reddit, etc. have decided the return on investment (ROI) associated with scaling up its RDBMS is not sufficient, therefore, they have decided on a different approach which is more cost-effective. In addition, because of the said companies' commitment to their customers, shareholders and core business practices, they are also sensitive to latency issues, therefore they cannot afford to wait 3 days for data to be processed. Therefore to enhance operations, accelerate decision making, maximize performance thereby increasing business value, companies such as eBay, Facebook, and others are committed to using new innovative technologies that go beyond RDBMS which in turn has enabled new types of data aggregation and analysis. Hence, the said businesses are able to obtain deeper and richer insights, which help management, make a decision that increases big data value which in turn increases revenue through cost-saving methods. The solution has been the development of new forms of data management and analytical techniques that rely on machine learning and new modes of visualization etc.

Consequently, big data revolution intertwines with analytics has substantially transformed business in the areas of culture, data architecture, management, security, etc., as such Big Data is a disruptive innovation. Therefore, using traditional methods on big data for data management and analysis is not a viable option. Consequently, businesses cannot afford to ignore Big Data, as it contains compelling and powerful information about evolving customer pain points, and recurring service issues. While there is no doubt that big data has created benefits to businesses and consumers alike, there are commensurate risks that go along with it. Moreover, many businesses currently do not understand the importance of Big Data or how to go about beginning to leverage it. At the Gartner Catalyst 2012 Conference in San Diego, it was stated "An understanding of when to use Big Data is lacking right now." That said the right Big Data solution for a particular enterprise depends on choosing the right use cases, tools, and staff, as well as making high-level decisions about investment and infrastructure.

Upon closer reflection and given the argument put forward in this paper, I posit that there is a need for academic institutions to revisit IT and Computer Science curricula, teaching tools, content, tools, methods, and outcomes vis-à-vis the said programs so that they will not be behind the curve of current methods, innovation and technology know how. For business is dictating the innovation in terms of innovative tools, methods and IT processes; which in itself is transformational because for most of the twentieth century, academia used to take the lead when it comes to information technology and computer science but now at best academia is partnering with business in which academia is the junior player in the areas of Information Technology, Computer Science, etc. So, is it time to play catch up?

References

Bakhshi H, Bravo-Biosca A et al (2014) Inside the Datavores: estimating the effect of data and online analytics on firm performance. Nesta, London

Bollier D (2010). The promise and peril of big data. The Aspen Institute. Available at: http://www.aspeninstitute.org/sites/default/files/content/docs/pubs/The_Promise_and_Peril_of_Big_Data.pdf. Accessed 1 Oct 2012

Brynjolfsson E, Hitt L et al. (2011) Strength in numbers: how does data-driven decision making affect firm performance. Available at SSRN 1819486

Columbus L (2014) Roundup of analytics, big data; business intelligence forecasts and market estimates, 2014. Forbes

Constine J (2012) How big is Facebook's data? 2.5 billion pieces of content and 500+ terabytes ingested every day. http://techcrunch.com/2012/08/22/how-big-is-facebooks-data-2-5-billion-pieces-of-content-and-500-terabytes-ingested-every-day

Goodridge P, Haske J (2015) How does big data affect GDP? Theory and evidence for the UK. Imperial College Business School, London

Information and Communications Technology Council (2015) Big data & the intelligence economy Canada's hyper connected landscape. Information and Communications Technology Council, Ottawa, ON. Available at http://www.ictc-ctic.ca/wpcontent/uploads/2015/12/BIG-DATA-2015.pdf

Kitchin R (2014) The real-time city? Big data and smart urbanism. Geo Journal 79:1–14

Lesk M (1996) How much data is in the world? at http://www.lesk.com/mlesk/ksg97/ksg.html or https://courses.cs.washington.edu/courses/cse590s/03au/lesk.pdf

Manyika J, Chui M et al. (2011) Big data: the next frontier for innovation, competition, and productivity. McKinsey Global Institute. http://www.mckinsey.com/~/media/mckinsey/.../mgi_big_data_exec_summary.ashx

Marz N, Warren J (2012) Big data: principles and best practices of scalable real time data systems. Manning, Westhampton

Mind Commerce. The big data market: business case, market analysis & forecast 2015–2020 September 2014. http://www.teleres.com.au/a/595.html

Miniwatts Marketing Group (2016). Internet World Stats Retrieved from http://www.internetworldstats.com/stats.htm

OCE (2012) IBM, Governments of Ontario and Canada, OCE and Seven Ontario Universities Work Together to Build a Smarter Ontario

OCE (2014) Agreement means big boost for big data start-ups. Ontario Centres of Excellence Inc., Toronto, ON

Open Data Center Alliance (2012). Big data consumer guide. http://www.opendatacenteralliance.org/docs/Big_Data_Consumer_Guide_Rev1.0.pdf

Press G (2014) 6 predictions for the $125 billion big data analytics market in 2015. Forbes, New York

Tambe, P. (2013). "Big Data Investment, Skills, and Firm Value." Skills, and Firm Value (May 8, 2013).

Walker B (2015) Every day big data statistics http://www.vcloudnews.com/every-day-big-data-statistics-2-5-quintillion-bytes-of-data-created-daily/

Facilitating the Exploration of Open Health-Care Data Through BOAT: A Big Data Open Source Analytics Tool

A. Ravishankar Rao and Daniel Clarke

Abstract Big Data Analytics is the use of advanced analytic techniques on very large data sets to discover hidden patterns and useful information. Many governments publicly release significant amounts of health data, including hospital ratings and patient outcomes. We propose applying Big Data Analytics to understand open health data. Ideally, citizens would use this data to choose hospitals or evaluate care options. There are major challenges, including merging data from disparate sources and applying interpretive analytics.

We are building an open-source tool to facilitate analytical exploration. Such a tool could enable researchers, hospitals, insurers, and citizens to obtain integrated global-to-local perspectives on health-care expenditures, procedure costs, and emerging trends. Our tool is based on the Python ecosystem, and contains a variety of modules from database analytics to machine learning and visualization. We analyzed data from the New York Statewide Planning and Research Cooperative System and determined the distribution of costs for hip replacement surgery across the state. The mean cost over 168,676 patients is $22,700, the standard deviation is $20,900, and 88% of these patients had hip replacement costs of less than $30,000. This provides the background to understand why in a state with similar demographics, The California Public Employees' Retirement System capped hip replacement reimbursements at $30,000, which resulted in significant medical savings. Obtaining transparency of medical costs is important to control expenditure. Even though such information is available, consumers have trouble utilizing it effectively. Our tool could be truly transformative, allowing consumers to fully use available data, and to perhaps demand access to data that ought to be made public.

Keywords Big data • BOAT • Open source • Health-care

A. Ravishankar Rao (✉) • D. Clarke
School of Computer Science and Engineering, Fairleigh Dickinson University, Teaneck, NJ, USA
e-mail: ravirao@fdu.edu

L. Tadj, A.K. Garg (eds.), *Emerging Challenges in Business, Optimization, Technology, and Industry*, Springer Proceedings in Business and Economics, DOI 10.1007/978-3-319-58589-5_7

Introduction and Motivation

One of the sustainable development goals (SDG) highlighted by the United Nations, SDG 16 (https://sustainabledevelopment.un.org/sdg16) aims to "Promote peaceful and inclusive societies for sustainable development, provide access to justice for all and build effective, accountable and inclusive institutions at all levels". One of the ways of achieving this goal is for institutions worldwide to release data about their functioning. The Open Data Barometer, a watchdog organization (http://opendatabarometer.org/) that keeps track of open data globally, notes that "Open data is essential to building accountable and effective institutions, and to ensuring public access to information — both goals of SDG 16. It is also essential for meaningful monitoring of progress on all 169 SDG targets. Yet the promise and possibilities offered by opening up data to journalists, human rights defenders, parliamentarians, and citizens at large go far beyond even these."

Jetzek (2015) investigated the value provided by the Open Data movement worldwide, and observes that Open Data Initiatives are yet to attain their true potential. A recent report (http://opendatabarometer.org/) highlights that open government data has not made an impact commensurate with initial expectations. This raises questions regarding whether we have the right methods and intellectual tools to both understand and measure the value that is contained in the data.

Our viewpoint is that we are still early in the value-determination phase. Until the right tools have been created, disseminated and utilized by the research community and concerned citizens, we cannot be sure that the appropriate value has been extracted. Open data has been successfully utilized in areas such as real estate, for instance by the company Zillow, that uses public records to estimate home prices. Another area that has garnered significant interest is health care, due to its enormous societal impact. In the USA, health care spending was $3.0 trillion in 2014, representing 17.5 percent of gross domestic product (Martin et al. 2016). As a percentage of GDP, the health care costs are approximately 11% in Canada, Germany, and France, 10% in Japan and 9% in Australia, Italy and the UK (Harding and Pritchard 2016). Hence, health care is high on the list of governmental responsibilities and expectations of citizens. Most governments are interested in making affordable and quality care available to all their citizens.

Given the importance of health care, the scope of the current paper is restricted to Open Data in the health care arena. We describe our approach and results in the creation of tools to analyze and derive insight from such data (Github; Rao and Clarke 2016). We expect our approach to spur innovation in the field of health care data analytics. The code for BOAT used in this paper is available freely through an open source repository on Github (Github).

A major challenge in extracting value from the available data lies in being able to organize and integrate the numerous datasets scattered across multiple Federal and State level agencies in the USA. The Center for Medicare and Medicaid Services (CMS) contains data about healthcare providers and hospital ratings (Martin et al. 2016; Harding and Pritchard 2016), the Center for Disease Control (CDC) has data about disease incidence (CDC), the New York State Statewide Planning and Research Cooperative System (SPARCS) initiative (SPARCS) has data about patient discharges in NY State, and the New York State Department of Education (http://www.op.nysed.gov/opsearches.htm) has information about graduation records for providers. The research presented in our current paper describes a viable approach to combine information from multiple datasets, and to answer specific questions about the relationship between seniority of practitioners and performance. Our research is also timely as there are several organizations including NIH (Department of Health R01; Department of Health R21), the Robert Woods Johnson Foundation and the Russell Sage Foundation (Russell Sage Foundation) that are offering grants to support the analysis of existing healthcare datasets and novel methods to analyze and interpret such data. Clearly, we are awash in data.

There is controversy in the medical field about the age and seniority level of providers performing different procedures on the patients, and outcomes (Stilgoe et al. 2014; Shadbolt et al. 2012; Borgman 2012; Bullinger et al. 2012). In order to investigate this issue, we used correlation and linear regression analysis in order to understand the relationship between seniority of health care professionals and performance. We applied these techniques separately to the Medicare Dataset (Martin et al. 2016; Harding and Pritchard 2016). This is addressed in further detail in the section “Discussion”.

There are several examples of the successful utilization of a data-driven approach to health care. A significant reduction in medical spending costs was achieved by the California Public Employees’ Retirement System (CALPERS) (Frakt 2016). Earlier, CALPERS beneficiaries were being reimbursed for hip replacement surgeries anywhere up to $100,000. A review of the costs at several hundred hospitals revealed that good quality surgery could be performed at a cost of $30,000. Based on this, CALPERS capped the beneficiary reimbursement at $30,000 with the patient paying the excess. A concerned citizen or patient may wonder where the above figure of $30,000 came from. We use our BOAT tool to perform analytics on an open dataset released by New York SPARCS, a state with similar demographics to California. We show that the mean hip replacement cost in New York State is $21,900 and only one in eight patients had hip replacement costs exceeding $30,000. Therefore, our analysis provides the context to understand decisions made by organizations such as CALPERS (Frakt 2016).

Related Work

Many governments worldwide are embracing Open Data and transparency. In the USA, the Center for Medicare and Medicaid Services (CMS) continues to release data quarterly about the performance of hospitals in the nation (https://data.medicare.gov/Physician-Compare/National-Downloadable-File/s63f-csi6; Medicare.gov) as well as the practitioners involved in providing care. Pharmaceutical companies are also releasing data to the public, through initiatives such as the Yale University

YODA project (Le and Kurd 2014). Rao et al. review many of the benefits provided by this open data movement for healthcare (2015). The quantification and measurement of health outcomes at multiple levels, from primary care to clinical trials leads to improved care delivery, cost reduction and efficiency (Schwartz et al. 2014).

The use of aspirin to prevent cardiovascular disease and colorectal cancer is now part of recommended medical practice in the USA (Bibbins-Domingo 2016). The roots of this recommendation go back to a meta-study (Baigent et al. 2009) where the results of several individual clinical trials were combined to yield a substantially larger pool of close to 90,000 patients. This illustrates the power of effectively using large datasets in health care. This meta-study (Baigent et al. 2009) was carried out by the Antithrombotic Trialists' Collaboration, involved international collaborations with researchers, and utilized large datasets containing anonymized data on individual patients rather than using less detailed summaries of trials.

Boulton et al. (2011) note the importance of making scientific data available to other researchers as this provides a mechanism to validate findings, and also enables re-use of the data for new advancements. Nisen and Rockhold from the drug maker GlaxoSmithKline (2013) made the following remark about their company's move to make clinical trial data available to qualified researchers. "We are taking this step because it is the right thing to do, both scientifically and for society, and it is in line with our company's commitment to transparency in clinical trial reporting". At the same time, Specks et al. made their clinical trial data available freely to all researchers without the need for approvals (2013). In 2013, these developments were hailed as the new frontier in clinical trial transparency (Zarin 2013). Since then, the Immune Tolerance Network has hosted data from 25 clinical trials, including 3200 patients and 72,000 study visits (https://www.itntrialshare.org/) and these are freely available.

The UK Biobank project has collected data from 500,000 British participants related to health outcomes with the goal of understanding complex diseases (Sudlow et al. 2015). This data is being made available to researchers through open access. There is a movement in the National Health Service in the UK and states in USA such as New York (SPARCS) to publicly release the outcomes of cardiac surgery. Bridgewater et al. (2007) conducted a study which showed that mortality rates were reduced in regions of the UK that reported cardiac surgery outcomes. Though causality was not established, there are many issues surrounding this association, including whether a surgeon's decision to operate on a high-risk patient is influenced by knowing that the outcome will be publicly reported.

The Center for Medicare and Medicaid Services (CMS) in the USA is publicly releasing data about payments made to doctors (https://openpaymentsdata.cms.gov/). This is being done under the Federal Open Payments Program (Fontenot 2013), which is intended to make transparent the relationship between the pharmaceutical industry and the medical community, where conflicts of interest have been frequently observed. Pharmaceutical companies responded by reducing their budget for physician meals and office visits by sales representatives (Fontenot 2013). A study even claimed that relatively cheap meals costing $20 provided by a drug company could influence a doctor to prescribe a drug made by that company (DeJong et al. 2016).

Martin et al. (2014) examine the experience of utilizing open health data in the state of New York. Public SPARCS data (SPARCS) was used by Crain's New York Business to identify cost disparities, such as the variation of the median cost of hip replacements from $103,725 at the New York University Hospitals Center to $15,436 at Bellevue Hospital Center. Such information is valuable to payer agencies such as Medicaid, which can determine appropriate reimbursement rates for all patients.

There is an entire journal devoted to exploring public engagement in science, called Public Understanding of Science, which contains interesting perspectives on the intersection of science, society, and politics (Stilgoe et al. 2014). Investigating these issues are important to understanding how citizen engagement can contribute to better governance. Open access to scientific literature and open data are two important paths that encourage citizen engagement. Davies and Perini (2016) highlight the progress made by the World Bank in evaluating the impact that the open data movement has had on developing countries. A key challenge is to create a common approach to identify factors that contribute to the success or failure of open data interventions.

Shadbolt et al. (2012) present an excellent overview of the experience faced by the UK Government and its citizens in effectively utilizing open government data. They mention several technology hurdles, including understanding the best join points for diverse datasets and building client applications that can provide meaningful output to real-world users, especially concerned citizens. Conradie and Choenni (2014) conducted an in-depth survey of the experiences of local governments that released open data. They observed that the aim of the local governments should not be just the release of data for its own sake, but should result in transparency, innovation, and increased participation. They acknowledged that this is a challenging task. Investigating the true impact of data sharing initiatives has turned out to be a complex endeavor. Borgman (2012) notes, "For the last 25 years, the need to share research data has been declared to be an urgent problem. Yet the discussion continues, policies proliferate, and evidence of data sharing is apparent in only a few research fields. Sharing research data is clearly a conundrum: an intricate and difficult problem".

In spite of these challenges that need to be overcome, we expect that the open health data movement will be a net positive for governments, societies, patients, and citizens. Bullinger et al. (2012) advocate an open innovation ecosystem for healthcare, with participation by multiple segments of society, spanning patients, caregivers, healthcare providers, practitioners, and the interested public. Open systems and architectures can be expected to lead to cooperation, improvement of interoperability, transparency, and increased innovation in the entire ecosystem (Estrin and Sim 2010). Public education has been recognized as being important in this endeavor (Safran et al. 2007). An increasing number of researchers are applying machine learning and advanced analytic techniques to analyze and interpret healthcare data (Rao and Clarke 2016; Krumholz 2014).

With these observations in mind, we present our work that addresses the design and implementation of a detailed framework, BOAT, which facilitates the exploration of open health-related datasets.

System Design and Approach

The data analysis framework (Harding and Pritchard 2016) used by BOAT (Github) is shown in Fig. 1, and consists of the following steps: data cleansing/ETL, data joining, feature engineering, clustering classification, and prediction, visualization of results, interpretation and reporting.

Our implementation of BOAT builds upon existing open source Python components, which include Pandas, Scikit-Learn and Matplotlib (Hunter 2007). Python Pandas is frequently used for big-data analytics in finance (McKinney 2012), but not as much in the healthcare industry. Python Pandas is advantageous as it integrates tabular and statistical modeling interfaces with a visualization and plotting interface via Matplotlib. The current paper shows that Python Pandas is readily applicable to healthcare datasets.

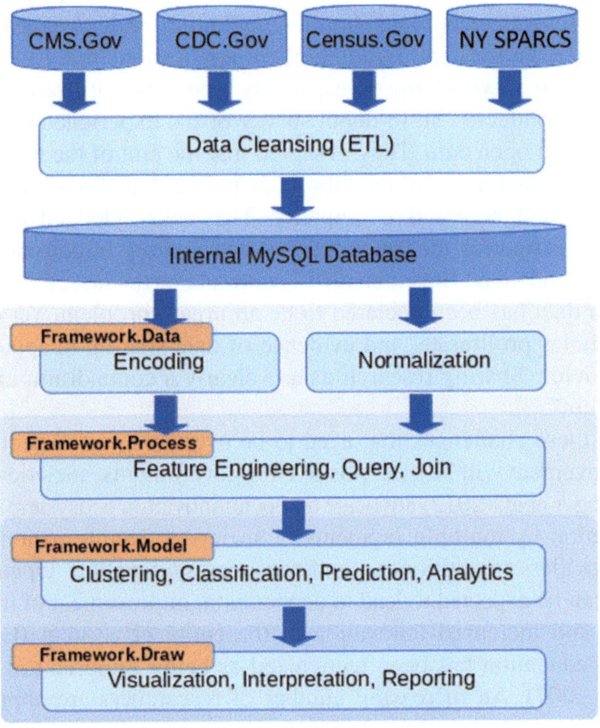

Fig. 1 Data analysis framework used by BOAT

Our development is conducted through the SciPy toolkit as it permits rapid exploration of datasets and algorithms. It is also popular in other fields like physics (Pérez and Granger 2007) and finance (McKinney 2010). The Scikit-Learn Python library (Pedregosa et al. 2011) provides several basic and advanced machine-learning capabilities including clustering, classification and prediction. Data and results can be visualized through packages such as Matplotlib and Graphviz.

Methods

We used two sources of public health data for our analysis, consisting of data from CMS and data from the New York SPARCS database.

Data from Medicare

We process data from CMS (Martin et al. 2016; Harding and Pritchard 2016) using the pipeline shown in Fig. 1. We found several errors in the CMS data that needed to be cleaned. Some of the errors include the following:

1. Incomplete or missing zipcodes for some of the rows of data. In this case, we either corrected the zipcode or deleted the row from subsequent analysis.
2. Duplicate rows. There were several rows of duplicate information, which were converted to unique rows.
3. Graduation years earlier than 1916. This would put the estimated age of the practitioners at 85 or above, which is due to a data-entry error (CMS). We eliminated these rows from our analysis. We also show in the section "Results" that the elimination of these results does not adversely affect our analysis and conclusion.

We join Medicare-provided data that resides in two separate files:

1. A file containing the hospital id and physician information: https://data.medicare.gov/Physician-Compare/National-Downloadable-File/s63f-csi6, henceforth referred to as "National-Downloadable-Physician-Compare".
2. A file containing the hospital id and hospital performance metrics provided by the CMS including the following: weighted clinical process of care domain score, weighted patient experience of care domain score, weighted outcome domain score, and total performance score. This can be found in http://www.medicare.gov/hospitalcompare/data/total-performance-scores.html.

Note that the description and interpretation of these fields are presented within this website, and a detailed explanation of the CMS methodology to obtain this data is outside the scope of this paper.

Data from 895,431 unique practitioners is joined with data from 3089 unique hospitals. We applied the K-means clustering algorithm (Fontenot 2013), available in Python Scikit, in order to understand the inherent groupings in the different specialties according to graduation year distributions. K-means clustering is an unsupervised learning technique, which automatically identifies clusters in data for a given number of clusters, denoted by the variable K. We chose $K = 7$ to find clusters among various specialties. The K-means clustering algorithm operates on an ensemble of objects, where each object is described by a feature vector. Let each specialty be considered as an object. For instance, we can have an object for "NURSE PRACTITIONER", and associate a feature vector with this object. The feature vector consists of 54 dimensions, where each dimension consists of the number of nurses that graduated in a given year in the range from 1960 to 2014. So the 54th dimension of the feature is the number of nurses that graduated in 2014, as determined by the "Graduation Year" field in the CMS database of practitioners. The feature vector is normalized so that the sum of all the normalized feature components equals 1.

The K-means clustering algorithm iteratively groups the feature vectors according to similarity, so after a given number of iterations, we arrive at a grouping of a pre-specified number of clusters, say $K = 7$.

Data from New York SPARCS

We use data about patient discharges and the cost of medical procedures in the state of New York as reported by SPARCS (SPARCS). This data was subjected to operations such as grouping by labels, binning, sorting, and statistical analysis to produce the results in the following section.

Results

We considered two separate sources for data: Center for Medicare/Medicaid Services (CMS) and New York State SPARCS. Information about these sources is shown in Tables 1 and 2.

Data from Medicare

We first examine the distribution of the different rows in "National-Downloadable-Physician-Compare". Each row represents a practitioner with an NPID (National Physician ID) and primary specialty. We plot the distributions of practitioners across primary specialties. Since there is a large variation across specialties, we show the results in two figures. Figure 2 shows the number of practitioners in each specialty

Table 1 Sizes of the datasets examined and used in this research

Source	Periodicity	Year range	Number of rows	Number of columns	Total number of entries
CMS Hospital Performance Scores	Quarterly	2009–2016	3089	17	52,513
CMS Healthcare Practitioners Database	Annual	2009–2016	1,976,455	44	86,964,020
New York State SPARCS Patient Diagnoses	Annual	2009–2014	14,028,434	40	561,137,360
New York Dept. of Education Medical Licenses of Cardiac Surgeons	Annual	2006–2010	156	10	1560
New York State SPARCS Cardiac Surgery Outcomes	Annual	2010–2012	1907	16	30,512

Table 2 Number of patient records released each year through SPARCS database

Year	Number of patient records
2009	2,665,414
2010	2,622,133
2011	2,589,121
2012	2,544,731
2013	2,426,516
2014	2,365,208

where there are at least 5000 practitioners, and Fig. 3 shows the number of practitioners in each specialty where there are less than 5000 practitioners. Figure 4 shows the relative proportion of different specialties in the dataset.

In Table 3, the column "Medicare count" shows the number of unique practitioners in the Medicare dataset analyzed in this paper. The column "AAMC Count" shows the number of medical practitioners by specialty as determined by the American Association of Medical Colleges in 2013 (Physician Specialty Data Book 2014). The third column "Percentage covered" is the percentage of the AAMC count that is covered by the current Medicare dataset for the given medical specialties. We use a few specialties for illustrative purposes, to show that the Medicare dataset in our analysis is representative of more than 75% of all medical graduates for several specialties.

Figure 5 shows the distribution of the total performance scores of practitioners in hospitals. All practitioners within a given hospital are assigned the total performance score corresponding to that hospital. The area under the curve is the total number of practitioners across all hospitals. The mean value for this distribution is 39.65 and the median value is 38.82, indicating that the distribution is skewed to the right. The skewness measure is 0.65 indicating a moderate skew. The kurtosis is 1.42.

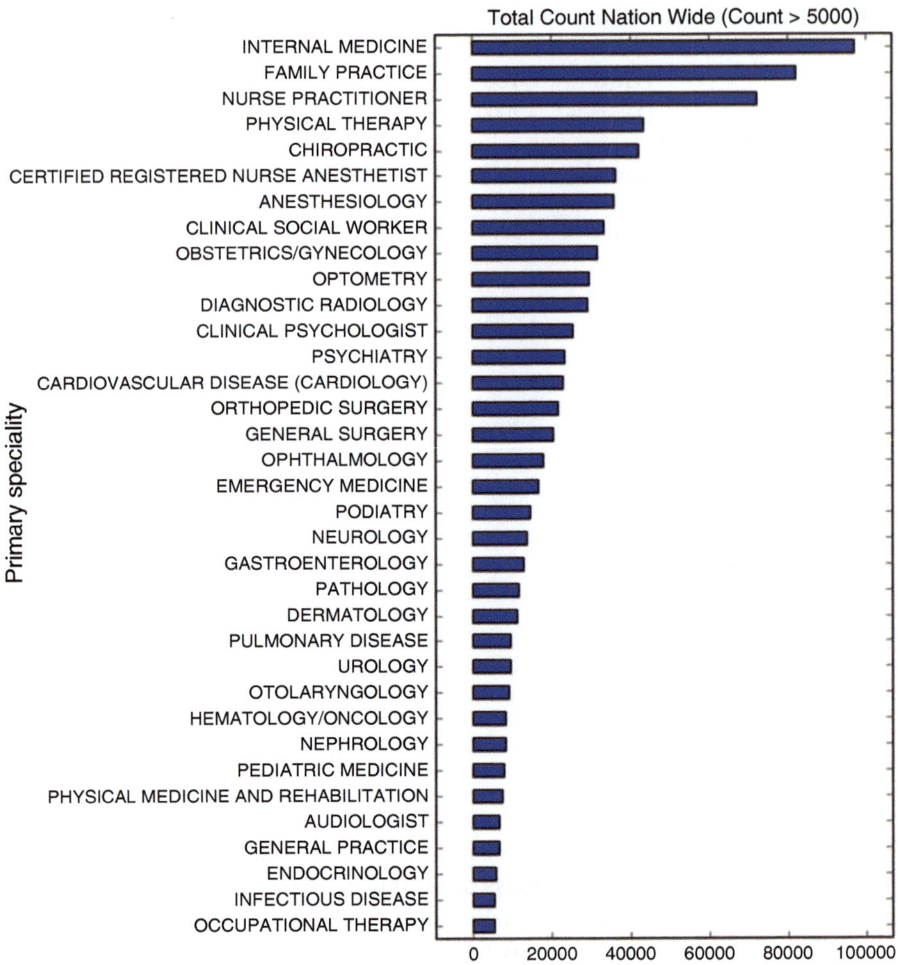

Fig. 2 Number of practitioners in each specialty with at least 5000 practitioners

Figure 6 shows the distribution of the total performance scores of all hospitals. The area under the curve is the total number of hospitals, which is 3090. The mean value is 41.7, and the median is 40.5. This indicates that the distribution is skewed to the right. The skewness measure is 0.7611 indicating a moderate skew. The kurtosis is 1.031.

Figure 7 shows the distribution of hospital sizes, by number of practitioners along *x*-axis. There are many small hospitals (of size <250 practitioners) and few large hospitals (of size >2000 practitioners).

Table 3 compares the number of medical practitioners in the current Medicare dataset to the actual number of medical practitioners in the USA determined by the AAMC (Martin et al. 2014). We have shown data for a few top specialties in our

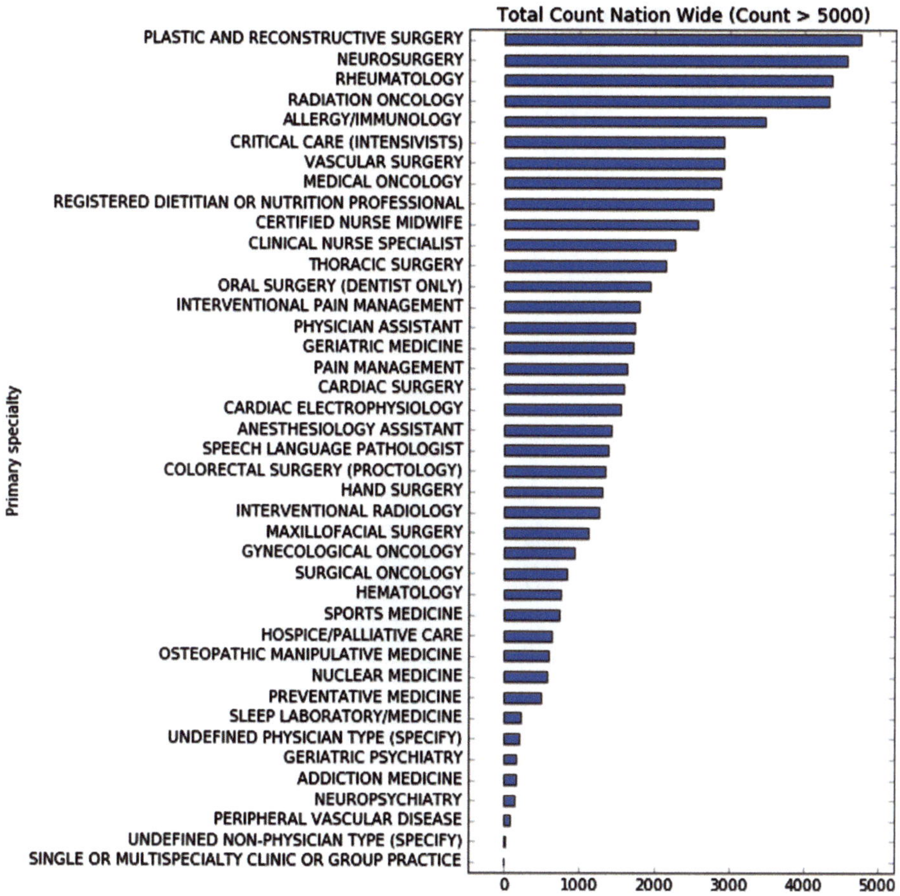

Fig. 3 Number of practitioners in each specialty with less than 5000 practitioners

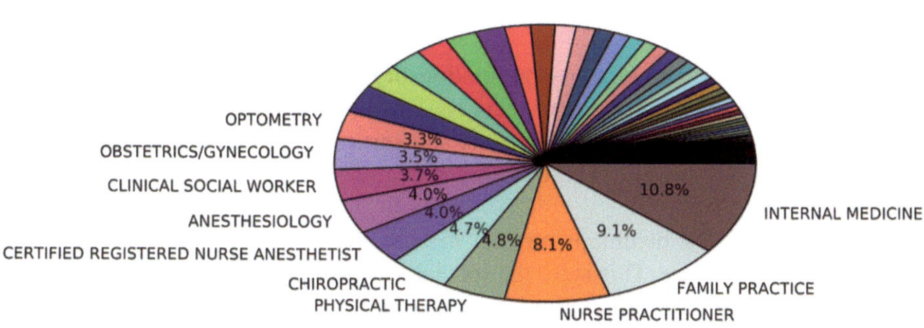

Fig. 4 Percentage of practitioners within each specialty

Table 3 From Medicare dataset

Specialty	Medicare count	AAMC count	Percentage covered
Internal medicine	96,975	111,047	87.33%
Family Practice	81,901	108,917	75.20%
Anesthesiology	35,667	40,758	87.51%
Obstetrics/Gyn.	31,399	40,826	76.91%

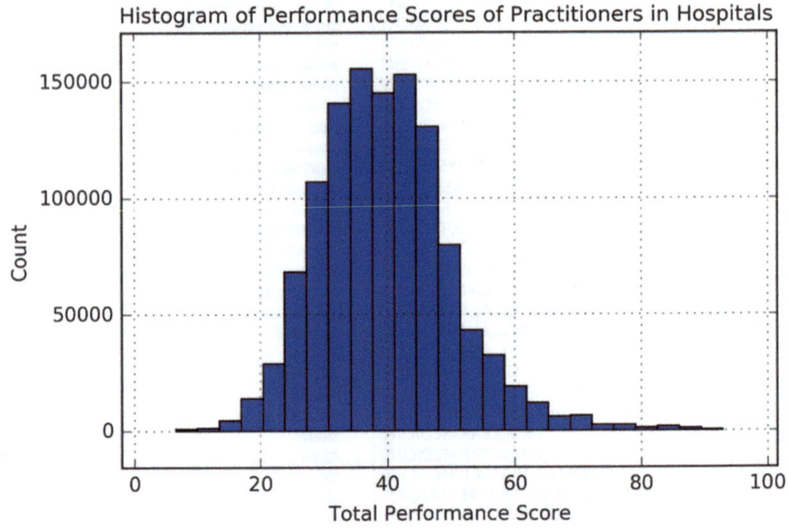

Fig. 5 Distribution of total performance scores of practitioners in hospitals

analysis, and there is a remarkably high coverage in the Medicare dataset of the total number of practitioners in the USA, exceeding 75%. The distributions shown in Figs. 5, 6 and 7 should orient the reader toward the spread of values contained in the dataset, and help form an intuition about the results we present subsequently. These distributions are calculated across all specialties and across all the hospitals in the dataset released by CMS. For instance, the means in Figs. 5 and 6 appear to be around 40.

A heatmap is used to explore the relationship between the graduation year and total performance score for each specialty. This provides a rich description of the variation between these two dimensions, and serves as a precursor to interpreting the correlation coefficient. Figure 8 shows heatmaps for four specialties over all hospitals.

Figure 8 depicts a heatmap showing the relation between graduation year and total performance score. This is for the specialties consisting of "Internal Medicine", "Family Practice", "Nurse Practitioner", and "Certified Registered Nurse Anesthetist". Practitioners across all hospitals were used. In subplot (a), $N = 191{,}774$ refers to the total number of relationships between Internal Medicine practitioners and hospitals. Similarly, "Med. Yr" represents the median graduation year for all

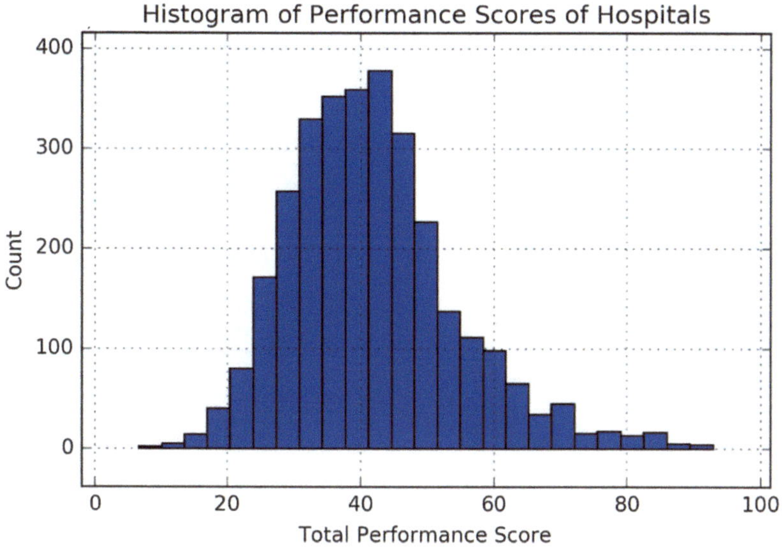

Fig. 6 Distribution of total performance scores of all hospitals

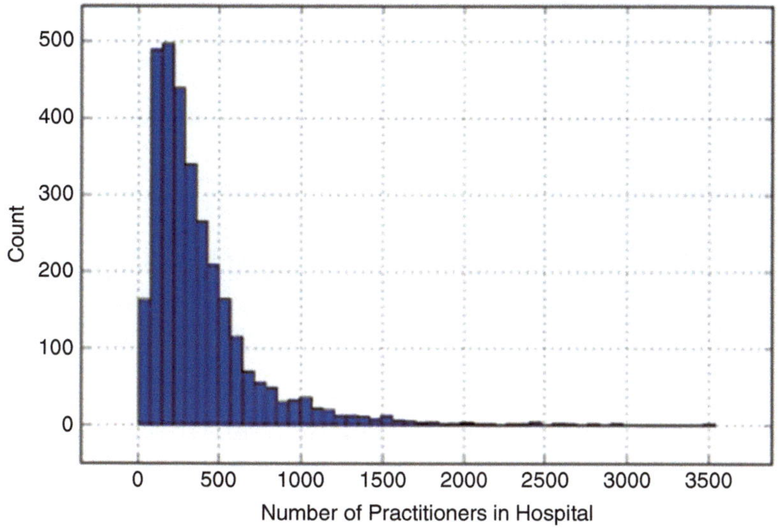

Fig. 7 Distribution of hospital sizes

Internal Medicine practitioners across all hospitals, which is 1993. Note that the colors in the map represent the counts at specific (x, y) locations corresponding to combinations of (Graduation year, Total Performance Score). We use different ranges for the counts to view the details within each image in the subplot. A single global range would render some of the details unviewable when the counts become small.

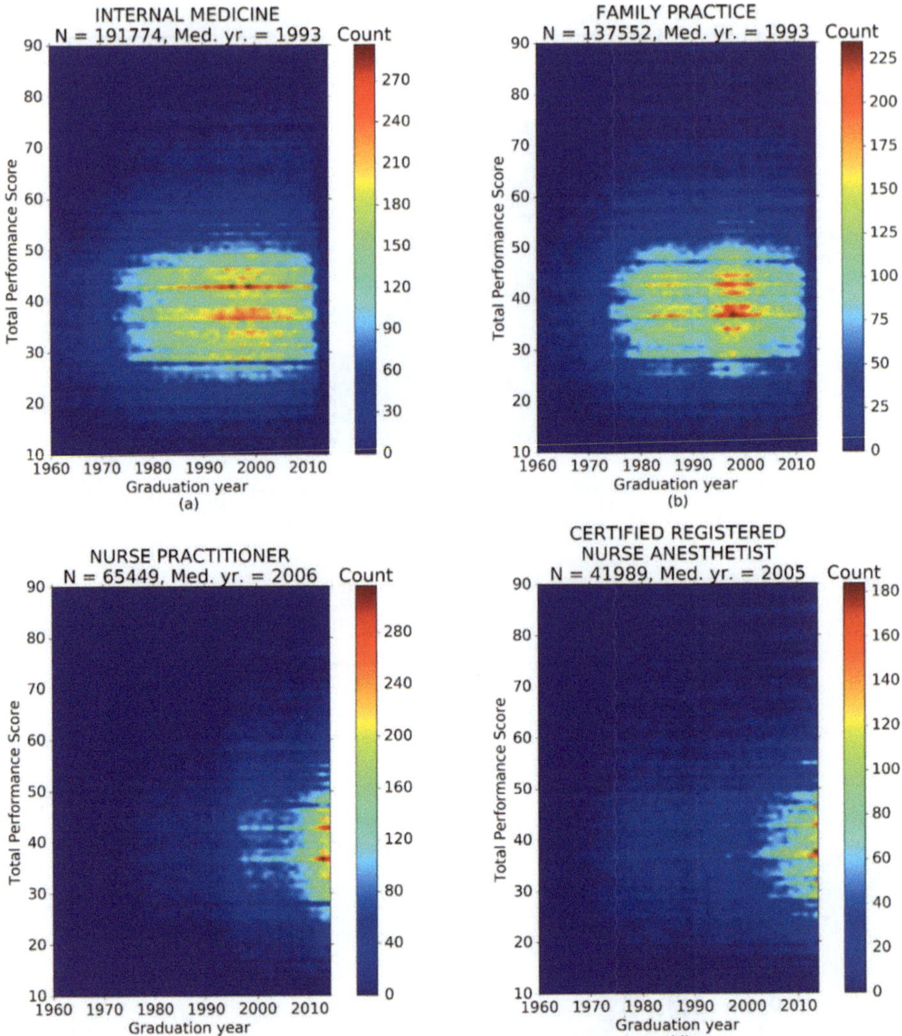

Fig. 8 Heatmap showing the relation between graduation year and total performance score

We compute the Spearman Rank correlation coefficient between the graduation years and total performance score across various specialties. We used the Spearman Rank correlation because the graduation years are discrete and non-continuous variables. Statistically significant correlations were found for 29 of 74 specialties, which were weak, with Spearman rank correlation values less than 0.164 ($p < 0.05$).

We also identified inherent clusters in the different specialties. The results of applying the K-means clustering algorithm (Fontenot 2013) are shown in Fig. 9. The feature vector for each specialty contains the normalized counts of practitioners

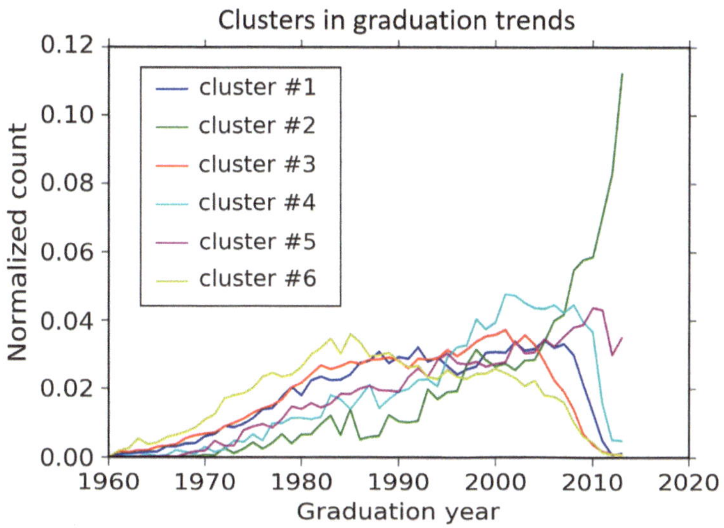

Fig. 9 Prominent clusters in the distribution of graduation years across specialties

for each graduation year. The K-means clustering algorithm identified several interesting trends, which are interpreted in the section "Discussion".

Figure 9 shows six prominent clusters in the distribution of graduation years across specialties. Cluster 2 shown in green consists of the specialties of certified registered nurse anesthetist, nurse practitioner, anesthesiology assistant, and physical therapy. Cluster 6 shown in yellow consists of specialties such as psychiatry and general practice.

Data from New York SPARCS

The precise distribution of hip-replacement costs from the New York SPARCS data is shown in Fig. 10.

Figure 11 shows the distribution of hip-replacement costs. The mean cost over 168,676 patients is $22,700, and the standard deviation is $20,900.

Figure 11 shows the distribution of costs for the three procedures with the lowest average costs per procedure. The average cost for "OPTHAML-/OT-OLOGIC DX" is $2384, for circumcision is $2612 and Prophylactic vaccination is $2905.

Figure 12 shows the distribution of costs for the three procedures with highest cost per procedure. The mean costs are higher than $155,000.

Figure 13 shows the distribution of costs for the three procedures with the smallest variance. The mean cost for episiotomy is $5226 with a standard deviation of $3128.

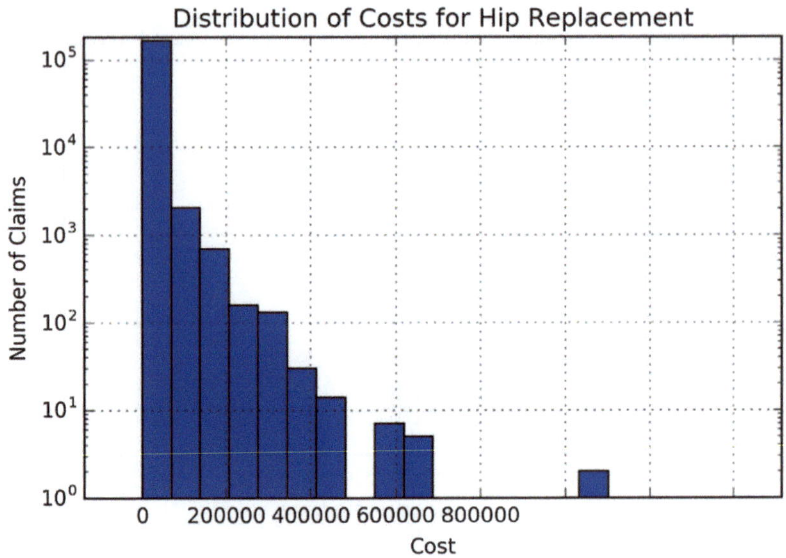

Fig. 10 Distribution of hip-replacement costs

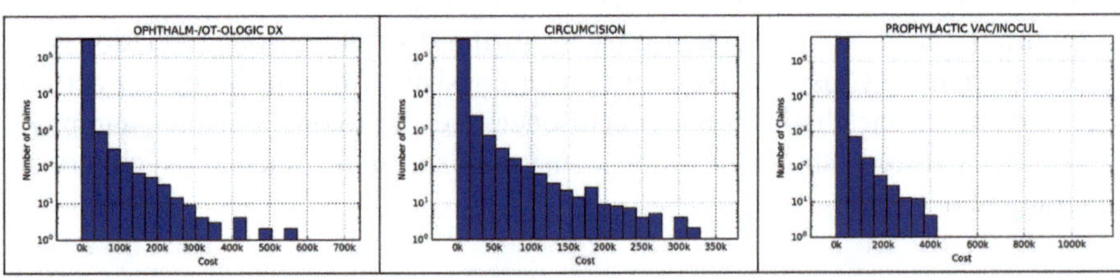

Fig. 11 Distribution of costs for the three procedures with lowest average costs per procedure

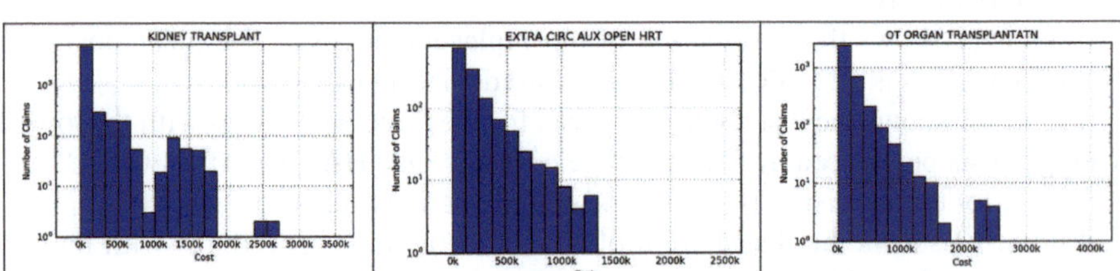

Fig. 12 Distribution of costs for the three procedures with highest cost per procedure

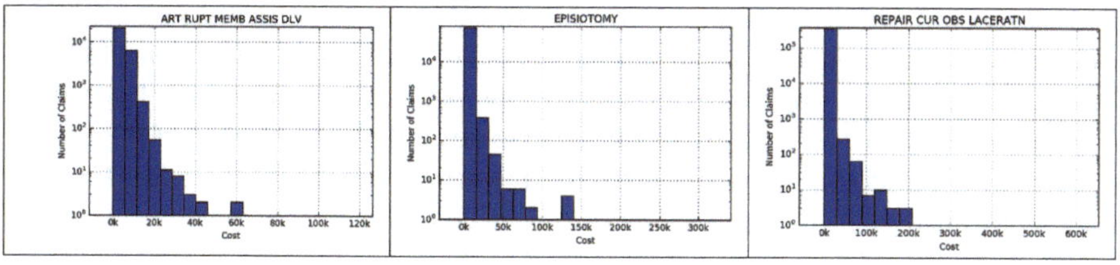

Fig. 13 Distribution of costs for the three procedures with the smallest variance

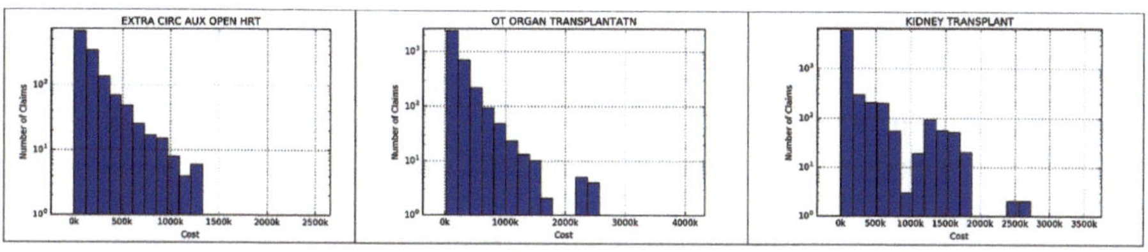

Fig. 14 Distribution of costs for the three procedures with the highest variance

Figure 14 shows the distribution of costs for the three procedures with the highest variance. The mean cost for "EXTRA CIRC AUX OPEN HRT" is $195,500 and the standard deviation is $222,000.

Discussion

The relationship between the age of a medical professional and the quality of care and outcomes is controversial and receiving increasing attention. On the one hand, researchers such as Choudhry et al. (2005) observed an inverse relationship between the number of years that a physician has been in practice, and the quality of care provided. A recent study by Jena and Romley (2015) showed that mortality rates for cardiac patients decreased when senior cardiologists were away for the National Cardiology Meeting in the USA. Schenarts and Cemaj (2016) survey a growing literature, which finds that more experienced physicians, and surgeons produce paradoxically worse clinical outcomes.

On the other hand, we could expect more experienced practitioners to provide better care. McAlister et al. (2015) did not find a negative association between physician experience and outcomes. Kupfer (2016) surveyed several studies and points out that many of them are limited by small sample sizes. This suggests that a national big-data approach like the one we are using has the potential to overcome such limitations. The presence of such seemingly conflicting studies indicates evidence of the need to synthesize significant findings from research in a user-friendly and readily available manner that can be used by practitioners to provide higher quality of care and achieve better outcomes for patients.

Prior research supporting observations of age-related cognitive decline in humans (Salthouse 2009) suggests that we would expect to see a positive correlation between graduation year and performance score, such that performance score declines with increasing age. This is countered by the observation that experienced practitioners could provide better care.

Our analysis indicates that seniority is not a significant factor. This is especially striking when this finding is contrasted with the relationship among seniority and job performance in other sectors of the economy. The workforce in more successful technology companies is significantly younger than the workforce in less successful companies (Hardy 2013; Thibodeau 2015).

Figures 2, 3, and 4 demonstrate that Nurse Practitioners are the 3rd largest group by total number among all the specialties. Figure 8 shows few Nurse Practitioners graduating around the year 1990, but shows a significant growth in the number of Nurse Practitioners starting around the year 2010. It is possible that this trend coincides with the advent of the 2010 Affordable Care Act. This may need to be verified by independent analysis of other data sources. This insight gained directly from the CMS data demonstrates the value of applying the right analytics and visualization techniques to the data.

We now interpret the results of the cluster analysis presented in Fig. 9. Cluster 2 shows an exponential increase, and consists of the specialties of certified registered nurse anesthetist, nurse practitioner, anesthesiology assistant, and physical therapy. Cluster 6 includes disciplines such as psychiatry and general practice and shows a gradual decline starting in 1980. These findings have policy implications in terms of capacity planning for the future of the workforce in these areas. Prospective students who wish to enroll in these specialties can use this data to make better-informed career choices. One advantage of using this data is that it is raw and has not been subject to any bias in reporting. It is possible that different organizations may impart their own spin in interpreting such data, and it is always reassuring for individuals to have the underlying data available to check the validity of interpretations that are offered.

Consider the costs of hip-replacement shown in Fig. 10. We used data from New York State SPARCS to determine that 148,000 patients were treated for a cost of less than \$30,000 and 20,676 patients were treated for a cost greater than \$30,000. Hence, 12 percent of the patients had hip-replacements that cost more than \$30,000. This indicates that a threshold of \$30,000 for reimbursable costs would affect about one in eight patients. This seems reasonable if we want to balance the objectives of making treatment affordable versus controlling costs. This level of analysis provides an insight into the decision by CALPERS (Frakt 2016) to use a threshold of

$30,000 for reimbursing hip replacements. By using BOAT, we can explore the ramifications of applying such a reimbursement law by examining the distribution of affected patients directly from the data. We need not wait for an article to be written about it, either in a newspaper or in a scientific journal. Perhaps such an article will never be written. Instead, we personalize our understanding of the original dataset.

CALPRERS utilized comparative medical cost data, known as reference pricing to reduce total costs for by $6 million (Frakt 2016). This move also led to several hospitals lowering their prices to match the reimbursable cost for hip replacement. Hence, there are multiple benefits that cost transparency can achieve, including lowering health care costs and making the health care system more efficient. However, it is hard to achieve such transparency, as many organizations and institutions do not want to share this information due to factors such as competitiveness and privacy.

Figures 2 and 3 show the mean costs per procedure for the most expensive and least expensive procedures. Organ transplants and heart surgery are the most expensive and circumcision and inoculation are among the least expensive. From Fig. 2, we see that though the mean cost for circumcision is $2612, there are hundreds of cases where the cost is greater than $50,000. Though there may be valid reasons, this aspect of the data may need further investigation. Figures 13 and 14 show the procedures with the smallest and largest variances. For episiotomy, the mean cost is $5226 with a standard deviation of $3128. This suggests that episiotomy is a procedure that could be subject to a closer analysis.

The framework, approach, and methods provided in our paper should close the gap between the availability of public healthcare data and our ability to extract meaning and value from this data. By making our tools and techniques open-source, we hope to spur further analysis, interpretation and understanding in this space and lower the barriers to conduct such research. BOAT uses iPython Notebooks (Bridgewater et al. 2007), which makes it easy for other researchers to understand and replicate our results. We note that one of the tools we used, Python Pandas (Sudlow et al. 2015) was released as an open source project in the finance world, and has spurred significant research and innovation therein. The world of healthcare could benefit by emulating such a model, with the release of open source projects. We have already witnessed the ongoing challenges in the use of Electronic Medical Records such as the lack of inter-operability between different vendor systems (Miller and Sim 2004). The wave of the future consists of greater transparency across all aspects of health care, including open health records (Walker et al. 2014). Nevertheless, the culture of the field needs to change, as noted by Friend in reference Roshan Paul (2011): “The “medical-industrial complex” is not incentivized to share among each other, let alone with patients.” We expect the combination of open data sharing as well as code sharing that we exemplify to further accelerate the pace of research and investigation in the health care arena. The current national outrage in the USA over escalating drug prices (Thomas 2016) only demonstrates how far we still need to go, as patient advocacy groups appear to be strait-jacketed by accepting significant funding from the same “medical-industrial complex” (McKinney 2010) that they are supposed to defend patients from. In this context, our current research represents a step in the right direction as open access to data and code will lower barriers to utilizing important healthcare data. By harnessing the well-documented advantages of open-source (Martínez-Torres and Diaz-Fernandez 2014) and utilizing attractive visualization front-ends in the future, such as the one created in (DATAUSA), we hope to reach a wide audience.

Conclusion

The value of the research presented in this paper lies in the creation of an open source toolkit that can be freely used by researchers to explore questions in healthcare by using voluminous sources of existing data. We have focused on techniques of Big Data Analytics, including the extraction and joining of data from multiple disparate sources, their processing and visualization to gain a deeper understanding of trends and relationships among variables that could potentially affect outcomes and other relevant metrics in healthcare.

Specifically, we presented an open-source toolkit based on Python, utilizing components such as Pandas, SciKit, and Matplotlib for analyzing and interpreting healthcare datasets. The relationship between seniority of practitioners and the quality of care they provide is controversial in the healthcare literature. We applied our framework to analyze data released by CMS, New York State SPARCS, and the New York State Department of Education to explore the relationship between seniority of practitioners and the quality of care they provide. In the CMS dataset, we found that the relationship between graduation year of practitioners and total hospital performance score is weak, based on the Spearman Rank correlation coefficient. Similarly, the relationship between the seniority of cardiac surgeons as measured by their graduation year and risk-adjusted mortality rate of their patients is weak, based on the Spearman Rank correlation coefficient. These results are significant because of the large dataset we used for the Medicare data, representing 7% of all healthcare workers in the USA. The data we used from the Medicare dataset representing medical specialties has a remarkably high coverage of the total number of medical practitioners in the USA as determined by the AAMC, and exceeds 75% for several medical specialties. Our results are also different from the norm in other sectors of the economy such as high technology, where there is a negative correlation between the age of workers in a company and the success of that company.

We provide a detailed visual exploration of the two-dimensional distribution of practitioners along the dimensions of graduation year and hospital total performance score using color heatmaps. This provides a more nuanced interpretation of the correlation scores, and illustrates the differences in population trends over a database of 1.2 million practitioners. We also performed unsupervised clustering of graduation trends among various specialties, and identified seven major groups, including specialties such as psychiatry that have a slow decrease of practitioners and specialties such as Nurse Practitioners that have an exponential increase in the number of practitioners.

We used data from New York State SPARCS to determine that the average cost of hip replacement surgery is $22,700 and that one in eight patients had hip-replacements that cost more than $30,000. This indicates that a threshold of $30,000 for reimbursable costs would seem reasonable if we want to balance the objectives of making treatment affordable versus controlling costs.

Our method generates promising results, and our tool BOAT can be used interactively to explore, analyze, interpret, and visualize large datasets. The application of this technique to data from multiple sources sheds light on factors and trends that can affect educational and health care policy. The free availability of our tools and techniques should prove valuable to other researchers and software developers in the healthcare arena, and eventually reach a broader audience. We expect our approach to serve as a new model for conducting healthcare research.

References

Baigent C, Blackwell L, Collins R, Emberson J, Godwin J, Peto R et al (2009) Aspirin in the primary and secondary prevention of vascular disease: collaborative meta-analysis of individual participant data from randomized trials. Lancet 373:1849–1860

Bibbins-Domingo K (2016) Aspirin use for the primary prevention of cardiovascular disease and colorectal cancer: US preventive services task force recommendation. Ann Intern Med 164:836–845

Borgman CL (2012) The conundrum of sharing research data. J Assoc Inf Sci Technol 63:1059–1078

Boulton G, Rawlins M, Vallance P, Walport M (2011) Science as a public enterprise: the case for open data. Lancet 377:1633–1635

Bridgewater B, Grayson AD, Brooks N, Grotte G, Fabri BM, Au J et al (2007) Has the publication of cardiac surgery outcome data been associated with changes in practice in northwest England: an analysis of 25,730 patients undergoing CABG surgery under 30 surgeons over eight years. Heart 93:744–748

Bullinger AC, Rass M, Adamczyk S, Moeslein KM, Sohn S (2012) Open innovation in health care: analysis of an open health platform. Health Policy 105:165–175

Centre for disease control and prevention. http://wwwcdcgov/DataStatistics/

Choudhry NK, Fletcher RH, Soumerai SB (2005) Systematic review: the relationship between clinical experience and quality of health care. Ann Intern Med 142:260–273

CMS.GOV, Private correspondence with the data vendor for CMS.

Conradie P, Choenni S (2014) On the barriers for local government releasing open data. Gov Inf Q 31:S10–S17

DATAUSA. https://datausa.io/about/

Davies T, Perini F (2016) Researching the emerging impacts of open data: revisiting the ODDC conceptual framework. J Commun Inform 12

DeJong C, Aguilar T, Tseng C-W, Lin GA, Boscardin WJ, Dudley RA (2016) Pharmaceutical industry–sponsored meals and physician prescribing patterns for Medicare beneficiaries. JAMA Intern Med 176:1114–1110

Department of Health and Human Services. Secondary analyses of existing data sets and stored biospecimens to address clinical aging research questions (R01)

Department of Health and Human Services. Secondary dataset analyses in heart, lung, and blood diseases and sleep disorders (R21)

Estrin D, Sim I (2010) Health care delivery open mHealth architecture: an engine for health care innovation. Science 330:759–760

Fontenot SF (2013) Understanding the affordable care act bit by bit: will transparency and sunshine shrink costs? Physician Exec 39:86

Frakt A (2016) How common procedures became 20 percent cheaper for many Californians. The New York Times 2016

github.com/fdudatamining/framework. Base Frame Work for Data Mining

Harding AJ, Pritchard C (2016) UK and twenty comparable countries GDP-expenditure-on-health 1980-2013: the historic and continued low priority of UK health-related expenditure. Int J Health Policy Manag 5:519

Hardy Q (2013) Technology workers are young (really young). The New York Times

Hunter JD (2007) Matplotlib: a 2D graphics environment. Comput Sci Eng 9:90–95

Jena AB, Romley J (2015) Changes in hospitalizations, treatment patterns, and outcomes during major cardiovascular meetings—reply. JAMA Intern Med 175:1420–1421

Jetzek T (2015) The sustainable value of open government data: uncovering the generative mechanisms of open data through a mixed methods approach. Copenhagen Business School, Institute for IT-Ledelse Department of IT Management

Krumholz HM (2014) Big data and new knowledge in medicine: the thinking, training, and tools needed for a learning health system. Health Aff (Millwood) 33:1163–1170

Kupfer JM (2016) The graying of US physicians: implications for quality and the future supply of physicians. JAMA 315:341–342

Le ME, Kurd MF (2014) A review and analysis of the YODA trials: what can we glean clinically? Curr Rev Musculoskelet Med 7:189–192

Martin EG, Helbig N, Shah NR (2014) Liberating data to transform health care: New york's open data experience. JAMA 311:2481–2482

Martin AB, Hartman M, Benson J, Catlin A, Team NHEA (2016) National health spending in 2014: faster growth driven by coverage expansion and prescription drug spending. Health Aff 35:150–160

Martínez-Torres MR, Diaz-Fernandez MDC (2014) Current issues and research trends on open-source software communities. Tech Anal Strat Manag 26:55–68

McAlister FA, Youngson E, Bakal JA, Holroyd-Leduc J, Kassam N (2015) Physician experience and outcomes among patients admitted to general internal medicine teaching wards. CMAJ 187:1041–1048

McKinney W (2010) Data structures for statistical computing in python. In: Proceedings of the 9th python in science conference, pp 51–56

McKinney W (2012) Python for data analysis: data wrangling with Pandas, NumPy, and IPython. O'Reilly Media, Inc

Medicare.gov. The total performance score information. https://www.medicare.gov/hospitalcompare/data/total-performance-scores.html

Miller RH, Sim I (2004) Physicians' use of electronic medical records: barriers and solutions. Health Aff 23:116–126

New York State Department of Health, Statewide Planning and Research Cooperative System (SPARCS). https://www.health.ny.gov/statistics/sparcs/

Nisen P, Rockhold F (2013) Access to patient-level data from GlaxoSmithKline clinical trials. N Engl J Med 369:475–478

Pedregosa F, Varoquaux G, Gramfort A, Michel V, Thirion B, Grisel O et al (2011) Scikit-learn: machine learning in python. J Mach Learn Res 12:2825–2830

Pérez F, Granger BE (2007) IPython: a system for interactive scientific computing. Comput Sci Eng 9:21–29

Physician specialty data book (2014). https://members.aamc.org/eweb/upload/Physician%20Specialty%20Databook%202014.pdf. Accessed 5 Jul 2017.

Rao AR, Clarke D (2016) A fully integrated open-source toolkit for mining healthcare big-data: architecture and applications. In: IEEE international conference on healthcare informatics ICHI, Chicago, vol 2016, pp 255–261

Rao AR, Chhabra A, Das R, Ruhil V (2015) A framework for analyzing publicly available healthcare data. In 17th international conference on E-health networking. Appl Services (IEEE HealthCom) vol 2015, pp 653–656

Roshan Paul AC (2011) An open source approach to medical research. Stanford Social Innovation Review
Russell SAGE Foundation Funding opportunity: the social, economic, and political effects of the affordable care act
Safran C, Bloomrosen M, Hammond WE, Labkoff S, Markel-Fox S, Tang PC et al (2007) Toward a national framework for the secondary use of health data: an American Medical Informatics Association White Paper. J Am Med Inform Assoc 14:1–9
Salthouse TA (2009) When does age-related cognitive decline begin? Neurobiol Aging 30:507–514
Schenarts PJ, Cemaj S (2016) The aging surgeon: implications for the workforce, the surgeon, and the patient. Surg Clin North Am 96:129–138
Schwartz AL, Landon BE, Elshaug AG, Chernew ME, McWilliams JM (2014) Measuring low-value care in Medicare. JAMA Intern Med 174:1067–1076
Shadbolt N, O'Hara K, Berners-Lee T, Gibbins N, Glaser H, Hall W (2012) Linked open government data: lessons from data.gov.uk. IEEE Intell Syst 27:16–24
Specks U, Merkel PA, Seo P, Spiera R, Langford CA, Hoffman GS et al (2013) Efficacy of remission-induction regimens for ANCA-associated vasculitis. N Engl J Med 369:417–427
Stilgoe J, Lock SJ, Wilsdon J (2014) Why should we promote public engagement with science? Public Underst Sci 23:4–15
Sudlow C, Gallacher J, Allen N, Beral V, Burton P, Danesh J et al (2015) UK biobank: an open access resource for identifying the causes of a wide range of complex diseases of middle and old age. PLoS Med 12:e1001779
Thibodeau P (2015) Median age at Google is 29, says age discrimination lawsuit. Computerworld
Thomas K (2016) Furor over drug prices puts patient advocacy groups in bind. The New York Times
Walker J, Darer JD, Elmore JG, Delbanco T (2014) The road toward fully transparent medical records. N Engl J Med 370:6–8
Zarin DA (2013) Participant-level data and the new frontier in trial transparency. N Engl J Med 369:468–469

Part III
Optimization Track

Optimal Production Planning Strategy for Deteriorating Items in Terms of Emission Tax, Pollution, and R&D Investment

Lotfi Tadj, Ajay K. Garg, and Abdelouahed Hamdi

Abstract Firms are faced with the question of what policies to implement to ensure efficient abatement behavior? In this paper, we aim to determine the optimal production rate and the optimal investment rate in pollution abatement technology. The situation is modeled as an optimal control problem with two state variables and two control variables. The optimal trajectories, the optimal control, and the optimal objective function value are obtained explicitly in both cases where the firm adopts either a continuous-review policy or a periodic-review policy. A numerical example is presented.

Keywords Optimal control • Production planning • Emission tax • Pollution abatement technology

Introduction

The traditional production planning has been revolutionized after the rising awareness and consciousness about the concept of Global warming. The environment and its perseverance has become a very important issue for the industry in general and manufacturing sector in particular. The industry has polluted the environment in a big way in the last two centuries. The emission of Green House Gases (GHG) has become a major issue of concern. The emission tax and Carbon credits' trading have become the major points of concern for every business and industry that cannot be

L. Tadj (✉)
Information Systems and Decision Sciences Department, Fairleigh Dickinson University, Vancouver, BC, Canada
e-mail: ltadj@fdu.edu

A.K. Garg
Administrative Sciences Department, Fairleigh Dickinson University, 842, Cambie Street, Vancouver, BC, V6B2P6 Canada

A. Hamdi
Department of Mathematics, Qatar University, Doha, Qatar

L. Tadj, A.K. Garg (eds.), *Emerging Challenges in Business, Optimization, Technology, and Industry*, Springer Proceedings in Business and Economics,
DOI 10.1007/978-3-319-58589-5_8

ignored now in the age of sustainable development and the preservation of environment. The Carbon Credits as a concept was discussed in length and formalized in the Kyoto Protocol. In December 1997, the Third Conference of Parties (COP) to the United Nations Framework Convention on Climate Change (UNFCCC) had adopted the Kyoto Protocol. The protocol requires developed and developing countries to limit their Greenhouse Gas (GHG) emissions to individual targets. The concepts of Emission Tax and Carbon Credits trading have become very important in production planning of manufacturing sector undertakings.

The Protocol agreed "caps" or quotas on the maximum amount of Greenhouse gases that each participating country can produce. Otherwise, the manufacturing organizations and countries have to bear with emission tax. Thus, the countries and then in turn the organizations have to work within set quotas on the emissions of installations. Thus to remain within the brackets of "Caps" or "Quota," the organizations have to invest in pollution control technology and its research or to engage themselves in Carbon Credits' trading. The third alternative is to pay heavy emission taxes, which in turn the organizations can lose the competitive advantage. In this paper, the production planning has been discussed at length with the limitations of "Emission Tax" and required investment to go for environment friendly technology.

The problem we are considering in this paper is that of a manufacturing firm that produces a single product. While on the shelves, items of the product are subject to deterioration. The firm also invests in pollution abatement technology. The goal is to determine the optimal production rate and the optimal investment rate in pollution abating technology. The problem is modeled an optimal control problem with two state variables and two control variables. The optimal trajectories, the optimal control, and the optimal objective function value are obtained explicitly. For applications of optimal control methods to production systems, see, for example, the survey of Sarimveis et al. (2008).

The rest of the paper is organized as follows. A literature review is presented in Section "Literature Review." The model is studied in continuous time in Section "Continuous-Review Policy" and in discrete-time in Section "Periodic-Review Policy." Each section contains a numerical example. Section "Conclusion" concludes the paper.

Literature Review

There are many researchers, who have contributed a great deal in the field of emission of gases, and reduction of global warming, but very few have contributed for production planning in terms of emission of Green House Gases and related investment on research and development. Some of these researches presented here are divided into three categories, which are as follows:

- Climate change regulation and carbon sequestration
- Emission market
- Carbon credits trading in the manufacturing sector

Climate Change Regulation and Carbon Sequestration

In the first section of the literature, most reviews are related to climate change regulation and carbon sequestration.

Kumar et al. (2016) focused on the performance of green supply chains and adding the green concept to it to emphasize the importance of environmental issues and the need for eco-friendly systems. They proposed a model for evaluating the effects of green policy on the performance of green supply chains. They show that supply chain collaboration is benefit enhancing only when the levels of green damage caused by pollution are low. This distorts the R&D decisions in ways that make the non-cooperative equilibrium benefit enhancing.

Gerigk et al. (2015) compared the conventional economic argument with reference to the contemporary one. The conventional economic argument favors the use of market-based instruments over "command-and-control" regulation. This viewpoint, however, is often limited in the description and characteristics of the latter; namely, environmental standards are often portrayed as lacking structured abatement incentives. Yet contemporary forms of command-and-control regulation, such as standards stipulated via benchmarking, have the potential to be efficient. The paper provides a first formal analysis of environmental standards based on performance benchmarks. It shows that under specific conditions, standards can provide efficient incentives to improve environmental performance.

Polonsky et al. (2011) describe that there are majorly of the issues, but at least four categories, i.e., scope, who pays, market or compliance-based mechanism and criteria must be considered for any type of climate change regulatory scheme. The "scope" used for carbon emission management system is global or regional. The concept "who pays" denotes the whole supply chain responsible for the cost of the carbon emission. The meaning of "market or compliance based mechanisms" is whether the carbon dioxide emission system is market-based or compliance-based regulatory system. The last concept "criteria" is the parameter to establish the credence of the remedy. Stevens et al. (2011) describe the protocols that tend to vary from very highly particular requirements to a comparative more general set of various recommendations. In this research no one set of protocols is the most opportunistic, but several protocols may have varying strength depending upon the type of project.

Lee and Cheong (2011) describe that the main action for implementing carbon management is basically to identify and calculate the carbon footprints of products and processes throughout the supply chain. By continuous monitoring and evaluating of the various suppliers' of carbon dioxide emissions performance, a focal company must avoid the various risks. Giddens (2010) describe the importance about the urgency of various actions to be taken to address the several critical issues of climate change and the action must be taken for reduction of emission. The researcher covers several types of aspects, which are related to global climate system, action plans, initiatives of organizations, role of United Nations, steps of emission trading and up to implementation program. Moore and MacCracken (2009) explained that reducing the emission of various greenhouse gases offers a cost-effective way of reducing the radiation in the environment, while at the same time there is an improvement in urban air. This research has been conducted both in high and low-income countries. The high-income countries work on reduction of greenhouse gas emissions whereas middle-income nations could make important contributions by controlling the emission of greenhouse gases.

Pan et al. (2004) describe in their article that the proposal of Kyoto Protocol in United Nations Framework Convention on Climate Change (UNFCC) is used to reduce the carbon or greenhouse gas emissions that have led to the global climate change. Ahonen (2004) describe in his article that for preventing the climate change, the emission of carbon dioxide must decrease, which is caused by human actions and it is more important that the information is provided about the various factors that affect the atmosphere and also provide some ways to act more environment friendly. Increase in the fuel consumption is basically the reason for many environmental problems like hazardous wastes and air pollution. Bates (2002) explained that it is not possible to neutralize the emissions. He also said that, if the fossil fuels are burnt then emission goes out in the environment and nobody can take it back. Miranda et al. (2002) describe in their article that forests are the main source for sequestration of carbon. This research also introduces the carbon credits, which can be traded in a global market. West and Marland (2002) describe in their research that the concentration of carbon dioxide in the atmosphere is regularly increasing due to the deforestation and various types of fossil fuel combustion. The sequestration of carbon in the field of agriculture required lots of change in the management practices for example, irrigation process, use of pesticides, and several types of farm machinery.

Emission Market

Wang et al. (2016) highlighted that to achieve the emission reduction target in 2020, China plans to establish a nationwide carbon trading market during 2016–2019. It is therefore an important but difficult task for policymakers to set emission allowances and allocate them among entities. Based on China's emission-abatement target, this paper examines the optimal investment and analyzes its implementation in different allocation rules. A new model is developed to formulate enterprises' emission reduction pathways and the cost-minimization problem with the emission cap. The results show that the magnitude of enterprises' emission reduction is positively related to their innovation potential; enterprise's individual emission-abatement investment is sensitive to efficiency, budget cap, and environmental benefit.

Wang et al. (2015) took two manufacturers in a duopoly market and studied the production decision after low-carbon regulations in a duopoly market, besides established revenue functions after taking green-tech input into consideration under none carbon emissions limit and carbon tax policy, thus getting manufacturers' optimal decisions. Through analysis above all, they found that manufacturers' optimal production decisions would be affected by the carbon tax policy, as a result, manufacturers should cooperate with each other and avoid the impact of carbon tax policy on profits as far as possible through centralized decision making in a duopoly market. Although green-tech input increased the manufacturer's cost, it improved products' green level and reduced the carbon emissions thus achieving the government's goal of developing low-carbon economy.

According to research conducted by Bond et al. (2004) that the overall reduction in the emission factors is partially offset by an increase in energy consumption. They found that the overall effect is decrease in emission especially in fossil fuel. Their research area is directly related to the Northern and Southern Hemisphere of the Globe.

Carbon Credits Trading in the Manufacturing Sector

This section covers the extensive literature with reference to the carbon credits trading for manufacturing sector.

Cao et al. (2016) proposed that from a sustainable development perspective, an index system is based on Sustainability Balanced Scorecard (SBSC), including the main index of Financial, Internal process, Customer, Learning and growth, Social and the sub-index which comprised 28 indexes to evaluate the Green Manufacturing (GM) of automotive industry.

Bergquist and Söderholm (2015) by employing historical case study methodology examined the transition toward renewable energy and increased energy efficiency in the Swedish pulp and paper industry (PPI) during the 1970s and 1980s. Between 1973 and 1990, CO_2 emissions were cut by 80% in this sector, and this was mainly achieved by substituting away from oil to biofuels in the form of by-products from the pulp manufacturing process. The CO_2 reduction was also a result of energy efficiency improvements and increased internal production of electricity through back-pressure turbine power generation. Sweden was highly dependent on oil at the advent of the first Oil Crisis in 1973, and the increased oil prices put pressure on the Swedish government and the energy-intensive PPI to reduce this oil dependency. Of central importance for the energy transition was the highly collaborative strategy of the PPI, both internally among pulp mills as well as between the sector as a whole and the corporatist Swedish state administration. The Swedish government chose a proactive strategy by emphasizing knowledge management and collaboration with the industry along with the substitution of internal biofuels for oil. The transition was also characterized by a strong focus on unutilized potentials in the PPI; a previous waste problem now could be transformed into energy savings and improved energy efficiency. Energy taxes and fees also played an important role in Swedish energy policy during the 1970s and the 1980s. The results point out at the importance of a more holistic understanding of the interplay between different policies and their impacts in the longer run.

Kopfle et al. (2007) emphasize on the protection of the environment from carbon emission. The focus of this research is on protecting the environment from various types of iron and steel products manufacturing organizations. If the organizations use natural gas in comparison to coal, as a fuel source, then the emission of carbon dioxide may be reduced. MIDREX Process is basically a natural gas-based direct reduction method. If the organizations use 80% hot charged Direct Reduce Iron (DRI) in the Electric Arc Furnace (EAF), then it is found that the carbon emission may be reduced up to 47% per ton of steel produced than the blast furnace. Several part of the world, such as Latin America, Middle East, Russia and several part of Asia use this MIDREX Process. Approximately 14 million tons of new MIDREX Plant capacity are started up recently and more than 20 million tons are under construction in the above part of the world. Singh (2008) describes that as per the Clean Development Mechanism of Kyoto Protocol, carbon credits or CERs are issued by United Nations Framework Convention on Climate Change to the developing countries such as India, China, etc. For reduction in carbon emission, these carbon credits can be purchased by the developed nation. The value of single carbon credit is equivalent to a one ton reduction of carbon dioxide or its corresponding greenhouse gas. Srinivas (2008) describes in light of decreasing price of fuels, like crude oil and coal, i.e., up to 60%, and in the perfect market conditions, the factories should use these fuels more. So that, they should, then need some more carbon credits to atone for the higher pollution. As per the prevailing conditions, the developing countries' manufacturing organizations need more liquidity and simultaneously should push up the prices of carbon credits or CERs. But the prices of carbon credits have also crashed because of the global recession and so compelling the factories to produce less.

Narasimham (2011) explained about the basic solution of infrastructure waste and fly-ash. The focus of his research is directly related to environmental issues. The researcher focuses on fly ash, which is generated from thermal power plants of India. The use of this fly-ash is as the raw material for manufacturing of pavement bricks and other construction materials. Therefore, the main focus of this research is on disposal of this dangerous fly ash, which is generated from thermal power plants. Dhingra and Dhingra (2010) describe that there is much evidence that shows that the climate of the earth is changing and the average temperature of the surface has risen. Therefore, the impact of this rise in temperature is that the glaciers have been melting and the level of the sea is rising. The industrialization is the main example of the human-caused emissions and there is no doubt in that the industries are the main source of generating greenhouse gases such as carbon dioxide, carbon monoxide, etc. McKinnon (2010) describes that the stock keeping unit level carbon auditing of the supply chains and the carbon labeling of products will be very costly. During the auditing process, the use of data inventories and the software support may assist. Jayaramiah (2009) describes two-wheeler manufacturers taking benefits through carbon credits for reducing the carbon dioxide emission. These benefits are available only if selling the green vehicles. These companies are in the process of registering themselves with UNFCCC, i.e., United Nation Framework Convention on Climate Change. According to her research, all these electric two wheeler manufacturers have signed the contract with Grutter Consulting. This consulting company is a Switzerland-based company and it works on clean development mechanism projects in the field of transportation. Sarkar and Manoharan (2009) describe in their research about the estimation of carbon in wooden products especially in harvested wooden handicraft products. The focus of their research is on small and medium-level enterprises. The research estimated that the average consumption of wood per SME unit has been estimated approximately 10,000 kg in a week. The research suggests that there is a need to develop some projects in the area for energy efficiency, reduction in waste and improving the quality of supply and sourcing wood from certified forests and trees outside the certified forests. Choudhary (2007) describes that the cement companies are taking two benefits from single step. The first benefit is that they are producing fly ash with linker to reduce their cost of production and another benefit is that they also earn carbon credits from cement production.

Continuous-Review Policy

We start by considering the case of a firm that adopts a continuous-review policy, that is, the firm continuously monitors its inventory level.

Model Formulation

Consider a manufacturing firm that invests in pollution abatement so that its productive technology is more environment-friendly. Denote by $b(t)$ the environment obsolescence rate of technology at time t (state variable) and by $k(t)$ the investment rate in pollution abating technology at time t (control variable). Then, according to Yi et al. (2014), the dynamics of the environment obsolescence rate of technology, over the planning horizon $[0,T]$, are governed by the following differential equation

$$\frac{db(t)}{dt} = -k(t) + \eta b(t), b(0) = b_0, \tag{1}$$

where η is a positive constant and b_0 is the known initial environment obsolescence rate of technology.

Improved quality can be realized through many means, one of which is benchmarking. Those involved in continuous improvement efforts rely on benchmarking to formulate goals and targets for performance, Ritzman et al. (2013).

Compared with a direct industry competitor renowned as a leading company, our manufacturing firm selects its goal environment obsolescence rate of technology $b(t)$ and its goal investment rate in pollution abating technology $\hat{k}(t)$. The goal $\hat{k}(t)$ should lead to the goal $\hat{b}(t)$ and therefore the pair $\left(b(t), k(k)\right)$ should satisfy the differential equation (1):

$$\frac{d\hat{b}(t)}{dt} = -\hat{k}(t) + \eta\hat{b}(t), \hat{b}(0) = \hat{b}_0. \tag{2}$$

Subtracting Eq. (2) from Eq. (1) yields

$$\frac{d"\, b(t)}{dt} = -"\, k(t) + \eta"\, b(t), "\, b(0) = b_0 - b_0. \tag{3}$$

We assume that the manufacturing firm produces a single product. Items of the product are sold to customers at a dynamic rate $D(t)$. While on the shelves, items of the product are subject to deterioration at a fixed rate θ. Denote by $I(t)$ the inventory level at time t (state variable) and by $P(t)$ the production rate at time t (control variable). The dynamics of the inventory level, over the planning horizon $[0,T]$, are governed by the following differential equation

$$\frac{dI(t)}{dt} = P(t) - D(t) - \theta I(t),\ I(0) = I_0, \tag{4}$$

where I_0 is the known initial inventory level.

Denote by $I(t)$ the goal inventory level (again acquired by competitive benchmarking) and by $P(t)$ the goal production rate at time t. Since $I(t)$ and $P(t)$ satisfy the differential equation (4), then

$$\frac{d\hat{I}(t)}{dt} = \hat{P}(t) - D(t) - \theta\hat{I}(t), \hat{I}(0) = \hat{I}_0. \tag{5}$$

Therefore,

$$\frac{d"\, I(t)}{dt} = "\, P(t) - \theta"\, I(t), "\, I(0) = I_0 - I_0. \tag{6}$$

Denote by h_1, h_2, K_1, K_2, the penalties incurrent by the firm when a state or control variable deviates from its goal. Then, the optimal state and control variables are obtained by minimizing the following objective function

$$\min_{P,k} J = \frac{1}{2}\int_{T}^{0}\left\{h_1 \Delta I(t)^2 + h_2 \Delta b(t)^2 + K_1 \Delta P(t)^2 + K_2 \Delta k(t)^2\right\}dt. \tag{7}$$

Optimal Control

To solve the problem stated in the previous section, we apply the maximum principle of Pontryagin, see Sethi and Thompson (2000). The necessary conditions for a solution to be optimal are that there should exist a continuous and piecewise continuously differentiable function $\Delta(t) = [\lambda_1(t), \lambda_2(t)]^T$ such that

$$\frac{\partial H}{\partial'' P(t)} = \frac{\partial H}{\partial'' k(t)} = 0, \tag{8}$$

$$\frac{\partial H}{\partial'' I(t)} = -\frac{d\lambda_1(t)}{dt}, \frac{\partial H}{\partial'' b(t)} = -\frac{d\lambda_2(t)}{dt}, \tag{9}$$

$$\lambda_1(T) = \lambda_2(T) = 0. \tag{10}$$

where the Hamiltonian H is given by

$$\begin{aligned} H = &-\frac{1}{2}\left\{h_1'' I(t)^2 + h_2'' b(t)^2 + K_1'' P(t)^2 + K_2'' k(t)^2\right\} \\ &+ \lambda_1(t)\left['' P(t) - \theta'' I(t)\right] + \lambda_2(t)\left[-'' k(t) + \eta'' b(t)\right]. \end{aligned} \tag{11}$$

Equations (8) are the control equations, Eqs. (9) are the adjoint equations, and Eqs. (10) are the transversality conditions.

The control equation (8) for $\Delta P(t)$ is equivalent to

$$\lambda_1(t) - K_1'' P(t) = 0, \tag{12}$$

i.e.,

$$'' P(t) = \frac{\lambda_1(t)}{K_1}. \tag{13}$$

Substitute Eq. (13) in Eq. (6):

$$\frac{d'' I(t)}{dt} = \frac{\lambda_1(t)}{K_1} - \theta'' I(t). \tag{14}$$

The adjoint equation (9) for $\lambda_1(t)$ is equivalent to

$$\frac{d\lambda_1(t)}{dt} = \theta\lambda_1(t) + h_1\text{''}\, I(t). \tag{15}$$

Differentiate Eq. (14) with respect to t. Then use Eq. (15) to eliminate $d\lambda_1(t)/dt$ and Eq. (14) to eliminate $\lambda_1(t)$ from the resulting equation:

$$\frac{d^{2\text{''}}\, I(t)}{dt^2} - \left(\theta^2 + \alpha_1^2\right)\text{''}\, I(t) = 0, \tag{16}$$

where $\alpha_1 = \sqrt{\frac{h_1}{K_1}}$ This is a homogeneous second-order differential equation with-constant coefficients. The auxiliary equation is

$$m^2 - \left(\theta^2 + \alpha_1^2\right) = 0. \tag{17}$$

It has two solutions of opposite signs m and $-m$, where

$$m = \sqrt{\theta^2 + \alpha_1^2}. \tag{18}$$

Thus, the general solution of Eq. (16) is

$$\text{''}\, I(t) = a_1 e^{mt} + a_2 e^{-mt}. \tag{19}$$

Also, differentiating Eq. (19) and using Eq. (14) we get

$$\lambda_1(t) = K_1\left[a_1(\theta + m)e^{mt} + a_2(\theta - m)e^{-mt}\right]. \tag{20}$$

Now, by Eq. (13), we have

$$\text{''}\, P(t) = a_1(\theta + m)e^{mt} + a_2(\theta - m)e^{-mt}. \tag{21}$$

To determine a_1 and a_2, we use the initial condition $I(0) = I_0$ and the trasversality condition $\lambda_1(T) = 0$. This yields the constants

$$\begin{aligned} \alpha_1 &= \frac{\text{''}\, I(0)(\theta - m)e^{-mT}}{(\theta - m)e^{-mT} - (\theta + m)e^{mT}}, \\ \alpha_2 &= -\frac{\text{''}\, I(0)(\theta + m)e^{mT}}{(\theta - m)e^{-mT} - (\theta + m)e^{mT}}. \end{aligned} \tag{22}$$

Finally, we obtain the optimal inventory level and the optimal production rate in closed form as

$$\Delta I(t)=\frac{\Delta I(0)\left[(\theta-m)e^{-m(T-t)}-(\theta+m)e^{m(T-t)}\right]}{(\theta-m)e^{-mT}-(\theta+m)e^{mT}},$$
$$\Delta P(t)=\frac{\Delta I(0)(\theta^2-m^2)\left[e^{-m(T-t)}-e^{m(T-t)}\right]}{(\theta-m)e^{-mT}-(\theta+m)e^{mT}}. \quad (23)$$

The control equation (8) for $k(t)$ is equivalent to

$$-\lambda_2(t)-K_2\Delta k(t)=0, \quad (24)$$

i.e.,

$$\text{"}\ k(t)=-\frac{\lambda_2(t)}{K_2}. \quad (25)$$

Substitute Eq. (25) in Eq. (3):

$$\frac{d\text{"}\ b(t)}{dt}=\frac{\lambda_2(t)}{K_2}+\eta\text{"}\ b(t). \quad (26)$$

The adjoint equation (9) for λ_2 is equivalent to

$$\frac{d\lambda_2(t)}{dt}=-\eta\lambda_2(t)+h_2\Delta b(t). \quad (27)$$

Differentiate Eq. (26) with respect to $_t$. Then use Eq. (27) to eliminate $d\lambda_2(t)/dt$ and Eq. (26) to eliminate $\lambda_2(t)$ from the resulting equation:

$$\frac{d^{2\text{"}}\ b(t)}{dt^2}-(\eta^2+\alpha_2^2)\text{"}\ b(t)=0, \quad (28)$$

where $\alpha_2=\sqrt{\frac{h_2}{K_2}}$ This is a homogeneous second-order differential equation withconstant coefficients. The auxiliary equation is

$$n^2-(\eta^2+\alpha_2^2)=0. \quad (29)$$

It has two solutions of opposite signs n and $-n$, where

$$n=\sqrt{\eta^2+\alpha_2^2}. \quad (30)$$

Thus, the general solution of Eq. (28) is

$$'' b(t) = c_1 e^{nt} + c_2 e^{-nt}. \tag{31}$$

In addition, differentiating Eq. (31) and using Eq. (26) we get

$$\lambda_2(t) = K_2\left[c_1(n-\eta)e^{nt} - c_2(n+\eta)e^{-nt}\right]. \tag{32}$$

Now, by Eq. (24), we get

$$k(t) = c_1(\eta - n)e^{nt} + c_2(\eta + n)e^{-nt}. \tag{33}$$

To determine c_1 and c_2, we use the initial condition $b(0) = b_0$ and the trasversality condition $\lambda_2(T) = 0$. This yields the constants

$$\begin{aligned} c_1 &= \frac{'' b(0)(\eta+n)e^{-nT}}{(\eta+n)e^{-nT} - (\eta-n)e^{nT}}, \\ c_2 &= \frac{'' b(0)(n-\eta)e^{nT}}{(\eta+n)e^{-nT} - (\eta-n)e^{nT}}. \end{aligned} \tag{34}$$

Finally, we obtain the optimal environment obsolescence rate of technology and the optimal investment rate in pollution abating technology in a closed form as

$$\begin{aligned} \Delta b(t) &= \frac{\Delta b(0)\left[(\eta+n)e^{-n(T-t)} - (\eta-n)e^{n(T-t)}\right]}{(\eta+n)e^{-nT} - (\eta-n)e^{nT}}, \\ \Delta k(t) &= \frac{\Delta b(0)\left(\eta^2-n^2\right)\left[e^{-n(T-t)} - e^{n(T-t)}\right]}{(\eta+n)e^{-nT} - (\eta-n)e^{nT}}. \end{aligned} \tag{35}$$

Substituting the optimal expressions (23) and (35) in expression (7) yields the explicit form of the optimal cost as

$$\begin{aligned} J^* = {} & \frac{'' I(0)^2 \left\{ \begin{array}{l} h_1\left[(\theta-m)^2\left(1-e^{-2mT}\right) + (\theta+m)^2\left(e^{2mT}-1\right) - 4mT\left(\theta^2-m^2\right)\right] \\ +K_1\left(\theta^2-m^2\right)\left[e^{2mT} - e^{-2mT} - 4mT\right] \end{array} \right\}}{2m\left[(\theta-m)e^{-mT} - (\theta+m)e^{mT}\right]^2} \\ & + \frac{'' b(0)^2 \left\{ \begin{array}{l} h_2[(\eta+n)^2\left(1-e^{-2nT}\right) + (\eta-n)^2\left(e^{-2nT}-1\right) - 4nT\left(\eta^2-n^2\right)] \\ +K_2\left(\eta^2-n^2\right)\left[e^{2nT} - e^{-2nT} - 4nT\right] \end{array} \right\}}{2n\left[(\eta+n)e^{-nT} - (\eta-n)e^{nT}\right]^2}. \end{aligned} \tag{36}$$

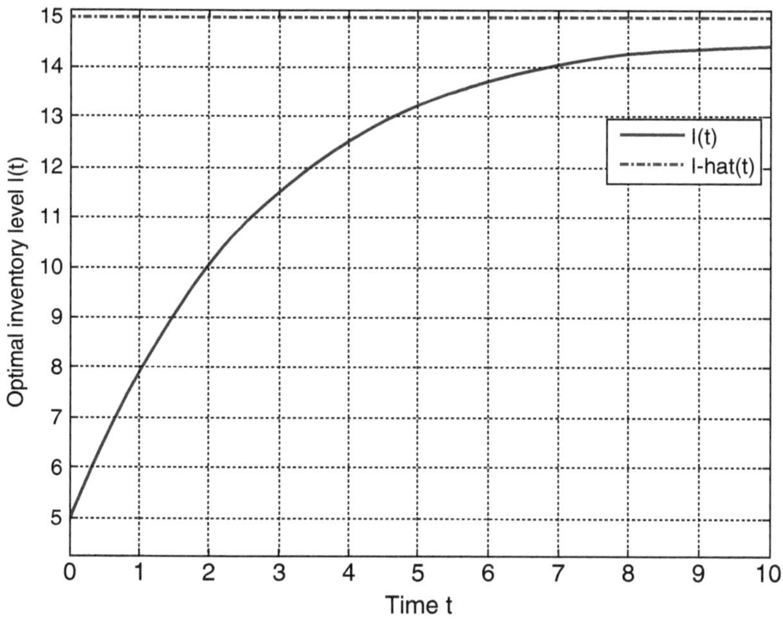

Fig. 1 Variations of the optimal inventory level $I(t)$

Illustrative Example

In the trivial case when $I_0 = \hat{I}$, the optimal inventory level and the optimal production rate are constant throughout the planning horizon interval [0, T]: $I(t) = \hat{I}$ and $P(t) = \hat{P}$. If, moreover, $b_0 = \hat{b}$, then the optimal environment obsolescence rate of technology and the optimal investment rate in pollution abating technology are also constant throughout the planning horizon interval $b(t) = \hat{b}$ and $k(t) = \hat{k}$.

Let us assume now that $I_0 \neq \hat{I}$ and $b_0 \neq \hat{b}$. Assume a planning horizon of length T = 10. The deterioration rate is θ = .01 and the goal inventory level is $\hat{I} = 15$. Assuming the demand rate $D(t)$ = 1 + sin t, the goal production rate is readily found to be $\hat{P}(t) = 2.5 + \sin t$. Assume now η = 0.8 and goal environment obsolescence rate of technology $\hat{b} = 10$. Then, the goal investment rate in pollution abating technology is found to be $\hat{k} = 8$. Finally, assume that initially, I_0 = 5 and b_0 = 5 and the various penalties are given by $h_1 = 5$, $K_1 = 40$, h_2 = 2, and K_2 = 50.

The graphs of the optimal state and control variables are shown in in Figs. 1, 2, 3, and 4. As can be seen, each variable converges to its goal by the end of the planning horizon. The optimal cost is J^* = 1701.64.

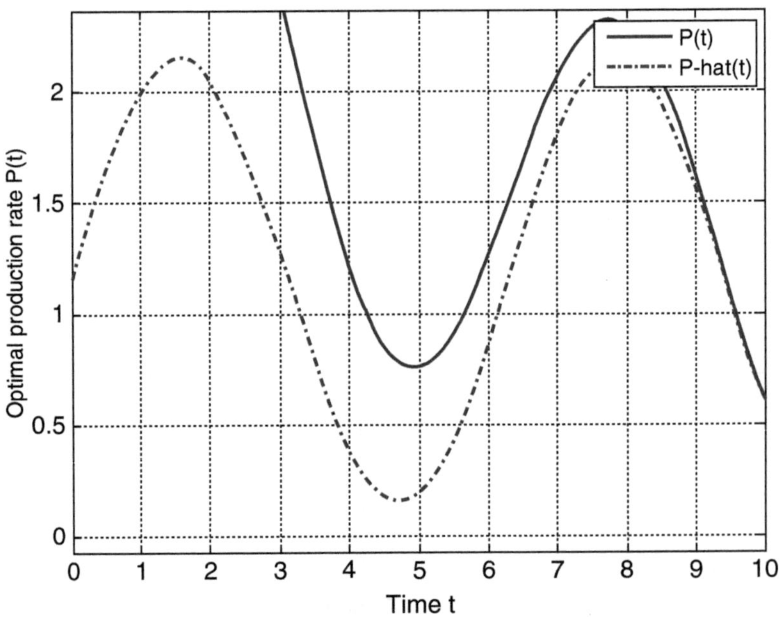

Fig. 2 Variations of the optimal production rate $P(t)$

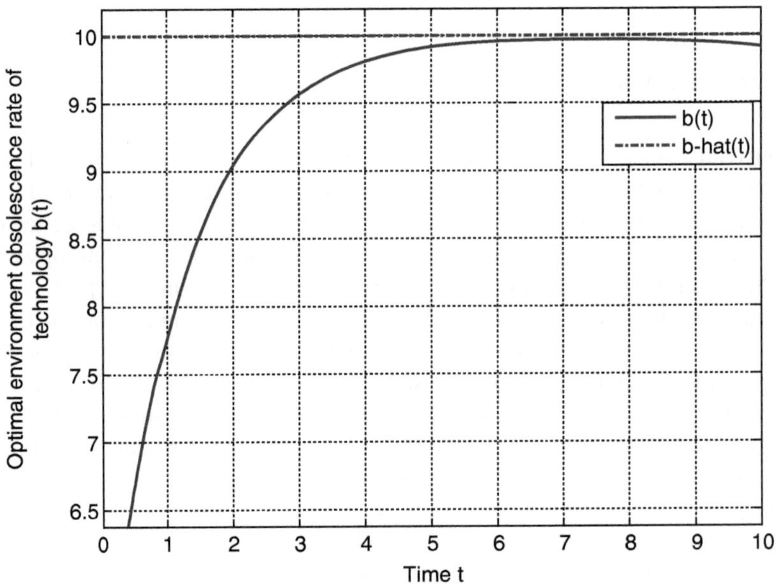

Fig. 3 Variations of the optimal environment obsolescence rate of technology $b(t)$

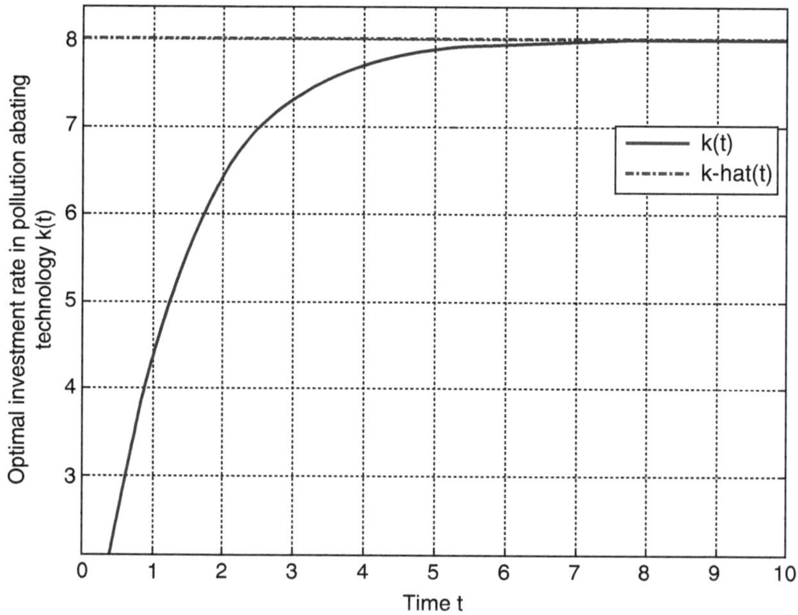

Fig. 4 Variations of the optimal investment rate in pollution abating technology $k(t)$

Periodic-Review Policy

We now turn to the case where the firm adopts a periodic-review policy, that is, the firm checks its inventory level periodically, for example at the end of the day, of the week, or the month, etc.

Model Formulation

To address the pollution abatement problem in discrete time, define $b(i)$ and $k(i)$, the environment obsolescence rate of technology during period i (state variable) and the investment rate in pollution abating technology during period i (control variable). Also, let $\hat{b}(i)$ and denote the corresponding goals. Then, the difference equation corresponding to the state equation (3) is given by

$$"\, b(i+1) = -"\, k(i) + (1+\eta)"\, b(i),"\, b(0) = b_0 - b_0 \tag{37}$$

Similarly, to address the production-planning problem in discrete time, let $I(i)$ and $P(i)$ represent the inventory level during period i (state variable) and the production rate during period i (control variable), respectively. Also, let $\hat{I}(i)$ and $\hat{P}(i)$

represent the corresponding goals. Then, the difference equation corresponding to the state equation (6) is given by

$$” I(i+1) = ” P(i) + (1-\theta)” I(i), ” I(0) = I_0 - I_0, \tag{38}$$

where $D(i)$ is the demand rate during period i. Finally, the optimal solution is obtained by minimizing the following sum of the deviations during the planning horizon:

$$\min_{P,k} J = \frac{1}{2}\sum_{N}^{0}\left\{h_1” I(i)^2 + h_2” b(i)^2 + K_1” P(i)^2 + K_2” k(i)^2\right\}. \tag{39}$$

Optimal Control

Introduce the Lagrange multipliers $\Lambda(i) = [\lambda_1(i), \lambda_2(i)]^T$ and the Lagrangian L as follows:

$$\begin{aligned} L = \sum_{N}^{i=0} \frac{1}{2}&\left\{h_1” I(i)^2 + h_2” b(i)^2 + K_1” P(i)^2 + K_2” k(i)^2\right\} \\ &+\lambda_1(i+1)\left[-I(i+1) + P(i) - D(i) + (1-\theta)I(i)\right] \\ &\quad+\lambda_2(i+1)\left[-b(i+1) - k(i) + (1+\eta)b(i)\right]. \end{aligned} \tag{40}$$

The optimality conditions are

$$\frac{\partial L}{\partial” P(i)} = \frac{\partial L}{\partial” k(i)} = 0, \tag{41}$$

$$\frac{\partial L}{\partial” I(i)} = \frac{\partial L}{\partial” b(i)} = 0. \tag{42}$$

The control equation (41) for $P(i)$ is equivalent to

$$\lambda_1(i+1) + K_1” P(i) = 0, \tag{43}$$

i.e.,

$$” P(i) = -K_1^{-1}\lambda_1(i+1). \tag{44}$$

The adjoint equation (42) for $\Delta I(i)$ is equivalent to

$$h_1 \Delta I(i) - \lambda_1(i) + (1-\theta)\lambda_1(i+1) = 0, \tag{45}$$

i.e.,

$$\lambda_1(i) = h_1 \Delta I(i) + (1-\theta)\lambda_1(i+1). \tag{46}$$

Using the sweep method of Bryson and Ho (1975), we let $\lambda_1(i) = s_1(i)\Delta I(i)$. The next step is to write $\Delta P(i)$ in terms of $\Delta I(i)$. We have

$$\begin{aligned} \Delta P(i) &= -K_1^{-1}\lambda_1(i+1) \\ &= -K_1^{-1}s_1(i+1)\Delta I(i+1) \\ &= -K_1^{-1}s_1(i+1)\left[\Delta P(i) + (1-\theta)\Delta I(i)\right]. \end{aligned} \tag{47}$$

Solving for $\Delta P(i)$ yields

$$\begin{aligned} \Delta P(i) + K_1^{-1}s_1(i+1)\Delta P(i) &= -K_1^{-1}s_1(i+1)(1-\theta)\Delta I(i) \\ \Delta P(i)\left[1 + K_1^{-1}s_1(i+1)\right] &= -K_1^{-1}s_1(i+1)(1-\theta)\Delta I(i) \\ \Delta P(i)\left[K_1 + s_1(i+1)\right] &= -s_1(i+1)(1-\theta)\Delta I(i). \end{aligned} \tag{48}$$

Therefore, we can write

$$\Delta P(i) = -\rho_1(i+1)\Delta I(i), \tag{49}$$

where

$$\rho_1(i+1) = \frac{s_1(i+1)(1-\theta)}{K_1 + s_1(i+1)}. \tag{50}$$

The elements $s_1(i)$ can be calculated through a recursive equation as follows:

$$\begin{aligned} \lambda_1(t) &= h_1 \Delta I(i) + (1-\theta)\lambda_1(i+1) \\ s_1(i)\Delta I(i) &= h_1 \Delta I(i) + (1-\theta)s_1(i+1)\Delta I(i+1) \\ &= h_1 \Delta I(i) + (1-\theta)s_1(i+1)\left[\Delta P(i) + (1-\theta)\Delta I(i)\right]. \end{aligned} \tag{51}$$

Thus,

$$s_1(i) = h_1 + (1-\theta)s_1(i+1)\left[-\rho_1(i+1) + (1-\theta)\right]. \tag{52}$$

Now all the elements $s_1(i)$ can be calculated recursively, starting from the boundary condition $s_1(N) = h_1$. Finally, the optimal solution for the production-planning problem is obtained since the optimal states are found by

$$\begin{aligned}\Delta I(i+1) &= \Delta P(i) + (1-\theta)\Delta I(i) \\ &= \left[-\rho_1(i+1) + (1-\theta)\right]\Delta I(i).\end{aligned} \tag{53}$$

and the optimal control is found by

$$\Delta P(i) = -\rho_1(i+1)\Delta I(i). \tag{54}$$

Going back to the pollution abatement problem, the control equation (41) for $k(i)$ is equivalent to

$$-\lambda_2(i+1) + K_2 \Delta k(i) = 0, \tag{55}$$

i.e.,

$$\Delta k(i) = -K_2^{-1}\lambda_2(i+1). \tag{56}$$

The adjoint equation (44) for $\Delta b(i)$ is equivalent to

$$h_2 \Delta b(i) - \lambda_2(i) + (1+\eta)\lambda_2(i+1) = 0, \tag{57}$$

i.e.,

$$\lambda_2(i) = h_2 \Delta b(i) + (1+\eta)\lambda_2(i+1). \tag{58}$$

Again, we use the sweep method of Bryson and Ho (1975) and let $\lambda_2(i) = s_2(i)$ $\Delta b(i)$. To write $\Delta k(i)$ in terms of $\Delta b(i)$, we have

$$\begin{aligned}\Delta k(i) &= K_2^{-1}\lambda_2(i+1) \\ &= K_2^{-1}s_2(i+1)\Delta b(i+1) \\ &= K_2^{-1}s_2(i+1)\left[-\Delta k(i) + (1+\eta)\Delta b(i)\right].\end{aligned} \tag{59}$$

Solving for $\Delta k(i)$ yields

$$\begin{aligned}\Delta k(i) + K_2^{-1}s_2(i+1)\Delta k(i) &= K_2^{-1}s_2(i+1)(1+\eta)\Delta b(i) \\ \Delta k(i)\left[1 + K_2^{-1}s_2(i+1)\right] &= K_2^{-1}s_2(i+1)(1+\eta)\Delta b(i) \\ \Delta k(i)\left[K_2 + s_2(i+1)\right] &= s_2(i+1)(1+\eta)\Delta b(i)\end{aligned} \tag{60}$$

Therefore,

$$\Delta k(i) = \rho_2(i+1)\Delta b(i), \tag{61}$$

where

$$\rho_2(i+1) = \frac{s_2(i+1)(1+\eta)}{K_2 + s_2(i+1)}. \tag{62}$$

As in the case of the production planning, we derive a recursive equation for $s_2(i)$ as follows:

$$\begin{aligned} \lambda_2(t) &= h_2'' \, b(i) + (1+\eta)\lambda_2(i+1) \\ s_2(i)'' \, b(i) &= h_2'' \, b(i) + (1+\eta) s_2(i+1)'' \, b(i+1) \\ &= h_2'' \, b(i) + (1+\eta) s_2(i+1)\left[{}'' \, k(i) + (1+\eta)'' \, b(i)\right]. \end{aligned} \tag{63}$$

Thus,

$$s_2(i) = h_2 + (1+\eta) s_2(i+1)\left[-\rho_2(i+1) + (1+\eta)\right]. \tag{64}$$

The boundary condition for the above recursion is $s_2(N) = h_2$. Finally, the optimal state is obtained by

$$\begin{aligned} {}'' \, b(i+1) &= {}'' \, k(i) + (1+\eta)'' \, b(i) \\ &= \left[\rho_2(i+1) + (1+\eta)\right]'' \, b(i) \end{aligned} \tag{65}$$

and the optimal control by

$${}'' \, k(t) = \rho_2(i+1)'' \, b(i). \tag{66}$$

Substituting the optimal expressions of the state and control variables in expression (39) yields the explicit form of the optimal cost as

$$J = \frac{1}{2}\sum_{N}^{i=0} \left\{ \begin{aligned} &\left[h_1 + K_1\rho_1(i+1)^2\right]\prod_{i}^{j=1}\left[1-\theta-\rho_1(j)\right]^2 {}'' \, I(0)^2 \\ &+\left[h_2 + K_2\rho_2(i+1)^2\right]\prod_{k}^{i=1}\left[1+\eta+\rho_2(j)\right]^2 {}'' \, b(0)^2 \end{aligned} \right\}. \tag{67}$$

Illustrative Example

For illustration, we use the same data as in the case of the continuous-review policy. The optimal state and control variables are depicted in Figs. 5, 6, 7, and 8. All variables converge toward their goal as in the continuous case. The optimal cost is $J^* =$ 73.08.

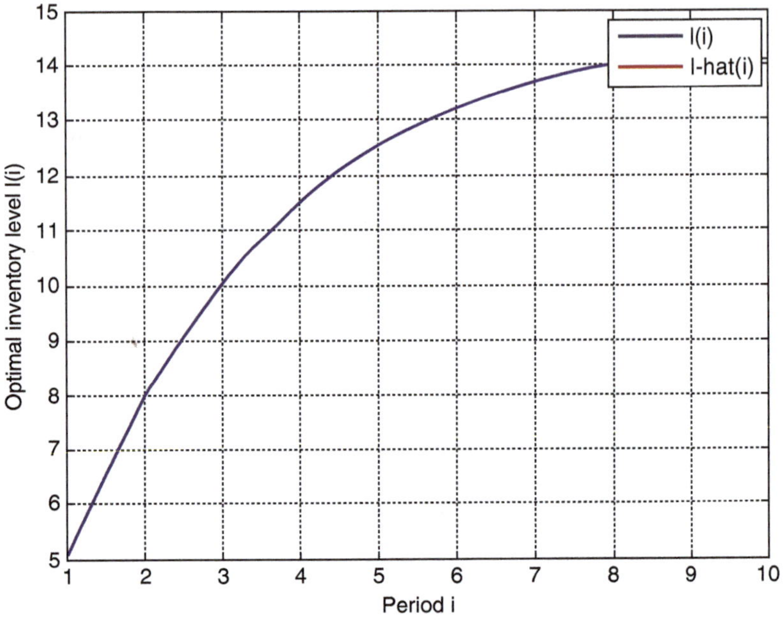

Fig. 5 Variations of the optimal inventory level $I(i)$

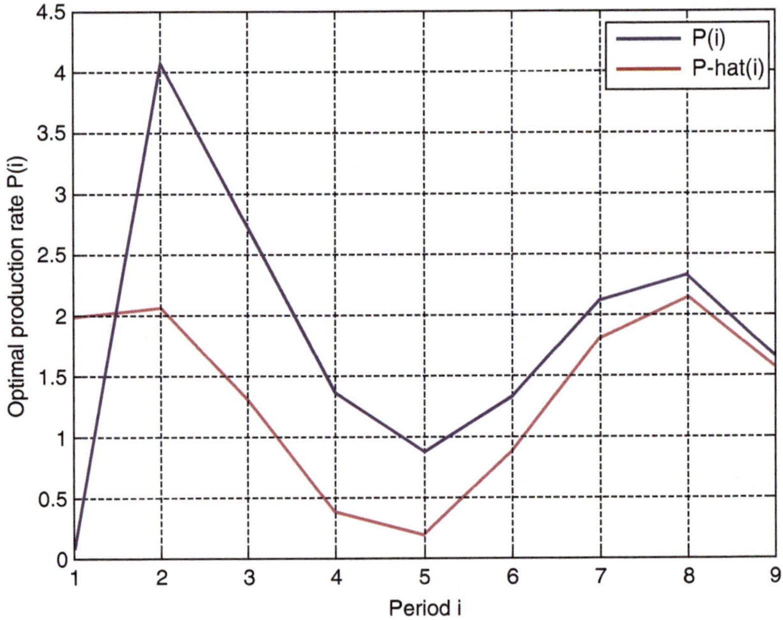

Fig. 6 Variations of the optimal production rate $P(t)$

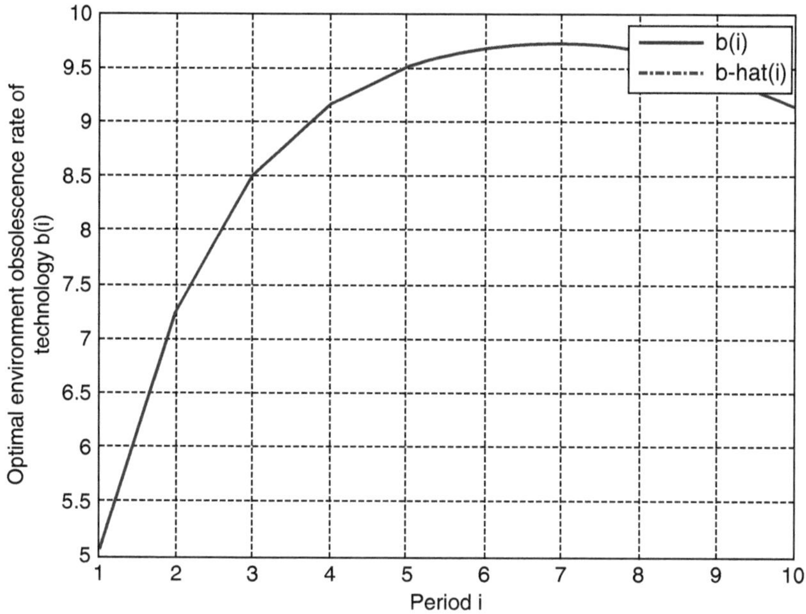

Fig. 7 Variations of the optimal environment obsolescence rate of technology $b(i)$

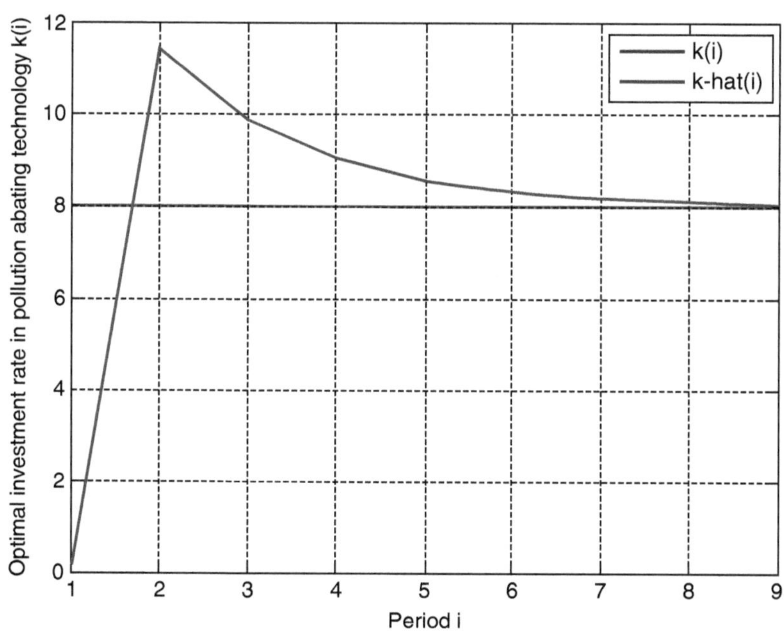

Fig. 8 Variations of the optimal investment rate in pollution abating technology $k(i)$

Conclusion

There are basically two types of market-based incentive policies for controlling emissions: (1) taxes and subsidies and (2) transferable emission permits, Field and Olewiler (2011). Under each policy, polluters make their own decisions about the amount of pollution to emit based on the prices per unit pollution they face. In this paper, we determine the optimal production rate and the optimal investment rate in pollution abating technology for a firm, given a target inventory level and a target environment obsolescence rate of technology. In a future research direction, one could combine this model with one where items of products are returned to the firm for remanufacturing. Remanufactured items could be as-good-as-new or as-good-as-old. Another research direction would be to assume a random demand rate.

References

Ahonen S (2004) Methods to reduce CO_2 emissions from offices and public events in Finland. Final thesis, Tampere Polytechnic, Environmental Engineering, Tampere, Finland

Bates R (2002) An economic analysis of sequestering carbon in forests grown on abandoned mine lands in West Virginia. Master's thesis, Austin State University, Nacogdoches, TX, pp 23–29

Bergquist A-K, Söderholm K (2015) Sustainable energy transition: the case of the Swedish pulp and paper industry 1973–1990. Energ Effic 9:1–14. doi:10.1007/s12053-015-9416-5

Bond TC, Streets DG, Yarber KF, Nelson SM, Woo J-H, Klimont Z (2004) A technology-based global inventory of black and organic carbon emissions from combustion. J Geophys Res 109(D14). doi: 10.1029/2003JD003697

Bryson AE, Ho YC (1975) Applied optimal control. Halsted Press, Washington, DC

Cao Y, You J, Wang R, Shi Y (2016) Designing a mixed evaluating system for green manufacturing of automotive industry. Prob Sust Dev 11(1):73–86

Choudhary S (2007) SRF raises Rs 500 crore from carbon credits sale. The Times of India. http://articles.economictimes.indiatimes.com/2007-04-09/news/28401606_1_ashish-bharat-ram-srf-carbon-credits. Accessed 28 July 2011

Dhingra N, Dhingra M (2010) Carbon credits: level of awareness in Indian SMEs. Viewpoint July-December, 25–35. http://www.tmu.ac.in/management/pdf/julydec2010/final_inner_08.pdf. Accessed 6 Mar 2016

Field BC, Olewiler ND (2011) Environmental economics, Third Canadian edn. McGraw-Hill, Ryerson, Canada

Gerigk J, MacKenzie IA, Ohndorf M (2015) A model of benchmarking regulation: revisiting the efficiency of environmental standards. Environ Resour Econ 62(1):59–82

Giddens A (2010) Can climate change modernize Russia? N Perspect Q 27(4):54–56

Jayaramiah J (2009) Carbon credits to boost electric 2-wheeler sector. The Financial Express. http://www.financialexpress.com/news/carbon-credits-to-boost-electric-2wheeler-sector/555546/. Accessed 26 July 2011

Kopfle JT, McClelland JM, Metius GE (2007) Green[er] steelmaking with the midrex direct reduction process. Millennium Steel 2007:19–22. http://www.spongeironindia.in/Midrex.pdf

Kumar M, Raman J, Priya (2016) The effects of green policy on the performance of green supply chains. Int J Integr Suppl Manag 10(1). doi:10.1504/IJISM.2016.074416

Lee K-H, Cheong I-M (2011) Measuring a carbon footprint and environmental practice: the case of Hyundai Motors Co. (HMC). Ind Manag Data Syst 111(6):961–978

McKinnon AC (2010) Product-level carbon auditing of supply chains: environmental imperative or wasteful distraction? Int J Phys Distrib Logist Manag 40(1/2):42–60
Miranda M, Dieperink C, Glasbergen P (2002) The social meaning of carbon dioxide emission trading institutional capacity building for a green market in Costa Rica. Environ Dev Sustain 4(1):69–86
Moore FC, MacCracken MC (2009) Lifetime-leveraging: an approach to achieving international agreement and effective climate protection using mitigation of short-lived greenhouse gases. Int J Clim Chang Strat Manag 1(1):42–62
Narasimham VL (2011) Issues with fly-ash and infrastructure waste: a techno-business solution, Naldehra Building Centre, Faridabad, India. Soc Bus Rev 6(2):157–167
Pan Y, Luo T, Birdsey R, Hom J, Melillo J (2004) New estimates of carbon storage and sequestration in China's forests: effects of age-class and method on inventory-based carbon estimation. Clim Chang 67(2):211–236
Polonsky MJ, Miles MP, Grau SL (2011) Climate change regulation: implications for business executives. Eur Bus Rev 23(4):368–383
Ritzman LP, Krajewski LJ, Malhotra MK, Klassen RD (2013) Foundations of operations management, Third Canadian edn. Pearson, Toronto, Canada
Sarimveis H, Patrinos P, Tarantilis CD, Kiranoudis CT (2008) Dynamic modeling and control of supply chain systems: a review. Comput Oper Res 35:3530–3561
Sarkar AB, Manoharan TR (2009) Benefits of carbon markets to small and medium enterprises (SMEs) in harvested wood products: a case study from Saharanpur, Uttar Pradesh, India. Afr J Environ Sci Technol 3(9):219–228
Sethi SP, Thompson GL (2000) Optimal control theory: applications to management science and economics, 2nd edn. Kluwer Academic Publishers, Dordrecht
Singh N (2008.) Carbon credit prices crash on falling crude. The Times of India. http://articles.economictimes.indiatimes.com/2008-12-06/news/27734074_1_cers-carbon-credits-crude-prices. Accessed 28 July 2011
Srinivas NN (2008.) Between global recession and carbon credits. The Times of India. http://articles.economictimes.indiatimes.com/2008-11-06/news/27711913_1_cer-prices-eu-allowances-carbon-credits. Accessed 28 July 2011
Stevens KA, DeAngelo G, Shenita B (2011) Comparative study of selected greenhouse gas offset protocols. Int J Clim Chang Strat Manag 3(2):118–139
Wang D, Fu T, Wang R, Anderson DE, Qi Y (2015) Production decision with carbon taxes and green-tech in a duopoly market. IEEE international conference on logistics, informatics, and service sciences (LISS), Barcelona 2015. http://ieeexplore.ieee.org/xpl/mostRecentIssue.jsp?punumber=7362949. doi: 10.1109/LISS.2015.7369735
Wang M, Wang M, Hu Y, Xie H (2016) Multistage investment actions with the emission cap. Math Probl Eng 2016: Article ID 9168765, 12 pages
West TO, Marland G (2002) A synthesis of carbon sequestration, carbon emissions, and net carbon flux in agriculture: comparing tillage practices in the United States. Agric Ecosyst Environ 91(1-3):217–232
Yi Y, Wang Z, Li S (2014) The optimal dynamic pollution control and optimal environmental taxation. Int J Eng Ind 5(3):37–45

Optimal Selection of Superlative Candidates for Open Positions Using Linear Programming

Abdelghani Bouras

Abstract Due to the extensions of businesses, companies have multi-positions to be filled every year. On the other hand, many experienced as well as fresh applicants are looking for new experiences that challenge their abilities, stimulate their knowledge, and increase their income. In a very robust competitive environment, leading organizations are looking for appropriate qualified people to cover the open positions that result from the business extension or from vacancies due to resignations and lack of capabilities.

The usual practice of originations is to hold nominee applications with the recruiting unit. Thus, the objective of the research is to provide the Human Resources Department with a valid systematic methodology to ensure that highly qualified employees are selected as soon as a department needs them, and then to guarantee the appropriateness of the final selection in terms of multi-qualifications criteria.

We develop a mathematical model to help the HR department of a local bank select candidates classified into three categories, experts, fresh graduates, and processors, based on the following criteria:

For experts, the model considers specialty, languages, interview feedback, residency, age, years of experience, and required packages.

Concerning graduates and processors, we consider major, languages, interview feedback, residency, age, bank's IQ test, and GPA.

The model, an integer program, is built to satisfy the following requirements:

- The minimum number of required employees, the field of experience, and the major
- Language constraints
- Interview score requirements
- Residency requirements
- IQ test related to the whole applicants
- Number of years of experience score
- Required package as opposed to other applicants
- GPA score

A. Bouras (✉)
Industrial Engineering Department, College of Enginineering, King Saud University, Riyadh, Saudi Arabia
e-mail: bouras@ksu.edu.sa

L. Tadj, A.K. Garg (eds.), *Emerging Challenges in Business, Optimization, Technology, and Industry*, Springer Proceedings in Business and Economics,
DOI 10.1007/978-3-319-58589-5_9

The minimization of the objective function consists of selecting the least number of candidates who satisfy all the constraints above.

The model is a very fast tool for helping the Bank to use rationally the existing resources and making the best decision in terms of selection of the most adequate candidates.

Keywords Human resources • Selection • Criteria • Linear programming

Social Implications of Carbon Credit Trading—A Case Study

Satyendra Arya, Ajay K. Garg, and Rakesh K. Mudgal

Abstract Carbon credits' trading is an emerging concept from which several organizations start earning financial and social status. The Climate change is the greatest challenge threatening the survival of humanity itself because of its malpractice and release of toxic gases resulting in pollution of ecological endowments caused by human behavior in pursuit of economic motives. This research paper will examine the conditions leading to the climate change and the issues which are directly or indirectly related to the carbon credits trading and its relevance in society. The basic concept of Carbon Credits Trading is generated from Kyoto Protocol and is basically used to control the greenhouse gas emissions. This research paper will be based on a case study on a training session conducted by a reputed university and it will show the calculation of carbon credits trading relevant for economic and social growth.

Keywords Carbon credit trading • Social implications • Global warning • Greenhouse gas emissions

Introduction

Carbon credits are an element used to aid in regulations of an amount of gases that are being released into the air. This is part of a larger international plan which has been created in an effort to reduce global warming and its effects. The plan works by capping an amount of total emissions that can be released by one company or business. If there is a shortfall in an amount of gases that are used, there is a

S. Arya (✉)
Research Scholar, Department of Management Studies, TMIMT, Teerthanker Mahaveer University, Moradabad, 244001, Uttar Pradeh, India
e-mail: satyendra_arya17@rediffmail.com

A.K. Garg
Administrative Sciences Department, Fairleigh Dickinson University, 842, Cambie Street, Vancouver, BC V6B 2P6, Canada

R.K. Mudgal
Vice Chancellor, Teerthanker Mahaveer University, Moradabad, 244001, Uttar Pradeh, India

L. Tadj, A.K. Garg (eds.), *Emerging Challenges in Business, Optimization, Technology, and Industry*, Springer Proceedings in Business and Economics, DOI 10.1007/978-3-319-58589-5_10

monetary value assigned to this shortfall and it may be traded. These credits are often traded between businesses. However, they also are bought and sold in international markets at whatever the determined market value for them is. There are also times when these credits are used to fund carbon reduction plans between trading partners.

Global Warming—The Issue

The earth has an atmosphere of the proper depth and chemical composition. About 30% of incoming energy from the sun is reflected back to space while the rest reaches the earth, resulting in warming the air, oceans, and land and maintaining an average surface temperature of about 15 °C. The chemical composition of the atmosphere is also responsible for nurturing life on our planet. Most of it is nitrogen (78%); about 21% is oxygen, which all animals need to survive and only a small percentage (0.036%) is made up of carbon dioxide which plants require for photosynthesis.

To mitigate the global warming, carbon credit is a major component at international and national levels. Carbon credits trading provides a way to reduce carbon emissions on an industrial scale at international and national levels by capping the total carbon emission annually and letting the global market by assigning a monetary value for any shortfall through carbon credits trading. These carbon credits can be traded between two or more business entities or brought from global market at a very nominal price. This amount can also be used to finance various carbon reduc-

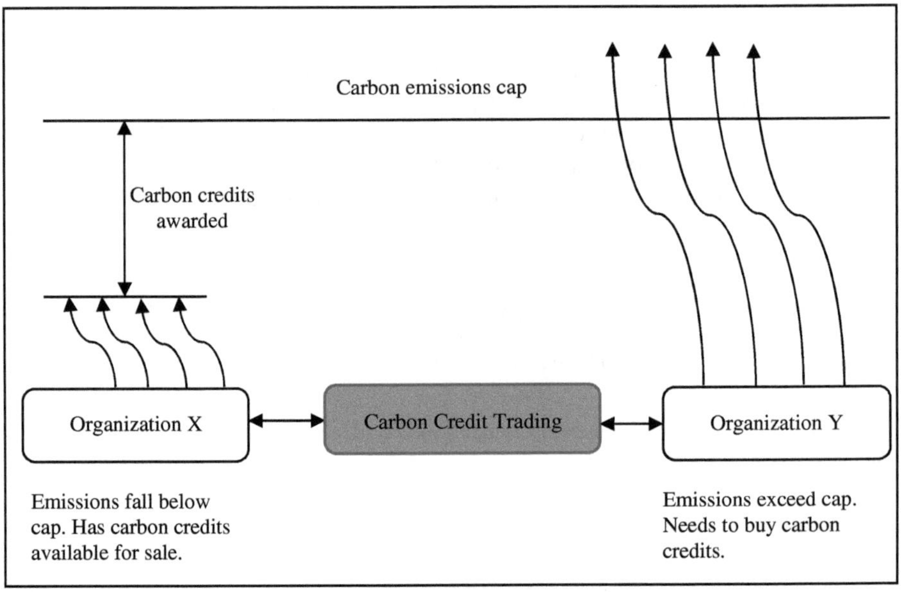

Fig. 1 How does carbon credit trading work?

tion schemes among the trading organizations around the globe. The framework of Carbon Credits Trading is shown in Fig. 1.

Carbon Credits

The means of Carbon Credits are as follows: 1 carbon credit (CER) = 1 ton of emission reduced.

- In the International Market, several companies can trade the carbon credit and now carbon credit has become an attractive model for industries, power plants, and consumers alike to gain additional income or reduce costs in the process of meeting their commitments toward controlling pollution and joining the drive to be eco-friendly.
- Many Indian companies and also companies in other developing countries must realize that the money could be generated by some eco-friendly initiatives.
- They would rapidly turn to clean technologies and would begin trading their carbon credits with companies in the US and in the European Union.

Example of a Carbon Credit Transaction

Suppose X (tons) represent the present emissions of a company and Y (tons) represent the emission quota for that same company. If X > Y, the company has two alternatives:

1. Install new machinery that will reduce the emissions from X to Y tons.
2. Purchase carbon credits worth (X–Y) tons of emissions.

Review of Literature

Sivasangari and Rajan (2016) opined that carbon credits trading was one of the fastest-growing markets and the worth of this market was around $100 billion and the expected worth after the ten years was around $1 trillion.

Ploss (2016) described in her study which is related to environmental assets i.e. greenhouse gas reduction projects. She explained that from establishments of greenhouse reduction projects companies would earn carbon credits and she advised that for trading, carbon credits must be quantifiable, real and verified by designated authority. She illustrated in her study that six greenhouse gases were eligible for carbon credits and these gases had different values which were totally depending on their global warming potential; methane was around 21 times more potentials than carbon dioxide. So, she advised to those organizations which were generating greenhouse gases like methane, carbon dioxide, etc. must think about carbon credits trading. She also described a procedure in her study, for the above organizations, to earn carbon credits.

Frunza et al. (2014) described in their study about measuring the value of the fraud and analyze the particular period where the carbon market was driven by MTF movements. After this, the government passed a law to reduce these types of fraud by applying the model. These authors also estimate the actual impact of the value added tax extortion at the carbon credits market at around $1.3 billion.

Horka (2012) emphasized his research on carbon credits for sustainable land use systems in an agriculture industry. He told that carbon credits were issued for reductions in greenhouse gas emissions and this can be traded globally. He pointed out the system in which an organization must go through a very lengthy approval process for earning carbon credits. He explained a number of factors need to be fulfilled for a project to become viable for a carbon credit project. He also described several Clean Development Mechanism (CDM) projects which were directly related to an agriculture industry.

Research Objectives

The main objectives of this research paper are as follows:

- To know the basic concept of carbon credit trading.
- To find out the social implications of carbon credit trading.
- To know the impact of organizations working on carbon credit trading.

Research Methodology

A research methodology is the way of defining the activity of research, the procedure of research, determining the elements of such research in terms of scientifically adopted models or approaches, designs, and tools. The present study has made an attempt to fulfil the impact of the organization's working on carbon credits trading.

In this research, the authors take the analytical and descriptive research approach. This research shows that, when an organization organizes an event then, how much carbon does it emit in the environment? The analytical approach of this research is based upon the 2 days International Conference that is held at Management Institute.

Case Study

The following case study will show the calculations of carbon credits. It shows how to calculate the carbon credits that are generated in organizing a 2 days International Conference.

Table 1 Energy consumption of working (per day)

Appliance	Units	Ratings (W)	Consumption (h)	K Wh
Fan	5	60	6	1.8
Tube light	20	40	6	4.8
Computer	5	80	6	2.4
Laptops	5	50	6	1.5
AC	2	2000	6	24.0
Miscellaneous	1	300	6	1.8
Total				36.3

Table 2 Energy consumption on the event day (single day)

Appliance	Units	Ratings (W)	Consumption (h)	K Wh
Fan	50	60	6	18.0
Tube light	100	40	6	24.0
Computer	20	80	6	9.6
Laptops	50	50	6	20.0
AC	15	2000	6	18.0
Miscellaneous	5	100	6	3.0
Total				254.6

Electricity Calculations

The following table represents the energy consumption for the conference. In this event, we assume that there are 5 fans, 20 tube lights, 5 computers, 5 laptops, 2 ACs, and 1 miscellaneous article that are working simultaneously. The electricity calculation of working and event day is as follows in (Tables 1 and 2):

We assume that we are planning this event since 4 months and total numbers of working days are 80.

Total electricity consumption on working days = 80 × 36.3 = 2904.3 K Wh.

Total electricity consumption on event days (two days event) = 2 × 254.6 = 509.2 K Wh.

Total Electricity Consumption = 2904.3 + 509.2 = 3413.5 K Wh.

$$\textit{Amount of } \mathrm{CO_2} \textit{release in atmosphere}(\textit{metric tons}) = (3413.55 \times 0.53)/(1000).$$
$$= 1.809 \, \textit{metric tons}.$$

(Source: http://www.carbonfootprint.com/calculator.aspx).

Transportation Calculation

In this case study, the authors assume three modes of transportation. The calculations for three modes of transportation are as follows:

1. Flights:
   1 person from flight = 0.17 metric tons of CO_2.
   5 person from flight = 5 × 0.17 = 0.85 metric tons of CO_2.
   Assumptions: Five members are from Mumbai and they travel through flight.
   (Source: http://www.carbonfootprint.com/calculator.aspx).
2. Cars/bikes:
   Assumptions: Team of 50 people travelling 30 km each on a vehicle with an approximate mileage of 30 km/L. Liters of petrol consumed = (30 × 50 × 80 days)/30 = 4000 L.
   Carbon footprint = 8.788 tons of CO_2.
   (Assume petrol car).
   (Source: http://www.carbon-calculator.org.uk/).
3. Trains:

Assumptions: Approximate number of people traveling by train: 50. (Different Places).
Average km traveled (back and forth): 400 kms.
Carbon footprint per person: 400 kms = 0.032 tons of CO_2.
Total carbon footprint 50 × 0.032 = 1.6 tons of CO_2.
Total carbon footprint generated due to transportation is as follows:

$$\textit{Carbon footprint generated from transportation} = (0.85 + 8.788 + 1.6)\,\textit{tons of}\ CO_2. \\ = 11.238\,\textit{tons of}\ CO_2.$$

(Source: http://www.carbon-calculator.org.uk/).

Energy Usage Due to Cooking

The authors assume that meals are arranged for 2 days (breakfast, lunch, and dinner). The total amount of LPG consumed will be around 20 commercial cylinders (20 L each).

Total LPG consumed = 20 × 20 = 400 L.
Emission of CO_2 per liters = 1.5 kg of CO_2.
Carbon footprint: (400 × 1.5) = 0.6 tons of CO_2.
(Source: http://www.carbonfootprint.com/calculator.aspx).

Table 3 Total carbon footprint generated during the international conference

Serial number	Categories	Amount on CO_2 emitted (tons)
1	Electricity	1.809
2	Transportation	11.238
3	Food	0.6
4	Miscellaneous (assuming 25% of total)	13.647 × 25% = 3.412
	Total	17.059

Carbon Footprint During International Conference

The total carbon footprint generated during the International Conference is as follows (Table 3):

Conclusion

Carbon credit trading is a concept that is used directly to protect our environment from dangerous gases. Several organizations are producing some dangerous and toxic gases in the environment regularly, and we need to reduce these gases from the environment. Therefore, there is a great impact of organization's profile on carbon emission, which was discussed in this research paper. The above case study shows that a 2-day conference generates 17.059 tons of CO_2. This is an eye-opening research for all because people emit lots of carbon in the environment and they are not aware about this. The challenge is now to find how to reduce carbon emission. This research paper examined the conditions leading to the climate change and the issues that are directly or indirectly related to the carbon footprint and its relevance in society.

References

Frunza MC, Guegan D, Lassoudiere A (2014) Missing trader fraud on the emissions market. http://www.emeraldinsight.com/journals.htm?issn=1359-0790&volume=18&issue=2&articleid=1923935&show=abstract. Retrieved 27 July 2014

Horka P (2012) Agriculture and the carbon market. https://www.fibl.org/fileadmin/documents/de/news/2012/calas/8_CaLas2011_Horka.pdf. Retrieved June 2016

Ploss S (2016) Introduction to carbon credits. http://www.soc.iastate.edu/sapp/soc415carboncredits.pdf. Retrieved Sept 2016

Sivasangari S, Vel Rajan T. (2016) Carbon trading—a financial incentive to pollute less. www.journalijar.com/uploads/388_IJAR-8787.pdf. Retrieved 29 June 2016

Measuring the Economic Integration of Immigrants—A Cross-National Comparison Between Canada and Germany

Isabella Krysa and Sharmistha Nag

Abstract This paper compares the economic integration of immigrants into the labor force between Germany and Canada. Both Canada and Germany rely on immigrants to remain competitive in the economy due to low birth rates and an aging population in both countries. Canada and Germany are based on two contradictory discourses in their consideration of immigration. While Canada has relied since its colonization by the British and French on immigrants for economic expansion and nation building, Germany never considered itself to be an immigrant country, but rather as a host of guest workers who would leave 1 day when their labor power was not needed any longer. Thus, a cross-national comparison between two opposing immigration discourses is a valuable contribution to the global research on immigration as it can highlight similarities and differences in the successful economic integration of immigrants. Further, it can point to determining factors that contribute to the economic integration of immigrants. In order to measure if the two countries have differences in the success of economic integration of immigrants, the measures of unemployment rates, field of work, and income of immigrants are compared and contrasted.

Keywords Integration of immigrants • Comparative analysis • Economic success of immigrants

---

I. Krysa (✉)
Management Department, Fairleigh Dickinson University, Vancouver, BC, Canada
e-mail: i.krysa@fdu.edu

S. Nag
Department of Economics, Fairleigh Dickinson University, Vancouver, BC, Canada

L. Tadj, A.K. Garg (eds.), *Emerging Challenges in Business, Optimization, Technology, and Industry*, Springer Proceedings in Business and Economics,
DOI 10.1007/978-3-319-58589-5_11

Part IV
Management and Global Issues Track

Educating for Change in Mindset and Worldview on Sustainability: One Teacher's Story

Kent D. Fairfield

Abstract Organizations around the world have become increasingly concerned about managing for sustainability. Educating undergraduates about sustainability presents the challenge of dealing with students with limited knowledge, politicized awareness, and modest understanding of business and sustainability issues. Traditional-aged students are at a stage of deriving their own worldview on many subjects, including their place in a broader world. Equipping them to be useful professionals in the future, or even specializing in sustainability-oriented careers, requires raising their awareness of the state of the world in environmental, societal, political, and business terms. A curriculum needs to get them acquainted with what the world needs to reach a more fruitful future, as well as the strategies that the business sector can pursue for that purpose. This study reports one professor's attempt to create a comprehensive pedagogy to produce highly qualified graduates and support them in acquiring a mindset and worldview that includes cognitive skills, fundamental values, and confidence to make an appreciable impact toward a sustainable planet.

Keywords Sustainability • Environment • Mindset • Global

Issues in sustainability have grown in importance far beyond early concerns about automobile gas mileage, plastic shopping bag use, and control of air pollution. The majority of the public around the world has come to believe in the severity of global climate change. Widespread income inequality has arisen, due to vigorous prosperity among the world's affluent, while, despite improvements, over 800 million stay mired in chronic poverty. As result, millions suffer from ill health, despair, early mortality, and civil unrest. Desertification and rising sea level have eroded the ability to scratch out even a subsistence living for a massive segment of the population.

K.D. Fairfield (✉)
Management Department, Fairleigh Dickinson University, Teaneck, NJ, USA
e-mail: kent@fdu.edu

L. Tadj, A.K. Garg (eds.), *Emerging Challenges in Business, Optimization, Technology, and Industry*, Springer Proceedings in Business and Economics,
DOI 10.1007/978-3-319-58589-5_12

Universities hoping today to equip undergraduates to become productive professionals are obliged to arm them with at least basic competence in dealing with sustainability issues. This paper will discuss the author's attempt at what can be done, starting with raising the awareness of students about the state of the world. It will then suggest some of the things that need to be done to move the planet toward a sustainable condition. The following section offers a review of what an educated business graduate needs to know about what businesses should do, what is already being done in many quarters, and what the business sector's potential is for powerful impact in the future. Finally, this paper describes the mindset and worldview that students should absorb if they are able to become serious critics, advocates, and executives in improving the sustainability of the world. I will include steps that I have taken to move toward these goals and indicate where my efforts have fallen short of ideal.

Understanding the State of the World

A starting point for educating about sustainability is to insure that all students have at least a modicum of knowledge about the world today. One challenge I have encountered is that our entering students vary widely in this regard. Some students come from highly educated families where world affairs make up a steady diet of conversation. Other households have been preoccupied with merely keeping food on the table. A sizable cohort comes from overseas to study, or are children of immigrants, where they have personal knowledge of two or more countries. Some of these are painfully aware of world poverty, water shortages, illiteracy, and devastating weather events that they have left behind. Still others have grown up with views that politicize issues like climate change, environmental regulation, and care for refugees or the poor.

Our beginning survey course is called "Managing Sustainability in a Global Context." I begin with readings that examine how to think about climate change, using Greg Craven's What's the Worst That Could Happen? A Rational Response to the Climate Change Debate. A high school science teacher, Craven, skillfully offers a risk management approach to thinking about climate change. He invites us to look on the decision about action on climate change as a matter of whether it is worth buying a kind of insurance policy. We are asked to think about the outcome if the world gears up to take care in case climate change is real, as opposed to the case of what disastrous results ensue if we do nothing. A useful section for undergrads discusses how scientific discovery takes place, along with the role of peer review and the range of credibility that may be attributed to eminent scientists, advocacy-based think tanks, or talk-radio commentators. The book also elaborates on common psychological limitations, like the confirmation bias and limiting one's research to a single finding. While Craven's own leanings eventually come through, he leaves the reader to make his or her own decision on the matter.

I also have students dip back into classics from the past. Reading the first few chapters of Rachel Carson's Silent Spring (and viewing a recently released biography on Public Broadcasting System) exposes them to the early days of the environmental movement. Carson's writing and eventual testimony in Congress and advocacy work rank as one of the first whistleblowing campaigns as she confronted large chemical companies about the perils of DDT and other toxic pesticides. Her message about how pesticides linger in the soil, infect other growing plants, then the animals that eat them, then the humans who ingest those animals, all offer a primer on the food chain and complex biological systems. Many traditional-age business undergrads, outside of the natural sciences, can experience an epiphany with such systemic learning.

Another stirring reading comes from Jared Diamond's Collapse. We read the chapter on the demise of the early civilization on Easter Island. Students learn how the inhabitants survived nicely for centuries by building wooden structures to live in and dug-out canoes for rowing great distances to reap a generous harvest of fish. Over time, however, inhabitants exhausted agricultural resources and devastated the forests, mostly for massive wasteful rituals as a show of strength against neighboring tribes elsewhere on the island. These actions rang the death knell for long-distance fishing, deteriorated nutrition and health, prompted vicious rivalries, and eventually caused bloody civil wars. The island's population shrank to an impoverished remnant, a far cry from the formerly prospering island. The accelerating decline over a relatively short time offers a lesson in vicious cycles and a caution to us today about short-sighted, parochial behavior that can undermine the larger community. I have allowed students to experience the temptation of over-consumption in the tragedy of the commons. Through an active exercise, they are invited to claim their share of a scarce resource—M&M's in this case—without exceeding the supply, the contents in a bowl. They invariably are too greedy, with total claims greater than the number available, disqualifying everyone from eating any (unless the instructor relents after an in-depth debriefing).

Occasional guest speakers from the sustainability field provide live stories to hear up-close how companies are actually behaving. When possible, they go on a field trip to visit a neighboring company. Students can glean other information about sustainability issues in the world. I encourage them to keep up with the New York Times, The Guardian, and other publications. We discuss convenient internet sites, such as Smartbrief on Sustainability, CSR Wire, and Smartbiz.com. I may require them to bring in and discuss in class some current events about the environment, employment abuse, or world poverty.

A traditional way of framing sustainability for many years is through the Triple Bottom Line and the importance of society, environment, and economy, or "people, planet and profit" (Elkington 1998). More recently, scholars have come to regard this approach as lending itself to concerns of sometimes competing priorities that only occasionally overlap and lead toward the same pursuits (Fig. 1). Instead, a more satisfactory conceptualization is to acknowledge that any company—or person, for that matter—resides inescapably inside society, which occupies space on the planet. It is unrealistic to consider that any action by us or our organization does

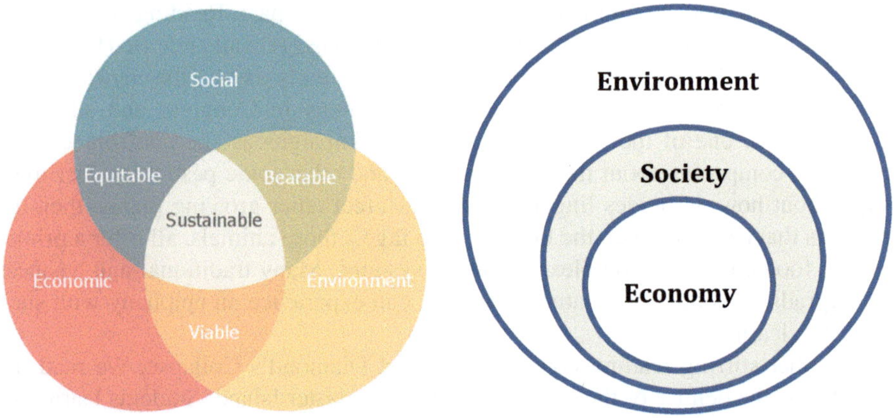

Fig. 1 Triple-bottom line concept (*left*) and nested domain concept (*right*)

not make up an element of society. Indeed, any organization derives inputs from society, whether employees, investors, manufactured components, or infrastructure. Similarly, society has an impact on the natural environment. Conversely, the environment provides a range of inputs, such as clean air, tillable land, biodiverse animal life, water, and the like. Even though it is natural to ignore such dependence on the environment, this framing is more complete, and it reminds us that we live in a nested existence, unable to separate ourselves from influences outside our door (Barbier 1987) (Fig. 1).

Addressing What Needs To Be Done

Once students begin to appreciate the extent of concern appropriate for the environment and society, they study some approaches to what needs to be done. One source of global challenge comes from the United Nations. In 2015, 193 member countries agreed to an ambitious list of 17 Sustainable Development Goals (SDGs) for 2030, covering a range of issues. This includes such things as No Poverty, Decent Work and Economic Growth, Good Health and Well-Being, Quality Education, Reduced Inequalities, and Climate Action (see Fig. 2). Several of these Goals can fall squarely on the responsibility of business, especially for those operating in developing countries; for example, Good Health and Well-Being, Reduced Inequalities, Gender Equality, and Clean Water and Sanitation.

As these Goals arose from the United Nations, they are now an explicit part of the expectations of all those business schools who have signed on for the UN's Principles of Responsible Management Education. Silberman College of Business has not only dedicated itself to infusing the business curriculum with the SDGs but has also helped promote the introduction of the SDGs to our sister colleges at the university, including those focused on liberal arts and sciences, hospitality,

Fig. 2 Sustainable development goals

engineering, healthcare, and the like. Students in all those disciplines will deepen their education if given an opportunity to study how the SDGs apply to the variety of human activity in their disciplines.

Another source for insight and encouragement for businesses striving to become more sustainable originates with the Future-Fit Foundation in its free, non-copyrighted electronic book. The "Future-Fit Business Benchmark" (2016) identifies 16 Global Challenges that threaten the future of the planet in our resource-constrained, environmentally endangered world. These include Climate destabilization, Ocean acidification, Access to mined materials, Health crisis, Governance failure, and Social instability (complete list, Table 1).

The authors of the Future-Fit Benchmark are among those objecting to the Triple Bottom Line insofar as it implies that part of business activity is separate from society and the environment. Instead,

Left unchecked, today's global challenges put in jeopardy Earth's natural processes, our social fabric, and economic activity as a whole. This creates an arguably huge moral imperative for collective action (Future-Fit, p. 13).

They urge a company interested in long-term success to "proactively explor[e] where its business model intersects with the global challenges—find ways to enhance its resilience and competitiveness.. ." so as to reap the possibility of three forms of payoff: increasing value, saving costs, and reducing risks (p. 13). The Benchmark lays out eight Future-Fit Business Principles to gird business's actions. The three principles pertaining to the environment prescribe that nature not be subject to (1) systematically increasing concentrations of substances extracted from the earth (e.g., fossil fuel), (2) substances produced by society (e.g., NOx, Chlorofluorocarbons), or (3) degradation by physical means (e.g., quality of soil, deforestation, over-fishing).

Table 1 Global challenges

1.	Climate destabilization
2.	Ocean acidification
3.	Biodiversity crisis
4.	Ecosystem degradation
5.	Access to mined materials
6.	Access to renewable materials
7.	Energy crisis
8.	Fresh water crisis
9.	Food crisis
10.	Health crisis
11.	Infrastructure crisis
12.	Governance failure
13.	Financial inequality
14.	Education crisis
15.	Social instability
16.	Erosion of trust

The five Principles related to society expect business actions will not subject people to obstacles in achieving health, influence, competence (e.g., education), impartiality, and meaning-making (e.g., cultural expression).

The authors of the Future-Fit Blueprint go beyond the idea of the trade-off thinking implied in the Venn diagram of People-Planet-Profits. In taking the more demanding standard of removing all forms of un-sustainability, they argue that businesses need to reduce every action that detracts from a sustainable world by using an adaptation of the notion of break-even. To achieve financial stability, a company needs to achieve financial performance of at least break-even. Analogously, they assert that a truly sustainable company must deliver at least "break-even" levels for social and environmental performance. For example, such a firm must not only reduce the rate of release of toxins in the workplace, or employee accidents, but also strive to actually do nothing that impairs the health of employees. Similarly, it must not only reduce the amount of metal and plastic in its products but also do nothing that adds to the waste stream after the product has been used and disposed of.

A useful textbook on more details on how to think about and execute constructive actions for sustainability is Laasch and Conaway's (2016) Responsible Business: A Textbook for Management Learning, Competence, and Innovation (for a more general model, see Fairfield et al. 2011). The authors lay out the underlying conditions of the world and some conceptual underpinnings of sustainability, with the endorsement of the UN PRME office. They expand upon what sustainable management practices would look like in the primary functions of logistics, operations and production, and the customer relationship management functions (marketing, sales, and service). This includes debunking some of the most "modern" practices today that in fact undermine environmental goals, such as undeniably efficient just-in-time shipping and individualized internet purchase and delivery, which may save costs but at the expense of excessive fossil fuel consumption and packaging. The book also covers what responsible management can do in various support functions, such as accounting, supply chain, and human resources.

I am convinced that, like most adults, undergraduate students often learn best and remember best by means of concrete examples. As a result, I supplement their reading list with articles and chapters that demonstrate some of the things that specific businesses are currently doing to advance their greening efforts. For example, Alcatel-Lucent (now part of Nokia) has made great strides in its own operations and as a leader in industry alliances to design electronic devices that reduce energy consumption by an order of magnitude or more (Wirtenberg 2014). Students read about Unilever's dogged efforts to seek organic ingredients for food products (Gelles 2015).

They read of the challenge companies face in taking responsibility for the behavior of their suppliers. One public shaming occurred in the aftermath of the many fatalities from the dreadful building collapse of an apparel manufacturing building in Bangladesh in 2013. Evidence of brand names on garments found in the rubble pointed to American and European retailers as the outlets that seemed to be benefitting from blatantly irresponsible working conditions. One was Walmart. It turns out that Walmart formerly contracted with a tenant in the ill-fated building, but months before, it terminated the contract due to concerns over inhumane conditions. Walmart did not realize, though, that its new contractor proceeded to contract with the original firm to continue to have the products made in the same creaky building. This is just one case of students learning some of the dilemmas and unintended consequences of efforts to improve one's sustainability.

One important element that needs to be part of a discussion about sustainability is the extent that one can hope to achieve in setting goals for improvement. Companies that make a well-intended effort to reduce carbon emissions, raise wages for the lowest earners, or cut back toxic chemicals in the residue of their products may think about dire predictions of global decline and wonder: Is it enough to just improve our performance? Compared to what? To simply slow down but not suspend worldwide deterioration? Or do we need to take steps that bring about absolute, long-term prospering of the world? How much is enough?

John Ehrenfeld is an emeritus professor from MIT, engineer, and thinker on such matters, stemming from his history in design. He asserts that almost all business and personal efforts that strive to increase sustainability are really concerned with only reducing un-sustainability (Ehrenfeld and Hoffman 2013). It does help, somewhat, when auto fleets consume less fossil fuel than they used to, or power plants use natural gas instead of coal, or world poverty is cut in half. The real goal in his mind, however, is that sustainability is "the possibility that human and other life will flourish on the planet forever." (Ehrenfeld 2009, p. 1). Three words stand out in this simple statement. First, he does not speak of improving life on earth, but of flourishing. This is a powerful word, whose force comes through in the comment from the forward to a book (author unknown) who observed, "When you ask someone, 'how's your marriage?', you don't expect him to brag, 'It's sustainable." Clearly, flourishing is a far higher standard. The second unexpected element is when Ehrenfeld includes not just humans but all forms of life. Most cultures in the world focus on humans as the dominant species and the only one that ultimately matters, not plants and other animal life. The third powerful idea is when this definition speaks of sustainability, not "in the future" or "in the next century" but forever. The authors of the Future-Fit Blueprint design their approach to pursue just such a standard (and to be explicated more thoroughly in a follow-on e-book, now in process).

This more ambitious level of behavior has been articulated by other scholars, who describe a continuum of behavior on sustainability (e.g., Landrum and Ohsowski 2017). Weak sustainability places an economic value on natural resources and is open to the substitution of economic resources for resources in nature. Strong sustainability, on the other hand, views natural resources as priceless and non-substitutable, given the many direct and indirect benefits of such resources. An example is clean water, which can lead to health and wellbeing plus irrigation downstream. Adequate clean water can also lead to the continuance of biodiversity, which can contribute to less rupture of the food chain or resources for pharmacological research. In addition, weak sustainability believes that continuous economic growth is necessary, bases decisions on cost-benefit analysis, and values progress measured by increasing gross domestic product. On the other hand, strong sustainability views growth as problematic and sees a future built around no growth, while prescribing decisions based on the environment and the welfare of living things (Landrum and Ohsowski 2017).

In their recent survey of teaching materials and readings in 51 American business schools of higher education, Landrum and Ohsowski posit a typology with gradations between the two poles of weak and strong sustainability. The five stages they describe are:

- Stage 1—*Compliance*, based on keying one's behavior on regulatory limitations, characteristic of Weak Sustainability (cf. "Legitimacy" in the classification from an early study by Bansal and Roth 2000).
- Stage 2—*Business-centered*, based on competitive advantage (also identified in Bansal and Roth 2000), Weak Sustainability.
- Stage 3—*Systemic*, based on businesses working collaboratively for systemic change, Intermediate Sustainability.
- Stage 4—*Regenerative*, based on businesses working to repair and restore social, environmental, and economic systems, Strong Sustainability.
- Stage 5—*Coevolutionary*, based on "creating integrated, harmonious partnerships with natural systems in an environment of coexistence and coevolution," Strong Sustainability (Landrum and Ohsowski 2017, p. 388).

These authors categorize an extensive list of written sources that are most often used for sustainability education today. One finding is that of the most frequently used readings for undergraduates, 55 percent are classified in Weak Sustainability and only 29 percent Strong Sustainability. Their database allows instructors to reflect on what sources they use and consider others to achieve the "strength" of sustainability desired for their students. While most of readings assigned in my class are not listed among the most popular, I would estimate that the bulk of them would fall in Stage 2. Only occasionally do I expose them to, and discuss in class, some in Stage 3 or, like Ehrenfeld, from Stage 4. I feel rather comfortable with this overall emphasis, though, in that most students enter this foundational class at a low level of awareness about the subject. It seems somewhat necessary to enlighten them on fundamental principles of sustainability before they can thoughtfully contemplate what strong sustainability could look like. While this might not apply to our students in MBA and Executive MBA classes, these undergraduates need to acquire a nuanced understanding of such issues and a mature mindset and worldview to appreciate the audacious aims of full-blown strong sustainability.

Engendering a New Mindset and Worldview

To truly internalize the stakes facing humankind today and consider the role of one's personal and business behavior in response to it, a person has to acquire a mindset or worldview that is complex. As Senge et al. (2008) has said, "All real change is grounded in new ways of thinking and perceiving." It has to be rooted in one's deep conception of self and relationship with others and community. The general tendency of Americans toward a more individualistic construal of self-militates against easily acquiring such a mindset compared to a more collectivistic orientation (e.g., Markus and Kitayama 1991). Arnett's seminal work on emerging adulthood points out that the cohort of traditional-aged undergraduates typically enter this stage of life attached to views of their parents (Arnett 2000, 2004). One of the markers of developing into adulthood is to acquire one's own worldview, which could imply that exposure to sustainability issues and literature in college may kindle an evolving, deepening interest that might not be possible earlier in life.

Psychologist Steve Schein interviewed 75 corporate executives working with sustainability, learning about the sources of their concern for the natural world (Schein 2015a, b). Reasons included early life experiences, such as family of origin, teachers, seeing poverty and natural degradation, as well as a sense of spirituality and service. Many respondents reported their awareness of being embedded in the natural ecology, the vulnerability of the earth, and the value of nature. Worldviews may be seen through the lens of moral and ego development. Brown (2012, cited in Schein 2015a, p. 99) asserts that worldviews become "more complex and encompassing" over time. They may be classified as "pre-conventional," related to the impulsive and opportunistic; "conventional," in tune with social conventions and short-term economic goals; or "post-conventional," with greater appreciation for reframing complex issues, interdependence of systems, and awareness of long-term implications of sustainability.

While Schein relates this typology of worldviews to executives, they may be equally applied to students. Most undergraduates would fit the first category, but some may be able to begin moving into conventional and post-conventional with powerful education techniques and experiences.

Bob Doppelt provides another insight into the mindset or worldview necessary to bring about sustainability. He describes the change of mindset required as converting one's primary focus "from me to we." To do so means the ability to make five "commitments" (Doppelt 2012):

1. See the systems you are part of.
2. Be accountable to all the consequences of your actions.
3. Abide by society's most deeply held universal principles of morality and justice.
4. Acknowledge your trustee obligations and take responsibility for the continuation of all life.
5. Choose your own destiny.

Rising to each of these commitments requires substantial change in consciousness and actions to fully absorb that mindset. For example, to perceive "all the consequences of your actions" means contemplating what was required to put gasoline in your automobile. One could think back to the geology of decay in prehistoric times, followed by today's infrastructure and action to explore and drill for oil and to refine and transport gasoline to a filling station. Each step triggers carbon emissions from the process—not to mention energy expended from the steel and other components that were required to build the drilling and transportation equipment. The downstream consequences, of course, involve carbon emissions from combustion and the fuel expended to return to refill the tank.

The commitment to abide by principles of morality (#3 above) is similarly multifaceted. Doppelt says this entails getting beyond a competitive perspective, subscribing to "do no harm," cutting material and energy consumption, and protecting the most vulnerable.

Educating our students to grow into all of these commitments is a demanding mission. Much of it may take a lifetime to achieve, if ever. I think profound experiences are necessary for many of them. For example, Schein points to the impact on his students—and himself—in learning more systems thinking at a deep level by immersing himself in "permaculture" near campus. "Permanent agriculture" is based on using nature's ways for growing crops and caring for the earth, caring for the people, sharing what one does not need, and returning waste to the earth. He also recommends greater exposure by students to eco-science, along with deep reflection and journaling.

At Fairleigh Dickinson we start students on their sustainability journey through service-learning. Everyone majoring in Management conducts at least one group service project for the benefit of some group or NGO. These have included such things as contributing to schools in rural Cambodia, underwriting a well in Ethiopia and Haiti, and exposing the campus to knowledge about the genocide in Darfur. They consistently report a deepening sense of compassion for the beneficiaries, while sharpening their cognitive and management skills. Some courses also require students to interview a social entrepreneur about the business that is set up to make money but also to serve the broader world. The analysis of their learnings is then submitted to the nonprofit Aim2Flourish (www.aim2flourish.org), which adds the inspiring stories to its open global library. This experience also provokes knowledge and inspiration for students' own future actions. They can occasionally hear outside speakers arranged by our Instituted for Sustainable Enterprise. These include provocative subjects of corporate actions, both on their values-based philosophy as well as best practices in their strategies.

Researcher and consultant Philip Mirvis has led fieldtrips of senior executives to impoverished third world countries. They report a powerful executive development experience engaging with the least fortunate inhabitants on the earth (Mirvis 2008). Participants increase self-awareness, understanding of others, and dealing with the larger world. The experiences have helped the executives connect global issues to areas pertinent to their companies. Similar experiential learning can have real impact on college students as well, as occurred with those who studied sustainability on trips to Costa Rica.

Conclusion

The results I would like to see required a long-term, complex process to educate undergraduates. Many of our school's graduates may be able to influence the sustainability actions of their future employers. Some may even work full-time in this domain. In any case, we can be proud if they can be equipped for a rewarding, purpose-driven career. Based on our results to date, and the gaps that are visible, several elements of the worthy destination stand out. I submit that instructors should aspire to guide students toward capabilities such as these:

- Understanding some of the science of environment and ecology;
- Comprehending truly complex systems and systems thinking;
- Feeling part of a larger world;
- Possessing the confidence to think really big, far beyond their comfortable horizon;
- Thinking truly long-term;
- Acquiring a mindset themselves to go "beyond me to we," considering their legacy as it affects their descendants, as well as the abject poor and endangered today; and
- Beginning to ascertain the kind of behavior they wish to exhibit in their personal and professional lives to contribute to a world worth leaving behind.

For business schools to fulfill their mission, incorporating sustainability into the curriculum and the overall experience is imperative. This multi-faceted effort requires creativity, rigor, and patience. At FDU, we have begun the journey, but we have an enormous amount ahead before we can have a broad impact. Guidance from the UN Sustainable Development Goals, other colleagues enrolled in PRME, and other scholars can help us a lot. As with any accomplishment of real merit, we have to vigorously persist toward this crucial goal for the future.

Acknowledgment The author expresses deep appreciation to his colleagues, Prof. Gerard Farias, for his thinking on many conceptual issues discussed, and Prof. Joel Harmon, Executive Director of the Institute for Sustainable Enterprise at FDU, for his continued insights and support for teaching and research on sustainability.

References

Arnett JJ (2000) Emerging adulthood: a theory of development from the late teens through the twenties. Am Psychol 55:469–480

Arnett JJ (2004) Emerging adulthood: the winding road from the late teens to the twenties. Oxford University Press, New York

Bansal P, Roth K (2000) Why companies go green. A model of ecological responsiveness. Acad Manage J 43:717–736

Barbier E (1987) The concept of sustainable economic development. Environ Conserv 14(2):101–110

Brown BC (2012) Conscious leadership for sustainability: how leaders with late-stage action logic design and engage in sustainability initiatives. Dissertation Abstracts International, UMI No 3498378, cited in Schein, S. (2015a). A new psychology for sustainability leadership: the hidden power of ecological worldviews. Greenleaf Publishing, Sheffield

Doppelt B (2012) From me to we: the five transformational commitments required to rescue the planet, your organization, & your life. Greenleaf Publishing, Sheffield

Ehrenfeld JR (2009) Sustainability by design: a subversive strategy for transforming our consumer culture. Yale University Press, New Haven

Ehrenfeld JR, Hoffman AJ (2013) Flourishing: a frank conversation about sustainability. Stanford University Press, Stanford

Elkington J (1998) Cannibals with forks: the triple bottom line of 21st century business. New Society Publishers, Gabriola Island

Fairfield KD, Harmon J, Benson S (2011) Influences on the implementation of sustainability: an integrative model. Organizational Manage J 8(11):4–20

Future-Fit Foundation (2016) Future-Fit Business Benchmark, Part 1: Concepts, Principles, and Goals Release 1, May

Gelles D (2015) Unilever finds that shrinking its footprint is a giant task. http://www.nytimes.com/2015/11/22/business/unilever-finds-that-shrinking-its-footprint-is-a-giant-task.html

Landrum NE Ohsowski B (2017) Content trends in sustainable business education: an analysis of introductory courses in the USA. International JNL of Sustainability Higher Educ, 18(3): 385–414

Laasch O, Conaway R (2016) Responsible business: the textbook for management learning, competence, & innovation. Greenleaf Publishing, Saltaire

Markus HR, Kitayama S (1991) Culture and the self: implications for cognition, emotion, and motivation. Psychol Rev 108(2):1711–1194

Mirvis P (2008) Executive development through consciousness-raising experiences. Acad Manage Learn Educ 7(2): 173–188

Schein S (2015a) A new psychology for sustainability leadership: the hidden power of ecological worldviews. Greenleaf Publishing, Sheffield

Schein S (2015b) Ecological worldviews: a missing perspective to advance global sustainability leadership. J Manage Global Sustainability 3(1):1–24

Senge P, Smith B, Kruschwitz N, Laur J, Schley S (2008) The necessary revolution: how individuals and organizations are working together to create a sustainable world. Doubleday, New York

Wirtenberg J (2014) Building a culture for sustainability: people, planet and profits in a new green economy. Praeger, New York

Social and Environmental Justice: The Management Challenge of Repurposing Business

Gerard Farias

Abstract We are all challenged today to deal with an unprecedented set of issues that are manifested in climate change, violence, poverty, rising inequality, resource depletion, biodiversity loss, water scarcity, and species extinction to name just a few. The responsibility for many of these pervasive problems has been placed at the door of an economic system that does not account for the negative externalities it generates and has a penchant for uncontrolled consumption and growth. The global population that now stands at about 7.5 billion is projected to grow to approximately 9.7 billion by the year 2050 and the likelihood of our finite planet adequately providing for a population of that size seems remote. It is in this context that important questions about role of business in the context of social, environmental, and intergenerational justice need to be answered.

The sustainability movement has gained tremendous momentum in the last few years, with many calling for a paradigm shift in the purpose and functioning of the business sector. This paper provides an overview of the evolution of the sustainability movement in business including the formation of the United Nations Global Compact and its academic counter-part, the United Nations Principles for Responsible Management Education (UNPRME). In particular, while many advocates for sustainability have used the notion of the business case as their primary argument, this paper will argue that a paradigm shift calls for a reexamination of the fundamental principles and values of business focusing on responsibilities not only toward shareholders, but also toward all stakeholders including those who are often invisible and voiceless. The paper focuses on the management challenges that both businesses and business schools that will need to address to not only ensure our survival as a species, but also that all species on the planet will flourish forever.

Keywords Sustainability • Justice • Responsibility • Flourishing

---

G. Farias (✉)
Management Department, Silberman College of Business, Fairleigh Dickinson University, Madison, NJ, USA
e-mail: gfarias@fdu.edu

L. Tadj, A.K. Garg (eds.), *Emerging Challenges in Business, Optimization, Technology, and Industry*, Springer Proceedings in Business and Economics,
DOI 10.1007/978-3-319-58589-5_13

Social and Environmental Justice: The Management Challenge of Repurposing Business

A recent OXFAM study (2017) indicates that eight men in the world have as much wealth as the bottom half of the world's population. OXFAM releases a report on poverty and (in)equality every year at the World Economic Forum in Davos. In 2015 and 2016, they reported that 80 and 62 people respectively held as much wealth as the bottom half of the world's population indicating a trend in the concentration of wealth. The trend is obviously in the wrong direction.

Inequality, however, while critical, is not the only measure of the state of our world. The United Nations 2015 estimate of the global population was 7.3 billion which is projected to grow to 8.3 billion by 2030 and 9.7 billion by 2050. The World Bank (2016a) reports significant reductions in global poverty, with extreme poverty dropping from 35% of the world's population in 1990 to 9.6% in 2015. These figures are based on the global poverty line of $1.9 per capita per day. While these achievements of the United Nations Millennium Development Goals are indeed laudable, they tend to obfuscate the challenges that lie ahead. First, we must note that it is extreme poverty that has been reduced. Even at this reduced level, the World Bank notes that there are still over 700 million people who suffer from extreme poverty. Obviously, this is unacceptable. Furthermore, it does not reveal the number of people who are just above the poverty line. According to Global Issues (2013), 3 billion people earn less than $2.50 per day suggesting that, while a large number of people have risen out of extreme poverty, they still hover just above the poverty line—needless to say, they are still poor. Some (e.g., Hickel 2015) argue that the $1.9 per day benchmark is too low, suggesting that it be raised to $5.00 per day to reflect a more reasonable assessment of poverty. If adopted, the impact on the number of people below the poverty line is obvious. In addition, there are inconsistencies in measurement in some countries. For example, India, one of the countries with very high levels of poverty, uses a much lower poverty line (between 48 and 70 cents a day) (Singh 2014), thus reporting inaccurate poverty levels based on the World Bank and United Nations benchmark.

Overall, the story on poverty is clear. Too many people suffer from poverty and live low quality lives. Even though wealth is being created, it is concentrated in the hands of a few. The severe poverty and disparities have associated consequences. According to UNICEF (2015), 683 million people do not have access to safe drinking water and 2.4 billion do not have access to sanitation. While this is a marked improvement due to the UN's Millennium Development Goals, fulfilling this basic human right represents a major challenge for humanity. Similarly, about 1.2 billion people do not have access to electricity and about 400 million do not have access to basic and minimal healthcare. It is important to note that there have been significant improvements in all these basic indicators of human well being in the last 15–20 years. However, it also important to note that these improvements need to be sustained even while the world's population grows to 9.7 billion by the year 2050. Furthermore, it is most likely that these significant improvements have been the easiest to make because they were the easiest to address. The challenges of the last kilometer lie ahead.

While poverty and economic development are major issues in themselves, environmental issues present yet another significant challenge. There is a clear consensus among scientists that human activity is a significant cause for climate change (Rockström et al. 2009; Steffen et al. 2015). Climate change is related to sea level rise that will devastate low-lying populated lands like Bangladesh and the Maldives. Furthermore, climate change causes ocean acidification that kills coral reefs, destroying an important aspect of the ocean ecosystem. This in turn has already begun to negatively impact ocean fish stocks endangering an important source of animal protein for half a billion people. 2014, 2015 and 2016, each, have been the hottest years measured until that time and scientists have associated these warming trends to severe weather events. The World Health Organization (2016) estimates that 250,000 additional people will die due to climate change every year by the year 2030. A Climate Vulnerability Assessment study by DARA (2015) estimates that 400,000 people die each year because of climate change and its associated problems. Most of these deaths take place in developing countries where the carbon footprint is relatively small. In effect, the high consumption, high carbon developed world is responsible for deaths in the low consumption, low carbon world. Yet, the world, particularly the developed world, continues to be addicted to fossil fuel and a life style that is incompatible with the capacity of planet earth.

Researchers from the Resilience Institute in Stockholm, Sweden (Rockström et al. 2009; Steffen et al. 2015) have identified nine planetary boundaries that are essential for the earth to maintain its ability to support life, as we know it. Their research indicates that we have crossed four of the nine boundaries. These include Land-use change, Concentration of Greenhouse gases, Phosphorous and Nitrogen concentrations and species extinction (Steffen et al. 2015). These outcomes of a "Take-Make-Waste" (Anderson and White 2011) industrial system not only endanger the quality of life for current and future generations, they also severely harm nature's inherent capacity to provide ecosystem services (Sukhdev 2009).

The above are just a few of the global indicators that suggest that there is a need for urgent and concerted action to bring us closer to even a semblance of global and environmental justice in the world. The injustice is manifested in Fig. 1 where the map on the left depicts countries' GHG emissions per capita and the map on the right depicts the expected impacts of climate change in the year 2030.

The Sustainability Movement

The concern about depleting resources and rising population gave rise to the idea that the emphasis on economic development alone, while essential, was undermining the prospects of future generations. The need for a sustainable approach to development gave rise to the Brundtland Commission. The commission defined sustainable development as "meeting the needs of current generations without endangering the ability of future generations to meet their own needs." This

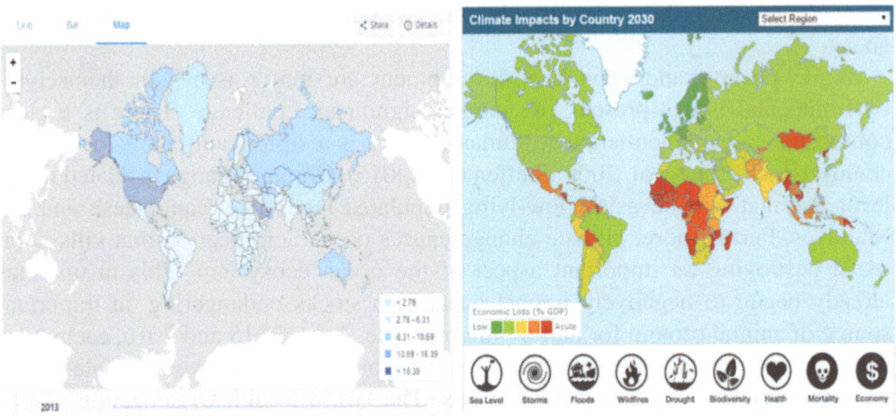

http://data.worldbank.org/indicator/EN.ATM.CO2E.PC?end=2013&start=2013&view=map (World Bank 2016b)

http://daraint.org/climate-vulnerability-monitor/climate-vulnerability-monitor-2012/indicators/

Fig. 1 Climate injustice

definition formulated in response to economic development at the expense of the environment is commendable. While it is appropriately a planetary level definition, it is fraught with problems. First, note the emphasis of meeting the needs of current generations. Nearly 30 years later, the needs of current generations are not being met with large parts of world's population not having access to basic needs like nutrition, energy, water, clothing, and shelter World Bank (2016b). While these problems may have been mitigated to some extent, they remain largely unresolved even while we contemplate the potential impact of a population of 9.7 billion people by the year 2050 (United Nations 2015). Seeing sustainable development as responsibility of governments, the business world barely paid any attention.

In 1999, Kofi Anan, the then General Secretary of the United Nations, proposed the formation of a "Global Compact," (United Nations 1999) where he invited business leaders to join with the United Nations to jointly commit to a set of ten principles that focused on Human Rights, Labor Rights, The Environment and Corruption. This was the first time, the United Nations engaged with the business sector to develop a partnership to meet the goals of sustainable development. Today, the Global Compact has over 9000 signatories and is a major vehicle for the implementation of the United Nations ambitious Sustainable Development Goals (United Nations 2016). The Global Compact initiative later led to several other initiatives like the "Principles for Responsible Management Education" and the "Principles for Responsible Investment."

In parallel, the United Nations launched its Millennium Development Goals at the turn of the century. These goals specified targets to meet by the year 2015. As noted earlier, the UN made significant progress on these goals. In 2016, the UN launched the Sustainable Development Goals (SDGs) not only to reflect the progress made, but also to address the challenges that lie ahead. The UN has launched a massive effort to enroll entities from all sectors, including the business sector to support the implementation of the SDGs.

The UN has also played a leading goal in its attempt to bring the nations of the world to commit to reducing their environmental footprints even while attempting to raise people out of poverty. These attempts are manifested in the Kyoto Protocol, Agenda 21 and many initiatives to address climate change, the most pressing and urgent problem of our time.

Sustainability and Business

While the UN has played a major role, bringing governments together to address environmental and social problems and has invited the business sector to be partners in these efforts, the business academia and practitioners have proposed a variety of philosophies, theories, approaches, and methods for the adoption of sustainability or against it over the years. For instance, Starik and Rands (1995) argued that the Brundtland commission definition focuses on current and future generations of humans and excludes other species. It is therefore anthropocentric in nature (Starik and Rands 1995). Sukhdev and Kumar (2008) argued that the definition is not reflective of the planet as an ecosystem and by implication does not demonstrate an understanding on the interdependence of species and the need to protect the biodiversity of the planet.

Environmentalists (e.g., Dietz and Neumayer 2007; Hediger 1999) have proposed defining sustainability in weak and strong terms. Their intention here is to respond to the commonly accepted perspective by traditional economists. This perspective supports the view that it is okay to convert natural capital into financial or manufactured capital as long as the sum of capitals remains the same. This view is highly problematic because it does not take into consideration the generative capacity and the ecosystem services that nature provides over time. Further, to be comparable to financial capital, it will be necessary to determine the net present value of nature if it is left undisturbed several years or centuries in the future. Natural capital is bound to be undervalued because we do not really understand the complete system well enough. For example, how would we determine the present value of a forest when it is very likely that we do not have a complete inventory of the biodiversity in the forests? If we do not have a complete inventory, it would be logically impossible to understand the systemic linkages between species and phenomena in the forest. To complicate matters even more, we have no time frame over which to compute the net present value of a natural asset—a hundred years? A thousand years? 10 thousand years? Environmentalists therefore argue that the conversion of natural capital into financial capital, even if done "sustainably," can only be weak sustainability at best. Strong sustainability on the other hand is based on the principle that natural capital must be maintained. To illustrate I point to the story of Niyamgiri in India based on an account by Padel and Das (2010). Niyamgiri is a bauxite-rich mountain range in Odisha,

India. A UK-based company, Vedanta, has applied for permits to exploit this valuable resource. However, the plan is to engage in mountain top mining, which means that the hills will be inundated with plant and equipment. The rich forests and their biodiversity on the hill slopes will be damaged or lost. Bauxite in its raw form is an ongoing source of value because it acts like a sponge-absorbing water from India's monsoon rains and releasing that water slowly for the rest of the year providing high-quality water to millions of people and the land downstream. The present value of the bauxite is obviously not comparable to the generative value of the bauxite and the ecosystem services it provides. This value can be generated for millennia if the bauxite is left undisturbed. Note that I have not even touched on the human impact of the proposed mining of bauxite at Niyamgiri. The area is home to the Dogra people, one of the many Adivasi (indigenous) communities in India. They have lived in harmony with the forests for centuries without a concept of property rights. They see a spiritual connection with the mountain and the forests. While they have been able to assert their rights under the Indian Forest Act, they are continually challenged to defend their homeland. From an environmental standpoint, it is clear that the manufactured capital in the form of aluminum from bauxite is nowhere near the value that the material will generate for generations if left undisturbed. Stories similar to Niyamgiri are common around the world. For example, in Canada, the extraction of tar sands oil will destroy or at the minimum severely damage the Boreal forest, a major carbon sink. It will also compromise the Athabasca river delta, which is a major source of water for wildlife and the human population that lives downstream (Lenz 2009). It also violates Treaty 8 signed in 1899 protecting the rights of the First Nations people. Adopting the weak sustainability approach converts regenerative capacity of nature that produces value through ecosystem services, which could potentially last forever into capital that is expended or dissipated rather quickly. Strong sustainability on the other hand behooves us to use the precautionary principle (Cameron and Abouchar 1991) in our decisions.

Ehrenfeld (2008) proposed the notion of "flourishing as sustainability." He defined sustainability as all living things flourishing on planet earth forever (Ehrenfeld 2008; Ehrenfeld and Hoffman 2013). This deceptively simple and elegant statement captures the essence of sustainability by bringing into focus an ecosystem perspective. It displays an understanding of the interdependence between different entities of the ecosystem and celebrates them. I see an alignment between flourishing and the call for strong sustainability.

It is generally accepted that the environmental problems we face are attributable to the system of industrial production we have adopted. For instance, Anderson and White (2011) lament the "take, make, waste" production system prevalent today. Environmental laws have been passed all over the world in response to issues that have emerged over time and corporations have been required to comply (Young and Dhanda 2012). For instance, the discovery of acid rain and its attribution to pollutants emitted into the atmosphere, resulted in laws to limit such pollution. Similarly, the discovery that chlorofluorocarbons (CFC's) caused a depletion of the ozone layer, which in turn had its health impacts resulted in the passing of laws to phase out the use of the culprit chemicals. Rachel Carson wrote Silent Spring in 1962 drawing attention to the use of dangerous chemicals and their impact on the environment. All these concerns and warnings about the human impact on the environment had an obvious connection with business and industry. They generated a compliance-driven response to environmental issues. As scientists understood the impact of industrial activity on the environment, laws and regulations were passed by the appropriate government and industry found ways to comply.

The idea that businesses may choose to pay close attention to the environment emerged later. For instance, Paul Hawken (1993) narrates his embarrassment that even though his company had done little that was meaningful for the environment, they still won an award for their work. Hawken took the position that industry had taken a path of destruction. He warned that unless industry reexamined its purpose to include the enhancement of the human condition humanity would be doomed. Despite his eloquent and brilliantly reasoned call to industry and business to change their ways, I am not aware of too many companies that truly understood and responded to the spirit of his call. One prominent exception is Interface Carpets' founder, the late Ray Anderson who committed his company to the specific and ambitious sustainability goal of "zero impact" by the year 2020 (Anderson and White 2011). The main point I wish to make here is that business and industry took a compliance-based approach to environmental issues, laws, and regulations. In some cases, industry found ways to manipulate the laws and standards or even hide the negative effects of their products and/or manufacturing process. For instance, Blake (2015) reports on DuPont's use of the toxic chemical C8 even while the company had knowledge of its high potential for harm. DuPont denied any culpability for the health impacts on its employees and the human and animal populations affected by the chemical till they were forced, because of legal proceedings to accept liability for the harm caused (Rich 2016). In contrast to the above, Hawken (1993) called for a commitment and values-based approach.

Starik and Rands (1995) indicate that the idea of an Ecologically Sustainable Organization (ESO) while gaining momentum was relatively new in contrast to the application of environmental sustainability to other fields of activity. They proposed a more comprehensive definition of sustainability; "Ecological sustainability is the ability of one or more entities, either individually or collectively, to exist and flourish (either unchanged or in evolved forms) for lengthy timeframes, in such a manner that the existence and flourishing of other collectivities of entities is permitted at related levels and in related systems" (page 909). Unfortunately, this definition, while cited somewhat frequently by academicians, is rarely seen in the practitioner-oriented literature. I consider this unfortunate because this definition captures the systemic, dynamic, and interdependent characteristics that make up our ecosystem. Starik and Rands (1995) elaborate their perspective by arguing for a multilevel approach to the development of the ESO and proposing a web of relationships between several levels; ecological, individual, organizational, political-economic, and socio-cultural. They rightly recognize and demonstrate that ecological sustainability requires organizations to develop strategies and act on them with the understanding that the scope of their activities and the impact of their actions reach far beyond their traditional boundaries.

Shrivastava (1995) emphasized the importance of incorporating issues of poverty and access to basic needs—food, water, and energy as critical in the development of ecological strategy. He raised the issue of meeting the projected needs of an increasing population in the context of the finite natural resources. He warned that the traditional model of economic growth through increasing levels of consumption will place untenable environmental pressure on the planet. Arguing that a compliance-based approach has only achieved incremental change, he calls on academicians and practitioners alike to reexamine the role of the corporation in society and bring to the forefront the need to both protect the environment and generate economic development for the world's poor. He also argues that it is the modern corporation that has both the capabilities and the financial resources to undertake the daunting task to make the paradigm shift. The key question is whether they have the values and the will.

Purser et al. (1995) argue that the linear perspective that drives anthropocentricism puts humans at the center of and in control of nature. They further argue that this perspective has manifested itself in the organization sciences through the view that technological knowledge provides an objective view of the world, which dominates and negates subjectivist perspectives. In addition, an egocentric perspective that celebrates self-interest is fundamental to the practice of business today even when it is at the expense of the environment and society.

The really interesting thing about the three articles cited above in combination with Hawken (1993) is that they all, either directly or by implication, call for a paradigm shift in the philosophy of management and business. All these authors argue convincingly that the current emphasis on maximization of shareholder wealth based on the foundational principal of self-interest is incompatible with the ecological perspective. Purser et al. (1995) in fact point to the fallacy of the argument of authors like Walley and Whitehead (1994) that shareholder value rather than regulations and compliance would encourage the adoption of sustainability. It also points to the parallel development of a perspective that involved the co-opting of the sustainability or green agenda. While it is likely and possible that there were good intentions behind these attempts to demonstrate a business case for sustainability, they ended up promoting business-as-usual (Ehrenfeld 2008; Ehrenfeld and Hoffman 2013).

The business case for sustainability received its greatest impetus with the proposition of the now ubiquitous triple bottom line (TBL) by Elkington (1998). He conceptualized it as a win-win-win for three dimensions; economy, society, and the environment. Representing the TBL by the diagram with overlapping circles, one for each dimension, he argued that the sweet spot could be found at their intersection where each of them was maximized without harming any of the others. I believe that the notion of the TBL, while important in drawing attention to the social and environmental impacts of a firm's operations, oversimplifies the very complex and holistic concept of sustainability. As noted by Norman and MacDonald (2004) measuring and reporting social and environmental bottom lines with any degree of accuracy would be unlikely and misleading. In fact, it can lead to the illusion that a business is operating sustainably when in reality it is not. In addition to measurement problems, social and environmental impacts are not just bottom line issues. They are also factors that are impacted upstream in the value chain. TBL gained tremendous momentum and has become the standard in conceptualizations and reporting about sustainability and was even endorsed by the United Nations in 2005 (Caradonna 2014).

Perhaps the most disturbing and contentious issue in relation to the TBL is that it equates society, environment, and the economy which implies a tradeoff between these dimensions. While the TBL is invoked with relative ease, in reality I believe that it is mostly driven by single bottom line thinking—society and environment are often compromised to achieve financial results. We do not need to look far for evidence of this phenomenon. Another ubiquitous idea that dominates the business literature and practice of sustainability is the aforementioned notion of the "business case" for sustainability. While the TBL provided a simple representation of sustainability, the business case evolved as a tool to communicate to the business world that not only was it okay to adopt sustainability—it would actually be profitable. The TBL and the business case are often used in conjunction with each other, which is illogical. The TBL ostensibly emphasizes the balance between social, economic, and environmental outcomes, while the business case places greater emphasis on economic outcomes. The academic and practitioner literature is replete with assertions that there is a business case for sustainability (e.g., Ambec and Lanoie 2008; Esty and Winston 2009; Porter and Kramer 2006, 2011; Prahalad and Hammond 2002). Most of the literature frames environmental and social issues as a crisis and/or an opportunity and it is in that framing that comprehensive and systemic solutions become elusive. The environmental crisis on our hands is really a symptom of a deeper malaise. We have a crisis of responsibility and values that are at the root of the environmental and social problems we face. Attempting to address these problems by leveraging the very paradigm that got us into this situation makes little sense.

Sustainability as Tensions

Hahn et al. (2015) argue that most scholars in the field of corporate sustainability adopt an instrumental logic (e.g., the business case), while in reality sustainable development, a normative concept, calls for addressing all three dimensions—economic, social, and environmental, simultaneously. The resulting integrative logic, they assert goes beyond the TBL because of a conscious effort to address the conflicting relationships between the three dimensions. As noted earlier, the TBL has been criticized for creating the impression of being balanced while in reality emphasizing the economic dimension. Jalal et al. (2013) referred to this as "mickey-mouse" model; when graphically represented it has a large economic circle with a small circle each for the social and environmental dimensions—mickey-mouse's ears.

A substantial body of research has been generated focusing on the tensions in corporate sustainability. Classifying research between 2003 and 2013, Van der Byl and Slawinski (2015) assert that tensions are viewed through four lenses—win-win; trade-off; integration, and paradox. They indicate that the bulk of the research focuses on the win-win and trade-off lenses. The win-win lens is based on the view that it is possible to devise business strategies where the corporation maximizes financial outcomes even while producing positive outcomes for society. This approach restricts sustainability initiatives to those where win-win is possible. The classic example would be improving efficiencies. For example, a firm that finds ways to reduce energy consumption and/or waste will achieve both, positive financial and environmental outcomes. In other words, it is possible to do well by or while doing good. Tensions are avoided by only focusing on those initiatives where a win-win is possible.

Trade-off's on the other hand suggest that in an attempt to focus on sustainability (environmental or social outcomes), firms make a choice to trade off some portion of their financial performance to achieve their environmental and/or social goals. The trade-off lens has been categorized by Van der Byl and Slawinski (2015) as following an instrumental logic. I see it as instrumental only when resultant decisions from following this logic are in favor of economic or financial outcomes. However, when managers make decisions that negatively impact economic outcomes in favor of social and/or environmental outcomes, it represents a values or principle-driven logic. Trade-off's of this kind represent the biggest challenges for managers. These are situations where the business case either does not exist or is not obvious. The win-win on the other hand represents a relatively easy decision. In reality, it is nothing more than business as usual. Achieving efficiency is one of the foundations of the management profession. As Karnani (2011) noted, the win-win strategy lies in the zone of opportunity where public good and firm performance align. Adopting sustainability in this context is a no-brainer. Karnani is less optimistic about those situations that lie in the zone of trade-off. He contends that it is unlikely that firms will adopt sustainable or responsible strategies unless they are forced by government regulations or social movements.

The integrative view (Gao and Bansal 2013; Hahn et al. 2015) involves rebalancing priorities to weighting each of the elements of the TBL equitably. While the win-win view essentially prioritizes financial outcomes and the trade-off view prioritizes any one of the TBL elements, the integrative view is an attempt to rebalance those outcomes (Van der Byl and Slawinski 2015). My position on this view is that while firms and their managers may have the intention to weight the elements equally, metrics in the context of the environmental and social elements are vastly underdeveloped and we have insufficient knowledge to achieve that balance. As a case in point, the costing and pricing of ecosystem services (Sukhdev 2009) is still in its infancy and very few firms have begun to even consider documenting and assessing their value to the firm and even more importantly to the planet and society. Similarly, firms rarely account for externalities and while attempts have been made to develop standards (e.g., Sustainability Accounting Standards Board; Integrative Reporting), the degree to which they have been adopted are limited. The integrative view is therefore likely to create the illusion of sustainability, but in reality fall short. Further, there are those situations where a trade-off is the only option. For example, toxic waste disposal costs money. In the case of DuPont and the chemical C8 (Blake 2015), the company was clearly presented with a trade-off. They chose a positive economic outcome over the negative environmental and health impacts—I doubt there was an integrative choice in this case. Similarly, Johnson and Johnson chose to market its antipsychotic drug, Risperdal, off label with full knowledge of the negative side-effects. The credo-driven company even manipulated the data to create the impression that the product was safe. These actions took place in violation of the law and over the Federal Drug Administration's objections (Brill 2015). Here again, the company had the choice to do the right thing and act on principle. The prospect of loss in market share and profits drove the company to knowingly make choices that had devastating effects on a segment of its customers. The recent manipulation of emissions testing by Volkswagen is yet another example. In each of these cases, the companies had a choice to act on principle. They chose not to. These examples are anecdotal evidence that supports assertions by Karnani (2011) and Slawinski and Bansal (2012) that firms will choose financial goals over social and environmental outcomes when faced with a choice.

More recently, scholars have begun to characterize the tensions in sustainability as paradox. Building on the work of Van de Ven and Poole (1988), Lewis (2000), and Smith and Lewis (2011), they argue that the tensions between the economic, social, and environmental dimensions of sustainability are best addressed by embracing and managing them. Smith and Lewis (2011) assert that embracing the tensions can lead to the development of creative solutions rather than the linear thinking that governs the more instrumental logics of the win-win and trade-off approaches. Van der Byl and Slawinski (2015) state that while the win-win and trade-off logics continue to dominate sustainability research, the integrative and paradox logics are evolving as a more sophisticated way to address the tensions in sustainability.

For instance, Hahn et al. (2014) compare the business case and paradoxical frames from a cognitive theory perspective. Here again, they emphasize the conflicting nature of the elements of sustainable development and the increasingly ambiguous situations they present. Overall, I have become increasingly uncomfortable with the notions of tensions and ambiguity that have been attached to sustainability. Instead, I suggest that we have been defining sustainability at the wrong level of analysis and will explore this idea in the following paragraphs.

Starik and Rands (1995) argued that sustainability is a multilevel phenomenon and Purser et al. (1995) explicitly discussed the tensions that exist between anthropocentricism, ecocentricism, and technocentricism. More recently, Whiteman et al. (2013) asserted that while there are many studies and articles on corporate sustainability, there is not much research that "investigates how corporate and industry actions affect, and are affected by each of the nine planetary boundary processes" (317). Hahn et al. (2015) argued that sustainability concepts are not the same at different levels of analysis and that actions at one level may not be in alignment with sustainability at a higher level of analysis. For instance, sustainability is often used by companies as a differentiating factor (Porter 1980) to earn a premium on their offerings. While such a strategy serves the firm's interests, it makes the product/service unaffordable to the poor suggesting that sustainable products are for the privileged. While such a perspective may be acceptable in the context of luxury products, it would clearly defeat the purpose in the context of sustainability.

I also see companies positioning the adoption of sustainability as a channel for growth—increasing consumption. Apple's strategy of launching a new iphone model every year is a case in point. Apple claims to be a sustainable company and emphasizes sustainability on its website. Tim Cook, Apple's CEO, was even lauded in the press for taking a stand against activist investors who questioned the company's expenditure on climate change initiatives (Shankelman 2014). However, the company is dependent on a large proportion of its customers purchasing new phones every year even when the old phone works perfectly well. This business model weakens the company's sustainability credentials.

Google's business model is driven by advertising. While the company proclaims that all the energy for its servers comes from renewable sources, its fundamental business model is dependent on increasing consumption. The point should be clear. Focusing on corporate sustainability is a distraction from planetary sustainability. By focusing on corporate sustainability, we are missing the forest for the trees.

The characterization of sustainability as win-win's, tradeoff's, integration, or paradox are also distractions—mainly because in the context of planetary sustainability, corporate sustainability is a non-concept. We believe some of the relatively early scholars like Gladwin et al. (1995), Purser et al. (1995) understood this. They clearly called for paradigm shifts. However, paradigm shifts do not take place while attempting to preserve some of the core principles and practices of the traditional business model that produced the problem in the first place.

We, academicians, are equally responsible for perpetuating the myth of corporate sustainability (there are some exceptions of course, e.g., Ghoshal 2005) by not asking the right questions and not challenging our underlying theories that have caused the situation in the first place. We have to understand that climate change is not the problem—rather it is the symptom of the underlying system and structure that created it. For example, Slawinski and Bansal (2015) report on the climate change mitigation strategies and tactics of firms engaged in the extraction of tar sands in Alberta, Canada. They discuss how different companies have different approaches to addressing climate change in the process of extraction and exploitation of the tar sands. It is well known that this oil is the world's dirtiest generating three times the greenhouse gases when compared to regular oil. In addition to mining the tar sands, these operations have a major impact on the First Nations of the area, who have been protesting the violation of the treaties between them and the government of Canada at the end of the nineteenth century (Farias 2015). Slawinski and Bansal report that each of the firms they studied had different approaches to engaging the First Nations people, with some being more inclusive than others. The question remains however whether the treaties and the rights of the First Nations people were ever respected in the process. Farias (2015) reports that the process for approval of mining in the area was developed without the consent of the First Nations people. Furthermore, the hearings followed the letter of the law, which gave no time to the First Nations leadership to mobilize the legal and substantial financial resources necessary to develop an informed position on the hearings. Slawinski and

Bansal do not report any interviews with the First Nations people—leadership or otherwise. By narrowing their focus on the climate change, they also did not address the plethora of impacts of tar sands extraction including the contamination of the Athabasca river, the deforestation (and the resulting carbon sink losses), the impact on the food chain, and the culture and lifestyle of the First Nations people. While we do understand the limitations of taking a holistic approach within the confines of a journal article, we think it really does a disservice to the notions of holism and systems thinking (Senge 1990) that are so consistently advocated by scholars of sustainability.

It is my position that we scrap the idea of Corporate Sustainability which is fraught with problems. We agree with Dyllick and Muff (2015) that there is a serious disconnect between corporate sustainability and sustainable development and assert that sustainability is a planetary concept and what we need are responsible and restorative enterprises (Waddock and Rasche 2011) with responsible and wise leaders (Maak and Pless 2009; Nonaka and Takeuchi 2011) who will lead the charge toward responsible corporations that not only eliminate harm but contribute to the well-being of humanity and the planet.

Instead of Corporate Sustainability, we need to advocate the development of the Responsible Enterprise (Sanford 2011; Waddock and Rache 2011). The Responsible Enterprise adopts a multiple stakeholder perspective carefully assessing its obligations to each of the stakeholders. These stakeholders must include the often invisible and voiceless and must be identified by carefully analyzing a company's value chain. In line with the definition of sustainability as flourishing, this analysis must take into consideration the impact of a firm's operations on all species and the earth (Ehrenfeld and Hoffman 2013; Sanford 2011; Starik and Rands 1995). This also means that all negative externalities must be accounted and paid for. When such negative impacts and/or their costs of mitigation are hard to assess, the company must adopt the precautionary principle to avoid permanent damage. Companies must search for and develop business models that seriously address the issue of consumption and design of products and services must follow the principles of the circular economy (MacArthur, 2015) eliminating waste from all production processes. Furthermore, business models must be designed to address the needs of the world's poor developing education and health services and the creation of economic opportunity. That was the promise of the business and the capitalist system. If it has to have any meaning, that promise needs to be restored.

References

Ambec S, Lanoie P (2008) Does it pay to be green? A systematic overview. Acad Manag Perspect 22(4):45–62

Anderson RC, White RA (2011) Business lessons from a radical industrialist. Random House Digital, Inc., New York, NY

Blake M (2015) Welcome to beautiful Parkersburg, West Virginia. http://highline.huffingtonpost.com/articles/en/welcome-to-beautiful-parkersburg/. Retrieved 9 Jan 2016

Brill S (2015) America's most admired law breaker. http://highline.huffingtonpost.com/miracleindustry/americas-most-admired-lawbreaker/. Retrieved 6 May 2016
Brundtland, G., & Khalid, M. (1987). UN Brundtland Commission Report. Our Common Future
Cameron J, Abouchar J (1991) Precautionary principle: a fundamental principle of law and policy for the protection of the global environment. Boston College Int Comp Law Rev 14(1)
Caradonna JL (2014) Sustainability: a history. Oxford University Press, Oxford
Carson R (1962) Silent spring. Houghton Mifflin, Boston, MA
Climate change and health (2016) Retrieved February 06, 2017, from http://www.who.int/mediacentre/factsheets/fs266/en/
DARA (2015) Climate vulnerability assessment. http://daraint.org/wp-content/uploads/2012/09/EXECUTIVE-AND-TECHNICAL-SUMMARY.pdf. Retrieved 22 Feb 2017
Dietz S, Neumayer E (2007) Weak and strong sustainability in the SEEA: concepts and measurement. Ecol Econ 61(4):617–626
Dyllick T, Muff K (2015) Clarifying the meaning of sustainable business introducing a typology from business-as-usual to true business sustainability. Organ Environ 29(2):156–174
Ehrenfeld J (2008) Sustainability by design: a subversive strategy for transforming our consumer culture. Yale University Press, New Haven
Ehrenfeld JR, Hoffman AJ (2013) Flourishing: a frank conversation about sustainability. Greenleaf Publishing, Shipley, England
Elkington J (1998) Partnerships from cannibals with forks: the triple bottom line of 21st-century business. Environ Qual Manag 8(1):37–51
Esty D, Winston A (2009) Green to gold: How smart companies use environmental strategy to innovate, create value, and build competitive advantage. John Wiley & Sons, Hoboken
Farias D (2015) Unstacking maps: the Athabasca Chipewyan first nation and the politics of place and identity, Unpublished Undergraduate Thesis, Princeton University
Gao J, Bansal P (2013) Instrumental and integrative logics in business sustainability. J Bus Ethics 112(2):241–255
Ghoshal S (2005) Bad management theories are destroying good management practices. Acad Manag Learn Edu 4(1):75–91
Gladwin TN, Kennelly JJ, Krause TS (1995) Shifting paradigms for sustainable development: implications for management theory and research. Acad Manag Rev 20(4):874–907
Global Issues (2013) Poverty facts and stats—global issues. http://www.globalissues.org/article/26/poverty-facts-and-stats. Retrieved 22 Feb 2017
Hahn T, Preuss L, Pinkse J, Figge F (2014) Cognitive frames in corporate sustainability: managerial sensemaking with paradoxical and business case frames. Acad Manag Rev 39(4):463–487
Hahn T, Pinkse J, Preuss L, Figge F (2015) Ambidexterity for corporate social performance. Organ Stud 37(2):213–235
Hawken P (1993) The ecology of commerce: how business can save the planet. Weidenfeld and Nicolson, London
Hediger W (1999) Reconciling "weak" and "strong" sustainability. Int J Soc Econ 26(7/8/9):1120–1144
Hickel J (2015). Could you live on $1.90 a day? That's the international poverty line. The Guardian. https://www.theguardian.com/global-development-professionals-network/2015/nov/01/global-poverty-is-worse-than-you-think-could-you-live-on-190-a-day. Retrieved 10 Nov 2015
Jalal A, Hoffman A, Nelidov T (2013) Sustainability in the Global Marketplace: Business-Almost-as-Usual? http://www.triplepundit.com/2013/10/sustainability-global-marketplace-business-almost-usual/. Retrieved 10 Jan 2017
Karnani A (2011) Doing well by doing good: the grand illusion. Calif Manag Rev 53(2):69–86
Lenz G (2009) The true cost of oil. http://www.ted.com/talks/garth_lenz_images_of_beauty_and_devastation. Retrieved 10 Jan 2017
Lewis MW (2000) Exploring paradox: toward a more comprehensive guide. Acad Manag Rev 25(4):760–776
Maak T, Pless NM (2009) Business leaders as citizens of the world. Advancing humanism on a global scale. J Bus Ethics 88(3):537–550

MacArthur E (Writer) (2015) The surprising thing I learned sailing solo around the world [Video file]. Retrieved February, 2017., from https://www.ted.com/talks/dame_ellen_macarthur_the_surprising_thing_i_learned_sailing_solo_around_the_world
Nonaka I, Takeuchi H (2011) The wise leader. Harv Bus Rev 89(5):58–67
Norman W, MacDonald C (2004) Getting to the bottom of "triple bottom line". Bus Ethics Q 14(02):243–262
Oxfam (2017). Just 8 men own same wealth as half the world. https://www.oxfam.org/en/pressroom/pressreleases/2017-01-16/just-8-men-own-same-wealth-half-world. Retrieved 22 Feb 2017
Padel F, Das S (2010) Out of this earth. East India Adivasis and the aluminum cartel. Oriental Black Swan, New Delhi
Porter M (1980) Corporate strategy. New York. New York, NY
Porter ME, Kramer MR (2006). Strategy and society: The link between competitive advantage and corporate social responsibility. Harv Bus Rev 84(12):78–92, 163
Porter ME, Kramer MR (2011) The big idea: creating shared value. Harv Bus Rev 89(1):2
Prahalad CK, Hammond A (2002) Serving the world's poor, profitably. Harv Bus Rev 80(9):48–59
Purser RE, Park C, Montuori A (1995) Limits to anthropocentrism: toward an ecocentric organization paradigm? Acad Manag Rev 20(4):1053–1089
Rich N (2016) The lawyer who became DuPont's worst nightmare. NY Times Mag 6
Rockström J, Steffen W, Noone K, Persson Å, Chapin III FS, Lambin E et al (2009). Planetary boundaries: exploring the safe operating space for humanity. Ecol Soc 14(2)
Sanford, C. (2011). The responsible business: Reimagining sustainability and success. John Wiley & Sons.
Senge P (1990) The fifth discipline: the art and science of the learning organization. Currency Doubleday, New York
Shankelman J (2014) Tim cook tells climate change sceptics to ditch apple shares. The Guardian. https://www.theguardian.com/environment/2014/mar/03/tim-cook-climate-change-sceptics-ditch-apple-shares. Retrieved 10 Mar 2016
Shrivastava P (1995) The role of corporations in achieving ecological sustainability. Acad Manag Rev 20(4):936–960
Singh MK (2014) New poverty line: Rs 32 in villages, Rs 47 in cities. http://timesofindia.indiatimes.com/india/New-poverty-line-Rs-32-in-villages-Rs-47-in-cities/articleshow/37920441.cms. Retrieved 22 Feb 2017
Slawinski N, Bansal P (2012) A matter of time: the temporal perspectives of organizational responses to climate change. Organ Stud 33(11):1537–1563
Smith WK, Lewis MW (2011) Toward a theory of paradox: a dynamic equilibrium model of organizing. Acad Manag Rev 36(2):381–403
Sanford C (2011) The responsible business: reimagining sustainability and success. John Wiley & Sons, San Francisco
Starik M, Rands GP (1995) Weaving an integrated web: multilevel and multisystem perspectives of ecologically sustainable organizations. Acad Manag Rev 20(4):908–935
Steffen W, Richardson K, Rockström J, Cornell SE, Fetzer I, Bennett EM et al (2015) Planetary boundaries: guiding human development on a changing planet. Science 347(6223):1259855
Sukhdev P (Writer) (2011) Put a value on nature [Video file]. Retrieved February, 2017, from https://www.ted.com/talks/pavan_sukhdev_what_s_the_price_of_nature
Sukhdev P, Kumar P (2008) The economics of ecosystems and biodiversity (TEEB). European Communities, Wesseling
UNICEF (2015) Water, sanitation and hygiene. https://www.unicef.org/wash/. Retrieved 22 Feb 2017
United Nations (1999) http://www.un.org/press/en/1999/19990201.sgsm6881.html. Retrieved 22 Feb 2017

United Nations (2015) World population projected to reach 9.7 billion by 2050 | UN DESA Department of Economic and Social Affairs. (n.d.). . http://www.un.org/en/development/desa/news/population/2015-report.html. Retrieved 10 Jan 2017
United Nations (2016) Sustainable development goals. Sustainable development knowledge platform. (n.d.). https://sustainabledevelopment.un.org/?menu=1300. Retrieved 10 Jan 2017
Van der Byl CA, Slawinski N (2015) Embracing tensions in corporate sustainability: a review of research from win-wins and trade-offs to paradoxes and beyond. Organ Environ 28(1):54–79
Van de Ven AH, Poole MS (1988) Paradoxical requirements for a theory of organizational change. In: Quinn RE, Cameron KS (eds) Paradox and transformation: toward a theory of change in organization and management, vol 19. Ballinger Pub. Co., Cambridge, p 80
Waddock S, Rasche A (2011) Building the responsible enterprise: where vision and values add value. Stanford University Press, Palo Alto
Walley N, Whitehead B (1994) It's not easy being green. Read Bus Environ 36:81
Whiteman G, Walker B, Perego P (2013) Planetary boundaries: ecological foundations for corporate sustainability. J Manag Stud 50(2):307–336
World Bank (2016a) Global monitoring report 2015/2016. doi:10.1596/978-1-4648-0669-8
World Bank (2016b) CO2 emissions (metric tons per capita). http://data.worldbank.org/indicator/EN.ATM.CO2E.PC?end=2013&start=2013&view=map. Retrieved 22 Feb 2017
Young ST, Dhanda KK (2012) Sustainability: essentials for business. Sage, Thousand Oaks

Understanding Factors Affecting University Student's Adoption of E-learning Systems in NCR

Sanjiv Mittal

Abstract Many Universities and Colleges of higher learning have started off late various courses online in India for various reasons. This shows that E-learning is becoming buzzword for tomorrow in terms of acquiring higher education, which in India is in nascent stage but will continue to grow in the future. However, little research has been done to verify the process how the University/College students of higher education will adopt and use E-learning. The present study took a sample of 200 University and College students in NCR to carry out the research. The proposed theoretical model that included Perceived ease of use (PEOU), Perceived usefulness (PU), E-learning self-efficacy (SE), Subjective norm (SN), System accessibility (SA), and their impact on E-learning Attitude and Behavioral Intension to use E-learning was developed based on the extended technology acceptance model (TAM). The results of the study statistically proved that Perceived Usefulness and Perceived Ease Of Use are the most important factors in user's acceptance of E-learning based on the correlation and regression tests. However, subjective norms were found to be the least important factor in influencing e-learners attitude and behavioral intensions.

Keywords E-learning • Technology acceptance model • Online course acceptability • Subjective norms toward (E-learning)

Introduction

There has been tremendous shift in imparting education in the university system and traditional face-to-face education is giving way to E-learning. The higher education institutions in India are rapidly adopting the concepts and factors of e learning. One of the biggest Universities offering online courses in India is IGNOU,

S. Mittal (✉)
School of Management Studies, Guru Gobind Singh Indraprastha University, New Delhi, India
e-mail: dr_sanjivmittal@yahoo.co.in

L. Tadj, A.K. Garg (eds.), *Emerging Challenges in Business, Optimization, Technology, and Industry*, Springer Proceedings in Business and Economics,
DOI 10.1007/978-3-319-58589-5_14

headquartered in Delhi. Practically, all types of Degree and Diploma courses are offered by this university, which has been branded as People's University. Many other Universities and institutions of higher learning have followed the suite and started offering technology-driven distance education (E-learning).

E-learning comprises all forms of electronically supported learning and teaching, facilitated through the Internet. Various studies have highlighted that E-learning as a medium allows the learner to access material, download the assignment, and even maintain contact with the professor and therefore ensure that the institution offering E-learning courses could deliver better information and education. Welsh et al. (2003) define E-learning as the "use of computer network technology, primarily over or through the Internet, to deliver information and instructions to individuals." Rosenberg (2001) shares a similar definition referring to E-learning as using Internet technologies to deliver various solutions to the learners. Holmes and Gardner (2006) simply state that E-learning provides us with access to resources that promote learning on anyplace and anytime basis. Bouhnik and Marcus (2006) stated that E-learning has four advantages: Freedom to decide, Lack of dependence on the time constraints of the lecturer, freedom to express thoughts, and the accessibility to the course online materials. Similarly, Capper (2001) listed the E-learning benefits as: any time, any place, asynchronous interactions, group collaboration, and a new educational approach.

Despite the perceived benefits of E-learning mentioned above, research studies have also shown that the students who commence E-learning courses, do not finish them (Dutton and Perry 2002). Bouhnik and Marcus (2006) have found out that students' E-learning dissatisfaction was based on the factors like lack of firm framework to encourage students to learn, absence of learning atmosphere, absence of self-discipline, lack of interpersonal, and direct interactions among students and less efficient learning process.

The present study is aimed to understand the factors affecting University Student's Adoption of E-learning Systems in NCR. Understanding the learner's attitude toward E-learning is important for improvement in E-learning usage; therefore, this research investigates the various factors in E-learning adoption among the students in NCR. There are five categories of E-learning implementation being evaluated, which are perceived ease of use, perceived usefulness, E-learning self-efficacy, subjective norm, and system accessibility. Studies have been conducted in developed and developing countries about acceptance of E-learning among students and to identify the factors that affect E-learning adoption (ELA).

Literature Review

Different factors have been enumerated as possible determinants of E-learning adoption. The following table illustrates selected studies on ELA, detailing the authors, the adoption factors that have been investigated, the country of study, and the research framework used (Table 1).

Table 1 Summary of literature review

Article	Theory	Country	Sample and methodology	Adoption determinants
Kuldip Kaur et al. (2004)	Assessment of E-learning readiness	Malaysia	A sample of 93 receivers and 35 enablers. E-learning Readiness Research Tool was used	Role of Regulatory body, Role of policy makers
Alaasadik (2007)	The readiness of faculty members to implement E-learning	Egypt	Academic staff of 100. Survey Method	Competencies, experience, Attitudes
Eslaminejad et al. (2010)	Assessment of instructors readiness for implementing E-learning	Iran	A sample of 70 faculty members. A factor analysis was employed to extract significant factors	Knowledge, attitudes, skills and habits toward E-learning in technology and pedagogy domain
Apitep Saekow et al. (2011)	E-Learning readiness	Thailand	30 online courses were compared between Thailand and USA Universities	Policy, technology, financial, human resource, infrastructure
Tagoe (2012)	The basic technology acceptance model	Ghana	Longitudinal survey of 534 university students, Descriptive analysis	Perceived usefulness, perceived ease of use, attitude toward use, Behavioral intention
Hassanzadeh et al. (2012)	Delone and McLean model measuring E-learning systems success (MELSS) model	Iran	Questionnaires completed by 369 instructors, students and alumni of 5 universities Structural equation modeling	Technical system quality Content and information quality User satisfaction Benefits of usage Goal Achievement
Raouf et al. (2012)	TOE framework Iraq	Iraq	Questionnaires Completed by 120 faculty members Structural equation modeling	IS expertise expected benefits It infrastructure competitive pressure Educational partners
Motaghian et al. (2013)	Technology acceptance model and IS model acceptance	Iran	Survey of 115 University Instructors	Perceived usefulness, perceived ease of use, system quality

(continued)

Table 1 (continued)

Article	Theory	Country	Sample and methodology	Adoption determinants
Patrick N. Mafenya et al. (2013)	An investigation of First-year students pedagogical readiness to E-learning	South Africa	Sample of 1st year students of five universities were taken and focus group and individual interviews were held to identify the factors	Skill, attitude, experience, organizational barrier, motivation
Oketch, Hada Achieng et al. (2013)	E-learning readiness assessment model	Kenya	A sample of 296 lecturers were taken	Technological, culture and content
Hamid Mohammad Azimi et al. (2013)	Readiness for implementation of E-learning in colleges of education	India	A sample of 35 receivers and 31 heads of college of education affiliated by University of Mysore. Survey method for assessing organizational readiness for E-learning	ICT infrastructure, human resources, budget and finance, psychological and content
Namisiko et al. (2014)	TAM and TOE	Kenya	Online questionnaires submitted to a total of 500 participants which included instructors, students and administrators both descriptive and inferential statistics	Availability of ICT infrastructure E-learning curriculum performance expectancy perceived usefulness. Perceived ease of use competitive pressure
(Amirkhanpour et al. 2014)	Conceptual framework	Cyprus	Online questionnaire distributed to all the public and private universities	Integration of social learning elements such as various social media tools

E-learning adoption has been studied from different perspectives in different countries using various research frameworks. E-learning is Technology based and is applicable in all spheres of Education. All the research studies pertaining to determining the readiness of E-learning were analyzed to identify the factors that are most widely used by the Researchers. The studies from developing countries have revealed that perceived influence (PI), perceived ease of use (PEOU) the variables of the TAM are important factors, which influence the adoption of E-learning (Al-Adwan et al. 2013; AlAmmary and Hamd 2008; Elkaseh et al. 2016). Further, perceived ease of use (PEOU) and perceived usefulness (PU) were found to be important factors to influence student behavioral intention in using E-learning in case of Libyan Higher Education (Elkash et al. 2016). Further studies have shown that perceived usefulness (PU), perceived ease of use (PEOU), and self-efficacy are important determinants of E-learning, Anderson (2002), Bean (2003), Chapnick (2000), Clark and Mayer (2003), Gold et al. (2001) (Teo et al. 2008). Further studies have highlighted that computer self-efficacy or E-learning self-efficacy (SE) had a significant influence on the actual use of computer and therefore E-learning (Bandura 1977, 1986, 1997), Compeau and Higgins (1995). It was also found that students with high Internet self-efficacy learn better than the students with low Internet self-efficacy in a web-based learning task (Tasai, 2003). For measuring E-learning self-efficacy scales are available developed by Compeau and Higgins (1995) to measure computer self-efficacy and Eastin and Larose (2000) developed Internet self-efficacy scale. In the meantime, Grandon et al. (2005) insisted that E-learning self-efficacy was found to have an effect on student intentions to adopt E-learning. It was also advocated that E-learning self-efficacy represents the personal confidence the students have in finding information and communicating with the instructor within the E-learning system.

As suggested in TAM2, subjective norm (SM) is important variable in influencing E-learning behavior (Ajzen 1991). A subjective norm is a social influence and it refers to how the person's perception is influenced by the people who are important to him or her. It is also one of the variables included in the theory of reasoned action and the theory of planned behavior; Abbasi et al. (2013) and Rivis and Sheeran (2003). Subjective norm was found to be significant factor in affecting university student's intentions to use E-learning in South Korea by Alshare and Kwan (2005). Subjective norm was found to be extrinsic motivational factors, which can encourage university students to self-regulate the use of E-learning Park (2009). Hence, subjective norm is positively related to intention to use E-learning and therefore it is used as important construct in this study.

Further System Accessibility was found to be an important organization context variable identified by the researchers which influence the use of information technology in the learning process (Thong et al. 2002). System accessibility also referred to as E-learning accessibility means the degree of ease with which a University student can access and use campus E-learning system as an organizational factor. University students will adopt E-learning when they think that system accessibility is there and they can use E-learning platform. To what extent this factor is going to influence the adoption of E-learning will depend upon the results of the study.

Research Model and Research Design

Technology acceptance model (TAM) was used as a guiding force to conduct the study. The present study seeks to understand factors affecting university student's adoption of E-learning systems in NCR, India, from the perspective of a developing country. Since E-learning involves individual adoption of a technology, it comes in

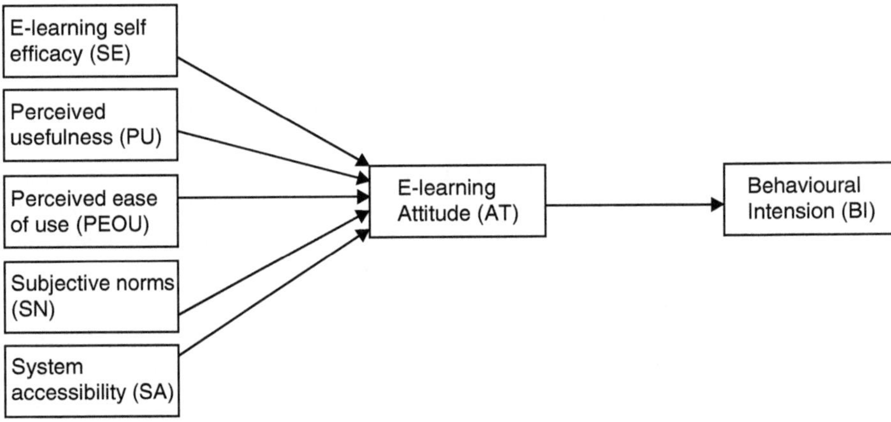

Fig. 1 Open-access tools

the domain of TAM. However, an extended version of TAM has been used to address the research purpose. Six factors as determinants of E-learning adoption from the developing country perspective have been used. These factors are E-learning self-efficacy (SE); perceived usefulness (PU); perceived ease of use (PEOU); subjective norms (SN); system accessibility (SA) and E-learning attitude (AT). These are shown in Fig. 1, which is a proposed theoretical model.

E-learning uses electronic devices and technological platforms to deliver the content of the courses sought by the students and therefore the ability of the students to use those devices and technology is important for its adoption. Hence, E-learning self-efficacy as a variable is taken in the present study. Various research studies have already shown that E-leaning self-efficacy has a significant effect on the use of adoption of E-learning from student perspective. Similarly, perceived ease of use (PEOU), perceive usefulness (PU), subjective norms (SN), system accessibility (SA) have influence on attitude of the students in the adoption of E-learning systems, so these variables are also taken in the study. Moreover, perceived usefulness, perceived ease of use, E-learning self-efficacy, subjective norms and system accessibility can be considered cognitive constructs, which are measurable, and E-learning attitude might be considered affective construct. In the same proposed model above behavioral intension that is intension to use could be regarded as behavioral construct.

Sampling Method and Procedure

The population in the study consisted of universities and college students in the NCR region where 20 universities and 20 college students were covered making a total population of around 1 lakh students. Among these 1 lakh, a sample size of 200 students was drawn by taking five students from each university and five students from each college using judgmental sampling. Precautions were taken to look in that these students were Internet users and have also heard about E-learning courses; they may or may not have taken them.

Instrument for Data Collection

The instrument for data collection was developed based on the literature review and the main objective of the study. For every construct that was used in the proposed model, minimum five statements were taken and after pilot testing the instrument with 25 students and 2 E-learning administrative staff and faculty members respectively, the content validity was established. The completed instrument consisted of two parts where part I was used to capture the demographical attributes of the respondents like age, gender, years of experience using the Internet and experience with E-learning. Part II was in the context of the factors affecting E-learning adoption and consisted of seven subsections as follows: (1) E-learning self-efficacy, (2) Perceive ease of use (PEOU), (3) Perceive usefulness (PU), (4) Subjective norms (SN), (5) System accessibility (SA), (6) E-learning Attitude (AT), (7) Behavioral Intension (BI). All statements in different constructs were measured on the 7-point Likert type scale, from 1 = strongly disagree to 7 = strongly agree. The instrument was tested for its reliability using Cronbach Alpha, which was found to be 0.89, which is found to be good.

Statistical Procedure

Data collected by questionnaire was coded and entered into SPSS window. Various types of statistical tests were performed like Descriptive statistics of Mean and Standard Deviation. Correlation and Regression were also performed.

Results and Discussions

Part-I: Demographical Analysis: The age distribution of the participants included in the sample showed that most of the students were in age bracket of 21–25 years with 70% of the sample, followed by students with ages between 26 and 30 years with 15% while in the age group of 30 years and above there were only 15%. In relation to gender distribution, the male participants were more than the females with 60% and 40% respectively. Further, with respect to experience of using Internet almost 98% asserted having used the Internet. With respect to experience with E-learning or having used E-learning studies, only 50% respondents said in the positive. Platforms such as Facebook, WhatsApp, Class emails, course websites, etc.

Table 2 Demographical analysis

Item	Category	Frequency	Percentage %
Gender	Male	120	60
	Female	80	40
Total		200	100
Age	21–25 years	140	70
	26–30 years	30	15
Total		200	100
Experience using the Internet	Yes	196	98
	No	4	2
Total		200	100
Experience with E-learning	Yes	100	50
	No	100	50
Total		200	100

were identified as platforms used for E-learning and that was the only E-learning experience they were having as shown in Table 2.

Based on the descriptive information given in Table 2, although students were highly experienced Internet users with 98% of the sample but they did not have much E-learning experience and were found to be only 50%. This result denotes a very positive message that in the future E-learning will be a potential learning tool for learners and University/College-based E-learning is going to be the potential market for the universities and college of higher learning.

Based on the descriptive statistics it can be seen from Table 3 that perceived usefulness having a mean score of 4.30, followed by perceived ease of use having a mean score of 4.23, than followed with E-leaning self efficacy having a mean score of 4.07, followed with system accessibility with score of 3.94 and followed with system accessibility having a mean score of 3.94 are the factors that influence E-leaning attitude which further leads to behavioral intension. So the most important factor that influences E-leaning adoption is perceived usefulness followed with perceived ease of use. It was found that a subjective norm has the least influence on E-learning adaptation, i.e., on learner's behavioral intension of using E-learning and higher education. Based on the findings it can be recommended that in order to enhance the use of E-learning the educators and the students' parents and other people who influence the E-learning behavior should encourage their students and wards to adopt E-learning.

Looking at the correlation analysis done in Table 4 it is found that the cognitive variables like Perceived ease of use (PEOU), Perceived usefulness (PU), E-learning self-efficacy (SE), Subjective norm (SN, System accessibility (SA) are having low correlation among themselves but are highly correlated with E-learning Attitude (AT) and Behavioral intension (BI). Perceived usefulness (PU) is found to be highly correlated with E- Learning Attitude (AT) and the lowest correlation is found between subjective norms.

Table 3 The mean, standard deviation, and Cronbach Alpha of the construct

Item	Mean	SD	α
Perceived ease of use (PEOU)	4.23	1.39	0.85
I find E-learning system easy to use (E1)	4.24	1.30	
Learning how to use an E-learning system is easy for me (E2)	4.25	1.39	ááã
It is easy to become skillful at using an E-learning system (E3)	4.23	1.41	
I find E-learning system friendly to use (E4)	4.23	1.42	
I find E-learning system easy to navigate (E5)	4.22	1.43	
E-learning facilitates its usage any time of the day (E6)	4.23	1.42	
Perceived usefulness (PU)	4.30	1.39	0.87
E-learning would improve my leaning performance (U1)	4.30	1.30	
E-learning would increase academic productivity (U2)	4.33	1.36	
E-learning could make it easier to study course content (U3)	4.27	1.41	
In order for me to prepare for the future job, it is necessary to take E-learning courses (U4)	4.28	1.42	
E-learning helps me to grasp the subject better (U5)	4.29	1.43	
I believe E-learning contents are informative (U6)	4.30	1.35	
I believe E-learning is a useful learning tool (U7)	4.30	1.44	
I believe E-learning contents are useful (U8)	4.31	1.41	
E- Learning Attitude (AT)	3.94	1.24	0.91
Studying through E-learning is a good idea (A1)	3.93	1.14	
Studying through E-learning is a wise idea (A2)	3.85	1.20	
I am positive toward E-learning (A3)	4.04	1.22	
I feel more comfortable toward E-learning (A4)	3.94	1.24	
E-learning adds to my confidence building (A5)	3.90	1.28	
If I am using E-learning system, I feel I am doing positive for myself (A6)	3.92	1.31	
I did not notice any inconsistencies in using E-learning (A7)	4.02	1.32	
E-learning does everything I would expect it to do (A8)	3.95	1.24	
Behavioral intension (BI)	4.10	1.31	0.92
I intend to check announcements from E-learning systems frequently (B1)	4.10	1.18	
I intend to be a heavy user of E-learning system (B2)	4.14	1.40	
I intend to use E-learning contents to assist my learning (B3)	4.13	1.39	
I intend to use E-learning as an autonomous learning tool (B4)	4.04	1.28	
I intend to use E-learning to improve my academic performance (B5)	4.05	1.31	
E-learning self-efficacy (SE)	4.07	1.42	0.91
I feel confident finding information in the E-learning system (S1)	4.07	1.39	
I have the necessary technical skills for using an E-learning system (S2)	4.11	1.41	
I feel confident using E-learning system (S3)	4.06	1.45	
I feel confident operating E-learning system (S4)	4.04	1.43	
I find it interesting in using E-learning contents (S5)	4.05	1.44	

(continued)

Table 3 (continued)

Item	Mean	SD	α
Subjective norm (SN)	3.50	1.31	0.89
What E-learning stands for is important for me as admired by my university/college senior (N1)	3.50	1.22	
I like using E-learning based on the similarity of my values to take E-learning courses (N2)	3.56	1.24	
Most people who are important to me think that I should take up E-learning (N3)	3.51	1.35	
It is expected of me that I take up E-learning program in near future (N4)	3.53	1.33	
The people in my life whose opinions I value would like that I take up E-learning program in the near future (N5)	3.55	1.36	
I feel pressure from Peers to adopt E-learning system (N6)	3.32	1.38	
I feel under social pressure to use E-learning system (N7)	3.57	1.27	
System accessibility (SA)	3.94	1.21	0.92
I have no difficulty accessing and using an E-learning system in the university/college (SA1)	3.93	1.14	
I am in a position to find the learning material on E-learning platform whatever is required (SA2)	3.95	1.15	
Internet speed is good enough for E-learning (SA3)	4.02	1.20	
Interacting on E-learning system is often user friendly (SA4)	3.94	1.21	
Interacting on E-learning system requires less of my mental efforts (SA5)	3.90	1.22	
E-learning system is found to be flexible to interact way (SA6)	3.92	1.28	
I find it easy to get knowledge through E-learning system whenever I want (SA7)	3.93	1.27	
Overall scale reliability			0.89

Table 4 Correlation analysis

Variables	2 (PU)	3 (AT)	4 (BI)	5 (SE)	6 (SN)	7 (SA)
1. Perceived ease of use (PEOU)	.52*	0.71*	0.67*	0.55*	0.51*	0.52*
2. Perceived usefulness (PU)		0.76*	0.70*	0.53*	0.50*	0.54*
3. E-learning Attitude (AT)			0.68*	0.67*	0.53*	0.67*
4. Behavioral intension (BI)				0.67*	0.52*	0.63*
5. E-learning self-efficacy (SE)					0.54*	0.53*
6. Subjective norm (SN)						0.51*
7. System accessibility (SA)						

*$p < 0.01$

Regression analysis was done which was a simple regression with E-learning Attitude as an independent variable and Behavioral Intension as a dependent variable. Similarly, multiple regressions were run with E-Learning attitude as a dependent variable and five independent variables as Perceived ease of use (PEOU), Perceived usefulness (PU), E-learning self-efficacy (SE), Subjective norm (SN), System accessibility (SA). Table 5 demonstrates that Perceived usefulness (PU) has the highest beta score (0.45) and therefore influences E-learning attitude the most. The second variable influencing E-learning attitude in order of importance is Perceived ease of use (PEOU) and E-learning self-efficacy (SE) with beta scores as 0.43 and 0.42 respectively. The other two independent variables like Subjective norm (SN) and System accessibility (SA) were not found to have much influence on E-learning attitude and they were found to be insignificant based on the p values. Similarly, the relationship between E-learning attitude and Behavioral Intension (BI) was found to be high having a beta score of 0.51. This indicates that perceived usefulness and perceived ease of use are critical for E-learning adoption among the students of the NCR region.

The coefficients of determination R2 showed that 47.8% variation in E-learning Attitude is explained by Perceived Usefulness. Overall, it was found that 57.8% variation in a dependent variable that is E-learning attitude is explained by independent variables out of which three independent variables were found to be significant which were Perceived ease of use (PEOU), Perceived usefulness (PU), E-learning self efficacy (SE). Similarly, 59.3% variation in Behavioral Intension is explained by E-learning Attitude. Hence, the results of this study revealed that there are two readiness dimensions which are found to be important and they are Perceived Usefulness and Perceived Ease Of Use for making the students of higher education for forming positive attitude toward E-learning. Moreover, if E-Learning attitude is formed it will also result in Behavioral Intension to start using E-Learning as a tool of learning. Faculty members will be required to help the students to develop self-directed learning and learner control skills for online learning contexts. The role of faculty will be very important for encouraging the students to vote for using online courses. Faculty members can create learning community through which experience sharing, instant feedback, and other methods can be used to keep the students

Table 5 Regression results of predicted path relations

Dependent variable	Independent variable	β	R2	R2	P
E- Learning Attitude (AT)	Perceived ease of use (PEOU)	0.43	0.285	0.578	< 0.001
	Perceived usefulness (PU)	0.45	0.478		< 0.001
	E-learning self-efficacy (SE)	0.42	0.112		< 0.001
	Subjective norm (SN)	0.26	0.031		< 0.078
	System accessibility (SA)	0.32	0.094		< 0.089
Behavioral Intension (BI)	E- Learning Attitude (AT)	0.51	0.593	0.593	< 0.001

taking interest in online courses. As more and more Internet penetration will increase and more and more universities/colleges will be offering courses through E-learning mode, it can expect that students would adjust to the use of online courses.

Conclusions

The purpose of the present study was to (1) understand E-learning Attitude of the students in higher education, (2) find out the factors that influence E-Learning attitude, and (3) investigate the relationship between E-Learning attitude and behavior intension to continue to enrol in online programs. The findings of the study have been quite meaningful and using the extended TAM model it was found that out of the five factors that were used to study the adoption of E-Learning Attitude the factors were found to be highly significant and were Perceived Usefulness and Perceived Ease Of Use. The influence of these variables was statistically tested using correlation and regression analysis. It was also found that once the attitude formation takes place toward E-Learning, it will result in the behavioral intension to E-learning adoption. Previous researchers have already provided support to the results which have come out of the study. This study has made some significant contribution to the research and practice. This study has contributed to the body of E-learning by validating the extended TAM model from the Indian perspective. Moreover, the study will provide practical guidance to University/College administrators and instructors to pay close attention to the factors, which have been used in the study when implementing E-Learning projects in their respective institutions.

Limitations and Recommendations for Future Research

This study revealed several limitations that should be taken up in future research. Limited independent factors as antecedents of adoption of E-learning were taken which can be increased from five to many more. The scale that was used for data collection was not any standardized scale and therefore might have some errors. Hence, the tests of validity may be conducted in future research to make the scale more meaningful. Future research can also take higher sample and conduct the study in different parts of the country to understand how E-Learning readiness varies in different states of India and can some model be proposed which can help in standardizing the results in terms of the factors that are found to be consistent in influencing the adoption of E-Learning among students of higher education. Moreover, the study can also be done to design better online courses for maximizing student's online learning experiences. The sample size that was taken was also small which could be further increased in future research. More sophisticated statistical techniques like Structure Equation Modeling etc. could be used to make the results more robust and statistically valid. However, the present research is the need of the hour as the future is going to be for online education.

References

Abbasi M, Stergioulas LK (2013) Hybrid wireless networks for e-learning and digital literacy: testing and evaluation. In Fostering 21st Century Digital Literacy and Technical Competency (pp. 233–245). IGI Global

Anderson T (2002) Revealing the hidden curriculum of e-learning. Distance education and distributed learning. pp. 115–134

Ajzen I (1991) The theory of planned behavior. Organ Behav Hum Decis Process 50:179–211

Albert Bandura, (1977) Self-efficacy: Toward a unifying theory of behavioral change.. Psychological Review 84 (2):191-215

Albert Bandura, (1986) The Explanatory and Predictive Scope of Self-Efficacy Theory. Journal of Social and Clinical Psychology 4 (3):359–373

Al-Adwan A, Al-Adwan A, Smedley J (2013) Exploring students acceptance of E-learning using technology acceptance model in Jordanian universities. Int J Educ Dev Inf Commun Technol 9(2):4–18

AlAmmary J, Hamd S (2008) Factors influencing the adoption of E-learning at University of Bahrain. Proceeding of the International Arab Conference on Information Technology ACIT'2008, Hammamet, Tunisia

Amirkhanpour M, Ruediger Kaufmann H, Garcia-Gallego A (2014) An extensive study of the E-learning practices within Cyprus universities. Int J Organ Anal 22(3):317–341

Azimi HM (2013) Readiness for implementation of e-learning in colleges of education. J Novel Appl Sci 2(12):769–775

Bean M (2003) Are you ready for e-learning. Assessing elearning readiness. MediaPro Newsletter: Tips and tricks of the trade, available at: http://www.mediapro.com/html/resources/news1-vol5-01.htm htm.

Bandura A (1977) Self-efficacy: toward a unifying theory of behavioral change. Psychol Rev 84(2):191–215

Bandura A (1986) The explanatory and predictive scope of self-efficacy theory. J Social Clin Psychol 4(3):359–373

Banduara A (1997) Self-efficacy: the exercise of control. Macmillian.

Bouhnik D, Marcus T (2006) Interaction in distancE-learning courses. J Am Soc Inf Sci Technol 57(3):299–305

Capper J (2001) E-learning growth and promise for the developing world. Tech KnowLogia, May/June. http://www.techknowlegia.org. Retrieved 20 July 2007

Chapnick S (2000) Are you ready for E-learning? http//www.astd.org/ASTD/Resources/dyor/article_archieves.htm. Retrieved 19 Dec 2004

Clark RC, Mayer RE (2003) E-learning and the science of instruction: proved guidelines for customers and designers of multimedia learning. Pfeiffer, San Francisco, CA

Compeau DR, Higgins CA (1995) Computers self-efficacy: development of a measure and initial test. MIS Q 19(2):189–211

Dutton J, Perry J (2002) How do online students differ from lecture students? J Manag Inf Syst 18(4):169–190

Eslaminejad T, et al. (2010) Assessment of instructors' readiness for implementing E-learning in continuing medical education in Iran. Taylor & Francis

Elkaseh AM, Wong KW, Fung CC (2016) Perceived ease of use and perceived usefulness of social media for e-learning in Libyan higher education: a structural equation modeling analysis. Int J Inf Educ Technol 6(3):192

Gasiewski JA, Eagan MK, Garcia GA, Hurtado S, Chang MJ (2012) From gatekeeping to engagement: a multicontextual, mixed method study of student academic engagement in introductory STEM courses. Res Higher Educ 53(2):229–261

Grandon E, Alshare O, Kwan O (2005) Factors influencing student intention to adopt online classes: a cross-cultural study. J Comput Sci Coll 20(4):46–56

Gold A, Malhotra A, Segars AH (2001) Knowledge management: an organizational capabilities perspective. J Manag Inf Syst 18(1):185–214

Hassanzadeh A, Kanaani F, Elahi S (2012) A model for measuring E-learning systems success in universities. Expert Syst Appl 39(12):10959–10966

Harold W. Webb, Grandon Gill, Gary Poe, (2005) Teaching with the Case Method Online: Pure Versus Hybrid Approaches. Decision Sciences Journal of Innovative Education 3 (2):223–250

Holmes B, Gardner J (2006) E-learning concepts and practice. Sage Publishing, Thousand Oaks, CA

H.A. OketchE-learning Readiness Assessment Model In Kenyas' Higher Education Institutions: A Case Study Of University Of Nairobi (Doctoral dissertationUniversity of Nairobi); (2013)

Kaur K, Zoraini Wati A (2004) An assessment of e-learning readiness at Open University Malaysia. In International Conference on Computers in Education. pp. 1017–1022

Mafenya PN (2013) An investigation of first-year students' pedagogical readiness to e-learning and assessment in open and distance learning: an University of South Africa context. Mediterr J Social Sci 4(13):353

Motaghian H, Hasanzadeh A, Moghadam DK (2013) Factors affecting university instructors' adoption of web-based learning systems: case study of Iran. Comput Educ 61:158–167

Namisiko P, Muniala C, Nyongesa S (2014) Towards an optimization framework for e-learning in developing countries: a case of private universities in Kenya. J Comput Sci Inf Technol 2(2):131–148

Oketch HA (2013) E-learning readiness assessment model. In Kenyas' higher education institutions: a case study of University Of Nairobi (Doctoral dissertation University of Nairobi)

Park SY (2009) An analysis of the technology acceptance model in understanding university students' behavioral intention to use e-learning. Educ Technol Soc 12(3):150–162

Raouf JB, Naser IS, Jassim BK (2012) Determinants of e-Learning implementation success in the Iraqi MoHE. Eng Tech J 30(4):659–671

Rivis A, Sheeran P (2003) Social influences and the theory of planned behaviour: evidence for a direct relationship between prototypes and young people's exercise behaviour. Psychol Health 18(5):567–583

Rosenberg MJ (2001) E-learning: strategies for delivering knowledge in the digital age, vol 9. McGraw-Hill, New York

Sadik A (2007) The readiness of faculty members to develop and implement e-learning: the case of an Egyptian university. Int J E-Learn 6(3):433

Saekow A, Samson D (2011) E-learning Readiness of Thailand's Universities Comparing to the USA's Cases. International Journal of e-Education, e-Business, e-Management and e-Learning, 1(2): 126

Tagoe M (2012) Students' perceptions on incorporating e-learning into teaching and learning at the University of Ghana. Int J Educ Dev Inf Commun Technol 8(1):91–103

Thong JYL, Hong WY, Tam KY (2002) Understanding user acceptance of digital libraries: What are the roles of interface characteristics, organizational context, and individual differences? Int J Hum-Comput Stud 57(3):215–242

Teo T, Lee CB, Chai CS (2008) Understanding pre-service teachers' computer attitudes: applying and extending the technology acceptance model. J Comput Assisted Learn 24(2):128–143

Webb HW, Gill G, Poe G (2005) Teaching with the case method online: pure versus hybrid approaches. Decis Sci J Innovative Educ 3(2):223–250

Welsh ET, Wanberg CR, Brown KG, Simmering MJ (2003) E-learning: emerging uses, empirical results and future directions. Int J Train Dev 7:245–258

Gender Differences and Perceived Efficacy of Humor Styles in the Workplace

Gwen E. Jones and Stephen E. Bear

Abstract Humor as a tool in the management toolkit has been underutilized and not well understood. Yet, humor has been found to result in many positive employee and organizational outcomes such as lowered stress and higher productivity. Further, it is asserted to be selectively and effectively applied by managers with the right knowledge of humor to enhance their relationships with subordinates. This paper specifically postulates how several types of humor can affect subordinate attributions of managerial competence and satisfaction with supervision. The proposed relationships are hypothesized to be moderated by gender.

Keywords Humor style • Affiliative • Self-enhancing • Mild aggressive • Self-defeating • Gender difference

"A Laugh Is the Shortest Distance Between Two People" John Cleese (2017)

Humor in the workplace has been of interest to the field of management and organizational effectiveness for some time (c.f. Blumenfeld and Alpern 1994), but the mechanism for how humor can be utilized to impact managers and their employees is not effectively understood (Dominic McCann et al. 2010; Robert and Wilbanks 2012). Despite numerous studies showing the positive effects of humor on individual stress levels as well as on organizational outcome variables, managers continue to fail to take humor seriously as a legitimate, useful tool in their managerial "toolkit" (Romero and Cruthirds 2006). This is partly due to increased workforce diversity coupled with discrimination and harassment law (Mesmer-Magnus et al. 2012), spawning questions about what is appropriate or inappropriate and possibly

G.E. Jones (✉) • S.E. Bear
Management Department, Fairleigh Dickinson University, Teaneck, NJ, USA
e-mail: gjones@fdu.edu

L. Tadj, A.K. Garg (eds.), *Emerging Challenges in Business, Optimization, Technology, and Industry*, Springer Proceedings in Business and Economics,
DOI 10.1007/978-3-319-58589-5_15

downright offensive. Hence, a manager may decide it is too risky to let out his or her humorous side in the workplace. This research examines the relationships between manager humor and subordinate attributions of the manager.

We can assume that there are good reasons to try to understand how we can effectively infuse a little levity. Much research has linked laughter and good health (O'Reilly 2007), and several studies have investigated the relationship between levels of humor and the moderating effects that it has on anxiety and stress. More specifically, multiple studies have reported that when a subject had a higher level of humor, they had lower levels of anxiety and stress (e.g., Abel 2002; Yovetich et al. 1990; Martin and Lefcourt 1983; Mesmer-Magnus et al. 2012). According to Farrell (1998, p. 4) "laughter lowers the blood pressure, relieves tension, improves blood flow and eases ailments of the digestive and intestinal tracts." It has been reported that rigorous laughter can provide many of the same cardiac, circulatory and respiratory benefits that one would receive from a physical workout. In fact, 1 h of belly-laughter can burn up to 500 calories (O'Reilly 2007).

In addition to these physical health benefits, there have been studies on humor and joking's positive effects on people within the working environment. It has been reported that when people are in a good mood, they organize data better and that humor helps people to develop both their negotiation and decision-making skills (Davidhizar and Shearer 1997). Another benefit of humor found in the workplace is greater commitment by the employees to the organization, which can lead to increased customer satisfaction (Brotherton 1996; Karl and Peluchette 2006). In addition, humor has been shown to have positive impacts on a variety of managerial challenges, such as increasing group cohesiveness (McGhee 1999; Holmes 2006), enhancing communications (e.g., Greatbatch and Clark 2002), boosting subordinate satisfaction (Decker 1987), and increasing productivity (Avolio et al. 1999), creativity (Brotherton 1996; Arendt 2009), and innovation (Tang 2008). In one study, top executives from Fortune 500 companies rated a sense of humor as the third most important requirement for success in business (Farrell 1998). Indeed, companies like Ben & Jerry's and Southwest Airlines are famous for integrating humor and fun into their organizational culture. Obviously, humor can lighten the mood and make work life more enjoyable. Humor can actually be a powerful, useful tool for embracing diversity and developing an inclusive, positive work environment, which in turn can enhance productivity and retention levels (O'Reilly 2007).

Typology of Humor Styles

Romero and Cruthirds (2006) assert that there is a science to humor that can be effectively and selectively applied by managers in organizations. However, there is little research addressing this aspect of the use in humor in the workplace. Humor is defined as a communication that is mutually amusing (Robert and Yan 2007) and elicits a "positive cognitive or affective response from listeners" (Crawford 1994). Humor is either intentionally amusing or is unintentionally seen as amusing

(Robert and Yan 2007; Evans and Steptoe-Warren 2015). Martin et al. (2003) developed a typology and measure of several humor styles, which we use in our model because of their useful and positive application for managers in the work environment. The first is affiliative humor. It includes nonthreatening kinds of funny stories about the group or group members, inside jokes, or good-natured kidding. Initiators of this style of humor are typically employing it to build social relationships and bring people together. The second type of humor is self-enhancing humor, in which the initiator exhibits a positive, humorous view of life where he or she can more easily deal with stress inducers. Initiators of this style employ it to enhance their self-image and manage tension and stressful situations. The third style is mild aggressive humor in which the initiator uses satire or teasing in a playful way, but may actually be delivering a forceful or reprimanding message. The last style is self-defeating humor, where the initiator employs amusing, self-ridiculing messages to seek acceptance or mitigate social distance from others. In this study, we will examine the effects of these four humor styles on subordinate attributions of managerial competence and satisfaction with supervision.

Gender Differences

In a survey, Myers et al. (1997) found that men rate themselves as engaging in humor more often than women engage, and also felt that their attempts were much more effective. The authors concluded that women do not incorporate humor into their communications with others as easily as men do, and may show that women are less likely to violate social norms, which prevent them from using humor more often. Bernard (1996) found in survey results that employees reported men used humor more frequently in the workplace than did women. He suggested that the reason for this finding might be that women are less willing to exhibit their sense of humor for fear of not being respected. However, supervisors who did make use of non-offensive humor were considered to be better managers than those who did not, regardless of gender. Thus, it is important for women to receive more guidance on how to effectively utilize humor as a management tool.

Romero and Cruthirds (2006) noted that the gender research on humor suggests that the effectiveness of the humor styles may be moderated by gender. For example, research by Hay (2000) suggests that women use humor to build alliances and men use humor to impress others. This is consistent with the two styles of humor, affiliative and self-enhancing respectively. Thus, we propose the following:

Proposition 1 When utilizing the Affiliative humor style, subordinate attributions of competence and satisfaction with supervision will be more positive for a female manager than for a male manager.

Proposition 2 When utilizing the Self-Enhancing humor style, subordinate attributions of competence and satisfaction with supervision will be more positive for a male manager than for a female manager.

Proposition 3 Subordinate attributions of competence and satisfaction with supervision will be more positive when a manager used the Affiliative or Self-Enhancing styles than if the manager used the Mild Aggressive or Self-Defeating humor styles.

Proposition 4 Female respondents will respond more negatively than will males to managers using Mild Aggressive Humor.

Proposition 5 Female respondents will respond more negatively to a female manager than to a male manager utilizing Self-Defeating humor.

Thus, it is proposed that the affiliative humor style will be more effective (gender role fit) and result in more positive subordinate outcomes (i.e., attributions of competence and satisfaction with supervision) for female managers and the self-enhancing humor style will be more effective for male managers. In addition, it is proposed that these two styles overall will be more effective on subordinate outcomes than the second two styles (mild aggressive and self-defeating). Furthermore, there may be moderating effects due to gender of the subordinate. Women may be less positively affected by mild aggressive humor than male subordinates. They might also be less impressed by women managers using self-defeating humor. These results are hypothesized based on more heightened status differential sensitivities (because of a history of inequalities) on the part of women in the workplace.

Conclusion

Humor in the workplace can be a powerful tool in the manager's toolkit. Much research has indicated that humor utilized by managers can have very positive outcomes. This research examined the relationships between manager humor and subordinate attributions of the manager. Specifically, different types of humor used by a manager are presented and relationships between subordinate attributions of managerial competence and satisfaction with supervision are proposed. Differences because of the gender of the manager and gender of the subordinate are also proposed, and future research should expand on this work by experimentally testing the above propositions.

References

Abel MH (2002) Humor, stress, and coping strategies. Humor 15:365–381

Arendt LA (2009) Transformational leadership and follower creativity: the moderating effect of leader humor. Rev Bus Res 9(4):100–106

Avolio BJ, Howell JM, Sosik JJ (1999) A funny thing happened on the way to the bottom line: humor as a moderator of leadership style effects. Acad Manag J 42(2):219–227

Bernard K (1996) Who makes a better boss? male or female, it's skills that count. Newsday B19

Blumenfeld E, Alpern L (1994) Humor at work. Peachtree Publishers, Atlanta, GA

Brotherton P (1996) The company that plays together.... HR Mag 44(12):76–82

Cleese J (2017. Quote taken from: New Jersey speakers' series presents John Cleese, Andrew McKay. www.fdu.edu

Crawford CB (1994) Theory and implications regarding the utilization of strategic humor by leaders. J Leadersh Stud 1(4):53–68

Davidhizar R, Shearer R (1997) Humor: don't manage people without it. Radiol Technol 69(1):83–88

Decker WH (1987) Managerial humor and subordinate satisfaction. Soc Behav Personal Int J 15(2):221–224

Dominic McCann P, Plummer D, Minichiello V (2010) Being the butt of the joke: homophobic humor, male identity, and its connection to emotional and physical violence for men. Health Sociol Rev 19(4):505–521

Evans TR, Steptoe-Warren G (2015) Humor style clusters exploring managerial humor. Int J Bus Commun 52(1):42–67

Farrell L (1998) You've got to be kidding: humor as a FUNdamental management tool. Rec Manag Q 32:3–4

Greatbatch D, Clark T (2002) Laughing with the gurus. Bus Strateg Rev 13(3):10–18

Hay J (2000) Functions of humor in the conversations of men and women. J Pragmat 32(6):709–742

Holmes J (2006) Sharing a laugh: pragmatic aspects of humor and gender in the workplace. J Pragmat 38(1):26–50

Karl K, Peluchette J (2006) How does workplace fun impact employee perceptions of customer service quality? J Leadersh Organ Stud 13(2):2–14

Martin RA, Lefcourt HM (1983) Sense of humor as a moderator of the relation between stressors and moods. J Pers Soc Psychol 45:1313–1324

Martin RA, Puhlik-Doris P, Larsen G, Gray J, Weir K (2003) Individual differences in uses of humor and their relation to psychological well-being: Development of the Humor Styles Questionnaire. J Res personal 37(1):48–75

McGhee PE (1999) The laughter remedy. www.thelaughterremedy.com

Mesmer-Magnus J, Glew DJ, Viswesvaran C (2012) A meta-analysis of positive humor in the workplace. J Manag Psychol 27(2):155–190

Myers SA, Ropog BL, Rodgers RP (1997) Sex differences in humor. Psychol Rep 81(1):221–222

O'Reilly S (2007) Laughing all the way to the bank. Pers Today 9:27

Robert C, Wilbanks JE (2012) The wheel model of humor: humor events and affect in organizations. Hum Relat 65(9):1071–1099

Robert C, Yan W (2007) The case for developing new research on humor and culture in organizations: Toward a higher grade of manure. In: Research in personnel and human resources management. Emerald Group Publishing Limited, Bingley, pp 205–267

Romero EJ, Cruthirds KW (2006) The use of humor in the workplace. Acad Manag Perspect 20(3):58–69

Tang YT (2008) The relationship between use of humor by leaders and R&D employee innovative behavior: evidence from Taiwan. Asia Pac Manage Rev 13(3):635–653

Yovetich NA, Dale A, Hudak MA (1990) Benefits of humor in reduction of threat-induced anxiety. Psychol Rep 66(1):51–58

How “Congruent” Are You?—University Seniors’ Sense of Self and Career Enactment

Özen Aşik-Dizdar

Abstract This paper explores the relationship between the sense of self of members of the young generation and their chosen occupation, with the expectation that the young workforce, given their generational characteristics, would be seeking a better match between themselves and their job. The brief qualitative research conducted for this purpose asked university seniors to comment on themselves and their future vision of the work they would be doing. The findings revealed that the ideal conditions for seniors' vision of themselves were mostly made up of a good match between their own characteristics and their chosen careers and work environments.

Keywords Young workforce • Career theory • Career models • Career enactment

Amidst the fast-changing context of the world of work with redefined conditions of employment, technological developments, and the changing nature of the labour force, a shift is being observed in the ways careers are perceived and experienced in the past several decades (DeFilippi and Arthur, 1996; Savickas, 2000; Storey, 2000). Compared to older generations, today's young workforce takes a more liberal outlook to careers and working in general, and ascribes a more subjective meaning to career development (Leach, 2015; Walton and Mallon, 2004). More specifically, today's generation of employees, with their confident and adaptable attitude, cares more about personal satisfaction and independence at work, appears less bound by authority, and wants to hold meaningful jobs where they can apply more discretion (Barney, 2002; Loughlin and Barling, 2001). Moreover, all these changes overlap with the age of “boundaryless careers” characterized by dissolving boundaries among functions, departments and organizations that require many more varied and flexible skills on the part of employees (Arnold, Cooper, and Robertson, 1998; Littleton, Arthur, and Rousseau, 2000).

Ö. Aşik-Dizdar, Ph.D. (✉)
Business Administration Department, Istanbul Altinbaş University, Istanbul, Turkey
e-mail: ozen.asik@kemerburgaz.edu.tr

L. Tadj, A.K. Garg (eds.), *Emerging Challenges in Business, Optimization, Technology, and Industry*, Springer Proceedings in Business and Economics,
DOI 10.1007/978-3-319-58589-5_16

Therefore, career theory has gradually moved away from traditional models, and adopted new approaches to entail and explain these changes.

The present paper explores these new career models from the perspective of young employees at the beginning of their careers. In other words, it aims to discover the congruence that young workers are experiencing between their sense of self and their current work. To do so, a brief qualitative study has been conducted and results have been discussed. This work attempts to be the first paper in a series of others to discuss the role of career enactment and construction of meaning in the work life.

Literature

Career can be defined as a series of positions, roles, activities, and experiences that pertain to one's working life (Arnold et al., 1998). Traditional models of career usually refer to a linear process of advancement, where individuals start working at entry-level positions, stay in the same organization for long periods of time, and gradually rise up in management hierarchy in return for job security (Peel and Inkson, 2004; Walton and Mallon, 2004). However, with changing times came increased use of flexible organizational structures, such as delayering/downsizing, outsourcing/contracting, and other flexible working arrangements (e.g., telecommuting, etc.) which led to the emergence of less hierarchy and more flat structures (Cappelli, 1999; Jacoby, 1999). These developments in organizations also led to new career models, such as "protean careers" (Hall, 2002), "boundaryless careers" (Arthur and Rousseau, 1996), and even "portfolio careers" (Mallon, 1999), where each approach describes careers as flexible, subjective experiences that, combined together, serve to enhance the individual's employability in today's flexible work environments in the long term (Cohen and Mallon, 2001; Mallon and Duberley, 2000).

In this context of high uncertainty where careers need to be defined in more subjective, integrative and flexible terms, interpersonal networks, and individual choice and sense-making have become major tools for individuals to determine their career path (Cohen and Mallon, 2001; Littleton et al., 2000). As such, the way in which careers are perceived and enacted has become intricately connected to the processes of identity-building and self-definition through work (Blustein and Noumair, 1996; Cappellen and Janssens, 2010). In addition, this turbulent environment seems to be a good match for members of today's young workforce who are rather free-spirited, and prefer work environments that allow them greater discretion in asserting their identities, values, and satisfactions for career enactment (Leach, 2015; Weick, 1996).

After all, the ultimate purpose of the young workforce today is to balance their career roles with their other life roles, and have congruence between their career objectives and their sense of self (Barney, 2002; Loughlin and Barling, 2001; Savickas, 1997; Sullivan, 1999).

As such, Donald E. Super's theory of career development may help us understand the behaviors of today's young workforce, as it presupposes a life-span, life-space approach to career development, and an active role for an adaptable self within it (Savickas, 1997). According to Super, career development is a process of asserting one's self and developing an identity through work. Individuals pursuing the aim of asserting oneself will look for opportunities to match their self and identity with their environment; therefore, they will better adapt to environmental changes, and hence, achieve greater satisfaction and harmony thanks to the relative congruence they will develop between their sense of who they are and their career as a whole (Savickas, 1997).

Research

The following brief research examined this very congruence with a qualitative approach. Twenty-four university seniors currently employed were asked open-ended questions as to whether they were indeed looking for some kind of match between their sense of self, and their occupation at the time. The purpose was to find out the outlook that the young workforce holds vis-à-vis working in general and their career in particular, and gain insight into how significant various kinds of influences (e.g., their sense of self, the pressure they may feel from parents, financial constraints, etc.) are when they are seeking jobs at this early stage of their working life. The following summarizes highlights from the findings.

- When asked about whether their career has started or not, about three quarters of seniors who participated in the study answered affirmatively.
- When asked to describe themselves, findings revealed that seniors accounted for their personal characteristics in both work-related terms, and in terms that describe their inner emotional world. That is, they were able to define themselves in a variety of ways, evidencing the fact that they had a pretty sound idea of who they are in and out the work environments. While this finding was nothing unusual in itself, it was significant that seniors were quite candid about themselves, with open self-expression and self-acceptance that seemed to lack any social desirability biases or other reservations.
- When asked about whether their personal characteristics had a defining influence over their career and how, seniors were found to identify hard work, perseverance, forward-looking attitude, and eagerness to learn as the most important characteristics to carry them forward in work performance, as well as interpersonal relationships. However, seniors did not stop here.
- Candidly again, they carried on a kind of self-criticism as to which of their characteristics helped them do things better or worse, or what potential jobs they thought they could fit in better and hence be more successful. Furthermore, they indicated the importance of psychological factors such as belief in oneself, happiness, and job satisfaction as the necessary conditions to boost work performance.

- Finally, when asked where/how they visualize themselves in the near future, aside from common answers that pertained to advancing in career positions, several seniors rather indicated not a future job/position, but various states of being they would aspire to—to be successful in one's job, to be a leading expert in one's field, or to engage in a brand-new endeavor that has not been tackled by anybody yet. Seniors emphasizing "what matters" for them in such clear terms, regardless of the future job or position they may hold, appears significant.

Discussion

The main research question at the foundation of this brief study was the following: If members of today's young workforce express themselves more openly, display a more free-spirited identity, and feel less bound by organizational limits and hierarchies, could it be more important for them to experience congruence between their sense of self, and characteristics of their work environment? If the answer is yes, this congruence can then be considered a first step to building meaning into one's work, and hence, enacting one's career. As such, this brief research tried to identify how central the sense of self was for university seniors as they have stepped into their careers, and whether they truly looked for the above-mentioned congruence.

The findings revealed that congruence was indeed observed between university seniors' chosen (or chosen-to-be) work environments, and their sense of self, operationalized as their self-defined personal characteristics. Consistent with the literature, the statements made by the young workforce to define themselves were pretty interesting, and were quite revealing as to the independent and free-spirited character they possessed. More importantly, seniors did not refrain from being frank, authentic, and true to themselves, as they appeared very accepting of their own characteristics (be it favorable or unfavorable), as well as showed awareness of the values that mattered to them, whichever work environment they may be in. Furthermore, it seemed that the young workforce attached greater importance to states of well-being, such as happiness, satisfaction, self-belief, and success, regardless of the future job or position they might occupy. All of these findings can be said to contribute to meaning-making at work, which is possible once self-and-work congruence is in place.

Although university seniors were able to define themselves quite openly, the characteristics they defined themselves with, not surprisingly, mostly pertained to performance, success, work, and careers, due to the context and content of the study. Despite this limitation of the research, seniors were still able to visualize themselves in their ideal working conditions, matching their own characteristics with their chosen careers and work environments. Another limitation of the study is the self-report format, where the findings must be evaluated with caution. Future research will have to employ more varied measurement methods and tools, which will help, assess the sense of self more thoroughly, and identify other potential factors that may influence career choice and enactment. In this regard, a follow-up study of the current participants several years from now would definitely reveal very interesting findings.

References

Arnold J, Cooper CL, Robertson IT (1998) Work psychology: understanding human behavior in the workplace, 3rd edn. Financial Times Prentice Hall, Harlow

Arthur MB, Rousseau DM (1996) Introduction: the boundaryless career as a new employment principle. In: Arthur MB, Rousseau DM (eds) The coundaryless career: a new employment principle for a new organizational era. Oxford University Press, New York, pp 3–20

Barney SM (2002) A changing workforce calls for twenty-first century strategies. J Healthc Manag 47(2):81–84

Blustein DL, Noumair DA (1996) Self and identity in career development: implications for theory and practice. J Couns Dev 74(May/June):433–441

Cappellen T, Janssens M (2010) Enacting global careers: organizational career scripts and the global economy as co-existing career referents. J Organ Behav 31:687–706

Cappelli P (1999) Career jobs are dead. Calif Manag Rev 42(1):146–167

Cohen L, Mallon M (2001) My brilliant career?: using stories as a methodological tool in careers research. Int Stud Manage Org 31(3):48–68

DeFilippi RJ, Arthur MB (1996) Boundaryless contexts and careers: a competency-based perspective. In: Arthur MB, Rousseau DM (eds) The boundaryless career: a new employment principle for a new organizational era. Oxford University Press, New York, pp 116–131

Hall DT (2002) Careers in and out of organizations. Sage Publications, Thousand Oaks, CA

Jacoby SM (1999) Are career jobs headed for extinction? Calif Manag Rev 42(1):123–145

Leach T (2015) Graduates' experiences and perceptions of career enactment: identity, transitions, personal agency and emergent career direction. Research in Post-Compulsory Education 20(1):50–63

Littleton SM, Arthur MB, Rousseau DM (2000) The future of boundaryless careers. In: Collin A, Young RA (eds) The future of career. Cambridge University Press, Cambridge, pp 101–114

Loughlin C, Barling J (2001) Young workers' work values, attitudes and behaviors. J Occup Organ Psychol 74:543–558

Mallon M (1999) Going "portfolio": making sense of changing careers. Career Dev Int 4(7):358–369

Mallon M, Duberley J (2000) Managers and professionals in the contingent workforce. Hum Resour Manag J 10(1):33–47

Peel S, Inkson K (2004) Contracting and careers: choosing between self and organizational employment. Career Dev Int 9(6):542–558

Savickas ML (1997) Career adaptability: an integrative construct for life-span, life-space theory. Career Dev Q 45(3):247–259

Savickas ML (2000) Renovating the psychology of careers for the twenty-first century. In: Collin A, Young RA (eds) The future of career. Cambridge University Press, Cambridge, pp 53–68

Storey JA (2000) 'Fracture lines' in the career environment. In: Collin A, Young RA (eds) The future of career. Cambridge University Press, Cambridge, pp 53–68

Sullivan SE (1999) The changing nature of careers: a review and research agenda. J Manag 25(3):457–484

Walton S, Mallon M (2004) Redefining the boundaries? Making sense of career in contemporary New Zealand. Asia Pac J Hum Resour 42(1):75–95

Weick KE (1996) Enactment and the boundaryless career: organizing as we work. In: Arthur MB, Rousseau DM (eds) The boundaryless career: a new employment principle for a new organizational era. Oxford University Press, New York, pp 40–57

Study of Driving Factors of Entrepreneurship Intention Among Management Students

Tushar Mahajan and Sonia Gupta

Abstract Entrepreneurship is the backbone of economic growth and development of any nation. It is a risk-taking activity and challenging task, and needs total commitment and sincerity with fullest involvement for personal and overall growth. It is crucial for the socio-economic transformation. From the perspective of management students, it is always a complicated decision to start a new firm due to high level of risk and uncertainties. There are many factors, which act as driving forces for entrepreneurial intention.

This study is an attempt to identify the various factors and the response of management students, especially in developing countries towards entrepreneurial intentions. Further, the study also explored comparison of entrepreneurial intentions among the students of metro and non-metro cities. Delhi-NCR (National Capital Region) and Dehradun in India was research study area. Students were found to have a high intention profile towards entrepreneurship in all the constructs namely self-confidence, need for achievement, risk-taking ability, and autonomy for both the samples but all are quiet high in Dehradun region in comparison to Delhi NCR.

Keywords Entrepreneurship • Entrepreneurship intention • Management students

Introduction

Entrepreneurship serves a significant role for developing economies as it is considered the engine of growth, economic development, employment creator and as a whole work for national development. Scarborough and Zimmerer (2003) reported that entrepreneurship is an important driver for new and creative revolutions in any nation to enhance economic growth and competitiveness. Various other studies like Kuratko and Hodgetts (2004) showed that there is a significant relationship between entrepreneurship and employment opportunities creation and technological change

---

T. Mahajan (✉)
Management Department, Institute of Management Studies, Ghaziabad, UP, India
e-mail: tushar.mahajan8@gmail.com

S. Gupta
Management Department, J.K. Business School, Gurugram, HR, India

L. Tadj, A.K. Garg (eds.), *Emerging Challenges in Business, Optimization, Technology, and Industry*, Springer Proceedings in Business and Economics,
DOI 10.1007/978-3-319-58589-5_17

in any economy. According to Schaper and Volery (2004), and Karanassios and Pazarskis (2006), entrepreneurship is important in the era of globalization as it is a significant development strategy for any country to grow and sustain in the competitive world. Brown (1999) and Henry (2003) in their studies suggested that many business graduates after completing their studies are unable to get a job, so the business education must equip the students with necessary entrepreneurial knowledge and skills to succeed in running businesses or to create employment from seizing existing entrepreneurial opportunities.

The main purpose of this research is to identify the various factors and the response of management students especially in developing countries, like India, toward entrepreneurial intentions. Hence, this research is an attempt to identifying the variables of entrepreneurial traits that influence students' intentions toward entrepreneurship specifically in Dehradun and Delhi NCR region in India, which is a developing country. This research primarily attempts to find out various drivers, which are entrepreneurial traits and their relationship with entrepreneurial intentions among management students. It is obvious that the culture of the city matters. Metro and non-metro cities have their own norms and values and it sets the different outlook of the students of these cities toward life. A comparative study of management students of metro and non-metro cities toward entrepreneurial intentions was also an objective of the study.

Literature Review

Literature review suggested that few personality traits are very significant factors for entrepreneurial intentions of any individual. The importance of personal traits in entrepreneurial intentions has been significantly discussed by many researchers. This study focused on the theoretical base of various trait theories, which discuss various drivers related to inborn traits and the environment which influence the entrepreneurial intentions among management students. Various trait theories suggested that entrepreneurs are born. According to a study by Allan Jacobwitz (cited in Cohen 1980), entrepreneurs possess some special personality traits like restlessness, independence, first mover, self-confidence, innovative, action oriented, high on need for personal control, and highly autonomous. Gartner (1989) in his study reported that situational factors such as the nature of the task and the environment are also significant than personality traits. The entrepreneurial intentions depend on how people construct the perceived opportunities. Some research studies for explaining and predicting entrepreneurial intentions are Shapero's "Entrepreneurial Event" model as well as Azjen's (1991) more general theory of planned behavior. Both the frameworks provide similar explanations of individuals' entrepreneurial intentions as being a function of the perceived feasibility and desirability of entrepreneurial behavior (Krueger and Brazeal 1994).

Many researchers have studied the reasons for the creation of new enterprises and the entrepreneurial characteristics of those individuals responsible for the emergence of new firms. An important question is why some individuals decide to pursue entrepreneurial endeavors while others do not. Few research studies have investigated the possible reasons behind this behavior from the perspective of the individual themselves as well as economic and other factors in their environment (Acs et al. 1994; Hofstede 2004). Recent work has also investigated the utility derived from choosing entrepreneurship over traditional career opportunities—it is argued that individuals will choose entrepreneurship as a career option if the utility derived from this choice exceeds the utility derived from formal employment (Douglas and Shepherd 2000). Through the literature review, it was found that while the utility derived from self-employment may exceed that derived from other career alternatives; it is generally not a sufficient condition for an individual to engage in entrepreneurial behavior. Rather, entrepreneurial behavior has three necessary conditions, these being: (1) the motive to pursue self-employment; (2) the perception of an apparently lucrative entrepreneurial opportunity; and (3) access to the means to pursue that opportunity. Without the simultaneous existence of these three prerequisite conditions, entrepreneurial behavior will not eventuate.

The motivation to behave entrepreneurially is explained by the utility-maximizing theory of entrepreneurial behavior. According to this the individual is motivated to become self-employed (or otherwise behave entrepreneurially) because that course of action promises the greatest psychic utility (Douglas and Shepherd 2000). Underlying this motivation is the strength of the individual's abilities (human capital) and his/her attitudes to elements provided by entrepreneurship, which include autonomy, risk, work effort, income, and net perquisites. In general, individuals desiring more income, more independence, and more net perquisites are more likely to want to engage in entrepreneurial behavior. Likewise, an individual with a higher tolerance for risk and less aversion to work effort should be expected to be more likely to want to engage in entrepreneurial behavior.

The decision to act entrepreneurially has been argued to be related to the utility derived from self-employment (Eisenhauer 1996) with individuals with more positive entrepreneurial attitudes and stronger entrepreneurial abilities being more likely to attain higher levels of utility in self-employment than in employment (Douglas and Shepherd 2000). Previous research has identified the role of risk tolerance, income, and preference for independence as being significant in the decision to be self-employed (Douglas and Shepherd 2002). Individuals with more tolerance for risk and stronger positive attitudes toward income and independence are more likely to want to pursue an entrepreneurial endeavor. Note that Douglas and Shepherd (2002) did not find attitude to work effort to be significantly related to entrepreneurial intentions, although their sample (MBA students) may not have been representative of the population in this respect. While individual attitudes to income, independence, risk, work effort, and net perquisites may vary, we would expect that individuals indicating higher expected utility (or lower disutility) from these factors would be more likely to have greater entrepreneurial intentions.

Self-concept represents those ideas the individual has of himself/herself that he/she learned in relationship with others. If self-concept is positive, a person tends to act and perceive the world positively. If self-concept is negative, a person feels dissatisfied and unhappy (Rogers 1980). The self and role we play interact. Since self strives for consistency, it selects those roles compatible with the self-concept. When the role and self-concept are incompatible, conflict arises. Character traits such as high self-concept, managerial competence, high commitment to work, favorable perception of work stress, aggressiveness, emotional stability, vigor, and self-reliance are necessary for entrepreneurial success (Akeredolu-Ale 1975; Carland et al. 1984; Meredith et al. 1982; Olakanpo 1968; Omololu 1990; Onah 1990; Schumpeter 1954).

Many studies have taken place on youth entrepreneurship intentions. Early research focused on exploring business students' interest in entrepreneurship and entrepreneurship courses, and identifying characteristics of entrepreneurs and variables that influence entrepreneurial intent (e.g., Hills and Barnaby 1977; Sexton and Bowman 1983; Hills and Welsch 1986; Hutt and Van Hook 1986; Hatten and Ruhland 1995; Ede 1998). Henderson and Robertson (1999) collected data from "young adults" aged 19 to 25 years who were studying entrepreneurship in Scotland, business students in England, and newly hired employees at a major U.K. bank, finding that 67% of those studying entrepreneurship expressed a desire for self-employment, compared to 5% among the rest. Urve Venesaar (2006) focused on identifying the attitudes and intentions of students at Tallinn University of Technology to start with business, their personality traits, and contextual factors of business environment, including the role of university in supporting students' entrepreneurial intentions. The objective of the study was to identify the students' attitudes and intentions toward entrepreneurship, their personal characteristics, and future plans in connection with entrepreneurship. They found that despite the considerable share of respondents thinking about starting a business, most of them do not want to undertake entrepreneurial activity after graduation, but postpone this to a more distant future. Strongly represented in the respondents' opinions was ambition for freedom followed by intention for self-realization and the strongest pushing factor is connected with searching for opportunity to earn better income. Those who attached higher importance to motivation factors intend to start with business in the near future.

Narendra (2006) conducted a study on a group of university students in India intended to do upon completion of their college education: start their own business (become entrepreneurs) or work for someone else. According to results of factor analysis, six variables (to lead other people, to be my own boss, to put my innovative ideas into practice, determination, personal challenge, and non-business education) were found to relate to the dependent variable. Mohammed and Aparna (2011) focused on entrepreneurship education, entrepreneurship intentions among students, the entrepreneurial self-efficacy of the students, and the perception/opinion of entrepreneurship among the students within an Indian setting. This study has provided some useful insights into the entrepreneurial intention among the students in the Hyderabad area of India. Most entrepreneurial self-efficacy or self-confidence lied with the students' perceived ability to manage money or be a leader. The results implied that self-efficacy may play an important role in shaping (or limiting) perceived career options as most respondents also indicated interest in corporate or government careers. Nabi (2010) identified three key outcomes: First, it establishes that across all years of the survey a substantial minority of students consistently hold relatively strong start-up intentions; Second, that despite considerable efforts to increase the numbers moving to start-up, little impact is discernible; Third, it fails to address critical questions around the impact of higher education on entrepreneurship and the transition from entrepreneurial intent to the act of venture creation.

Maalu et al. (2010) found that the goals in entrepreneurial ability are influenced by factors such as: maximum utilization of own skills and talents; full control of own future; achievement of what one values personally; being "my own boss"; the freedom/opportunity to make own decisions; the opportunity to learn new things; financial security; performing challenging and exciting work; having peace of mind with a peaceful and stress-free life; allocation of enough free time for family, hobbies, leisure, and other interests; an opportunity to extend one's range of abilities, a goal to accumulate wealth; desire to live an adventurous and exciting life; the goal to start own business, striving for an idea to own business, an ultimate goal to be self-employed and the wish to become an influential person to the future. Bernstein (2012) concluded that self-confidence for having a successful entrepreneurship career increases interest in entrepreneurship majors and electives. Students in general, regardless of their levels of Self-confidence, perceived both the entrepreneurship major and elective as increasing their likelihood of success as an entrepreneur. Students with lower levels of self-confidence agreed at similar levels that an entrepreneurship major or non-entrepreneurship major along with an entrepreneurship elective would both increase their likelihood of success as an entrepreneur. Students with higher levels of self-confidence agreed at similar levels that an entrepreneurship major or non-entrepreneurship major would both increase their likelihood of success as an entrepreneur. However, these students did not perceive an entrepreneurship elective would increase their likelihood of success as an entrepreneur over non-entrepreneurship major alone.

Thus, review of literatures suggested that there has been growing interest in entrepreneurship intentions among business students in various countries including India. The majority of published studies to date have focused on the identifying drivers or personality traits of students who were interested in entrepreneurship. Thus, the present study focused on driving factors or personality traits of management student toward entrepreneurial intentions.

Objectives of the Study

This study is an attempt to know the relationship of various factors with entrepreneurial intentions of management students in India as developing country. The research examined four drivers (traits or factors) connected with entrepreneurial intentions, namely the need for achievement, autonomy, risk-taking, and self-confidence. These four constructs represent only some aspects of entrepreneurship. Hence, the objectives of the study are:

1. To study relationship between self-confidence and entrepreneurial intention.
2. To analyze relationship between need to achievement and entrepreneurial intention.
3. To examine relationship between risk taking and entrepreneurial intention.

4. To determine relationship between autonomy and entrepreneurial intention.

Based on the above objectives, for the present study, the following hypotheses were formulated:

1. There is significant and positive relationship between self-confident and entrepreneurial intention.
2. There is significant and positive relationship between need to achievement and entrepreneurial intention.
3. There is significant and positive relationship between risk and entrepreneurial intention.
4. There is significant and positive relationship between autonomy and entrepreneurial intention.

Research Methodology

The present study focused on management students' entrepreneurial intention. Data were collected through self-designed structured close-ended questionnaire based on Likert scale. Respondents were management students in self-financed colleges at Delhi-NCR and Dehradun regions doing Masters of Business Administration course. The sample technique was convenient sampling. After validating, the final total sample size was 100, consisting of 50 students for each region. SPSS 21 was used for data analysis. The questionnaire was tested for reliability and the Cronbach alpha value was found to be 0.82, indicating higher reliability of the data collection instrument.

Results

This section of the research paper presents the detailed results. The respondents were the management students pursuing MBA course from self-financed colleges. The first sample was from the Delhi NCR region, which consists of 50 respondents out of which 15 were females and 35 were males. The second sample was from the Dehradun region, which consists of 50 respondents of which 14 were females and 36 were males.

Descriptive Analysis

The students were asked a few questions about the constructs. According to the responses, the overall perception of the respondents of the Delhi NCR region is as follows:

As shown in Table 1, the questionnaire feedback for each construct from the respondents showed a high intention profile level, as the mean score values ranged from 4.22 to 4.52. The high level of each of these constructs resulted in a high overall intention profile toward entrepreneurship among the participants, with a mean value of 4.355.

According to the responses, the overall perception of the respondents of the Dehradun region is as follows:

As shown in Table 2, the questionnaire feedback for each construct from the respondents showed a high intention profile level. This is seen from the mean score values ranging from 4.38 to 4.66. The high level of each of these constructs resulted in a high overall intention profile toward entrepreneurship among the participants, with a mean value of 4.465.

On comparing the intention profile level of the respondents, it is clear from Table 3 that every construct has a high degree in the Dehradun region and a comparative low degree in the Delhi-NCR region:

Table 1 Overall perception of respondents of Delhi NCR

Construct	Mean	Standard deviation	Level
Self-confidence	4.520	0.580	High
Need to achievement	4.220	0.545	High
Risk-taking	4.360	0.525	High
Autonomy	4.320	0.471	High
Total	4.355	0.530	High

Table 2 Overall perception of respondents of Dehradun

Construct	Mean	Standard deviation	Level
Self-confidence	4.660	0.479	High
Need to achievement	4.380	0.490	High
Risk-taking	4.440	0.501	High
Autonomy	4.380	0.490	High
Total	4.465	0.490	High

Table 3 Comparative detail of overall perception of respondents of Delhi NCR and Dehradun

	Delhi NCR		Dehradun	
Construct	Mean	Standard deviation	Mean	Standard deviation
Self-confidence	4.520	0.580	4.660	0.479
Need to achievement	4.220	0.545	4.380	0.490
Risk-taking	4.360	0.525	4.440	0.501
Autonomy	4.320	0.471	4.380	0.490
Total	4.355	0.530	4.465	0.490

Hypotheses Testing for Dehradun Region

Hypothesis 1
The first hypothesis showed that students who have self-confidence would have more positive entrepreneurial intentions. There is a significant relationship between self-confident and entrepreneurial intentions of management students. The following regression output tables (Table 4) summarize the relationships between self-confidence and entrepreneurial intention. The ANOVA table (Table 5) shows that the F value is significant.

Hypothesis 2
The second hypothesis indicated that students who have need to achievement will have more positive entrepreneurial intentions. There is a significant relationship between need to achievement and entrepreneurial intentions. The following regression output tables (Table 6) summarize the relationships between need to achievement and entrepreneurial intentions. The ANOVA Table 7 shows that the F value is significant.

Hypothesis 3
The third hypothesis showed that students who have risk-taking ability will have more positive entrepreneurial intentions. There is a significant relationship between risk-taking ability and entrepreneurial intention. The following regression output table (Table 8) summarizes the relationships between risk taking ability and entrepreneurial intention. The ANOVA table (Table 9) shows that the F value is significant.

Hypothesis 4
The fourth hypothesis indicated that students who have autonomy will have more positive entrepreneurial intentions. There is a significant relationship between autonomy and entrepreneurial intention. The following regression output tables (Table 10) summarize the relationships between autonomy and entrepreneurial intention. The ANOVA table (Table 11) shows that the F value is significant.

Table 4 Model summary

Model	R	R square	Adjusted R	Standard error
1	0.211[a]	0.044	0.024	0.27

[a]Predictors: (Constant), self-confidence

Table 5 ANOVA[b]

	Df	SS	MS	F	Sig. F
Regression	1	0.164848	0.164848	2.251034	0.140075[a]
Residual	48	3.515152	0.073232		
Total	49	3.68			

[a]Predictors: (Constant), self-confidence
[b]Dependent variable: entrepreneurial intention

Table 6 Model summary

Model	R	R square	Adjusted R	Standard error
1	0.224[a]	0.050	0.030	0.269

[a]Predictors: (Constant), need to achievement

Table 7 ANOVA[b]

	Df	SS	MS	F	Sig. F
Regression	1	0.185942	0.185942	2.554402	0.11655[a]
Residual	48	3.494058	0.072793		
Total	49	3.68			

[a]Predictors: (Constant), need to achievement
[b]Dependent variable: entrepreneurial intention

Table 8 Model summary

Model	R	R square	Adjusted R	Standard error
1	0.184[a]	0.033	0.013	0.272

[a]Predictors: (Constant), risk-taking ability

Table 9 ANOVA[b]

	Df	SS	MS	F	Sig. F
Regression	1	0.124805	0.124805	1.685041	0.200459[a]
Residual	48	3.555195	0.074067		
Total	49	3.68			

[a]Predictors: (Constant), risk-taking ability
[b]Dependent variable: entrepreneurial intention

Table 10 Model summary

Model	R	R square	Adjusted R	Standard error
1	0.224[a]	0.050	0.030	0.269

[a]Predictors: (Constant), autonomy

Table 11 ANOVA[b]

	Df	SS	MS	F	Sig. F
Regression	1	0.185942	0.185942	2.554402	0.11655[a]
Residual	48	3.494058	0.072793		
Total	49	3.68			

[a]Predictors: (Constant), autonomy
[b]Dependent variable: entrepreneurial intention

Hypotheses Testing for Delhi-NCR Region

Hypothesis 1
It showed that students who have self-confidence will have more positive entrepreneurial intentions. There is a significant relationship between self-confidence and entrepreneurial intentions of management students. The following regression output table (Table 12) summarizes the relationships between self-confidence and entrepreneurial intention. The ANOVA table (Table 13) shows that the F value is significant.

Hypothesis 2
The second hypothesis showed that students who have need for achievement will have more positive entrepreneurial intentions. There is a significant relationship between need to achievement and entrepreneurial intentions. The following regression output table (Table 14) summarizes the relationships between need to achievement and entrepreneurial intentions. The ANOVA table (Table 15) shows that the F value is significant.

Table 12 Model summary

Model	R	R square	Adjusted R	Standard error
1	0.066[a]	0.004	−0.016	0.598

[a]Predictors: (Constant), self confidence

Table 13 ANOVA[b]

	Df	SS	MS	F	Sig. F
Regression	1	0.076117	0.076117	0.21237	0.646997[a]
Residual	48	17.20388	0.358414		
Total	49	17.28			

[a]Predictors: (Constant), self confidence
[b]Dependent variable: entrepreneurial intention

Table 14 Model summary

Model	R	R square	Adjusted R	Standard error
1	0.231[a]	0.053	0.034	0.583

[a]Predictors: (Constant), need to achievement

Table 15 ANOVA[b]

	Df	SS	MS	F	Sig. F
Regression	1	0.928834	0.928834	2.726658	0.105214[a]
Residual	48	16.35117	0.340649		
Total	49	17.28			

[a]Predictors: (Constant), need to achievement
[b]Dependent variable: entrepreneurial intention

Hypothesis 3
There is no significant relationship between risk-taking ability and entrepreneurial intention. The following regression output table (Table 16) summarizes the relationship. The ANOVA table (Table 17) shows that the F value is not significant.

Hypothesis 4
There is no significant relationship between autonomy and entrepreneurial intention. The following regression output table (Table 18) and ANOVA table (Table 19) summarize the relationships between autonomy and entrepreneurial intention.

To compare the entrepreneurial intentions of both the samples, the Z-test was applied to compare the variance between two samples. Variable 1 stands for the Delhi-NCR region and Variable 2 stands for the Dehradun region. The results are as follows:

Table 16 Model summary

Model	R	R square	Adjusted R	Standard error
1	0.382[a]	0.145	0.128	0.554

[a]Predictors: (Constant), risk-taking ability

Table 17 ANOVA[b]

	Df	SS	MS	F	Sig. F
Regression	1	2.522604	2.522604	8.205036	0.006179[a]
Residual	48	14.7574	0.307446		
Total	49	17.28			

[a]Predictors: (Constant), risk-taking ability
[b]Dependent variable: entrepreneurial intention

Table 18 Model summary

Model	R	R square	Adjusted R	Standard error
1	0.443[a]	0.196	0.179	0.537

[a]Predictors: (Constant), autonomy

Table 19 ANOVA[b]

	Df	SS	MS	F	Sig. F
Regression	1	3.397647	3.397647	11.7478	0.001259[a]
Residual	48	13.88235	0.289216		
Total	49	17.28			

[a]Predictors: (Constant), autonomy
[b]Dependent variable: entrepreneurial intention

According to Table 20, there is significant difference between the two samples for the self-confidence.

According to Table 21, there is significant difference between the two samples for the need to achievement.

According to Table 22, there is significant difference between the two samples for the risk-taking ability.

According to Table 23, there is significant difference between the two samples for the Autonomy.

According to Table 24, there is significant difference between the two samples for the entrepreneurial intentions.

Table 20 z-Test: two sample for means: self-confidence

	Variable 1	Variable 2
Mean	4.52	4.66
Known variance	0.336327	0.22898
Observations	50	50
Hypothesized mean difference	0	
z	−1.316651555	
P(Z < = z) two-tail	0.187955449	
z critical two-tail	1.959963985	

Table 21 z-Test: two sample for means: need to achievement

	Variable 1	Variable 2
Mean	4.22	4.38
Known variance	0.297551	0.240408
Observations	50	50
Hypothesized mean difference	0	
z	−1.542518552	
P(Z < = z) two-tail	0.122947633	
z critical two-tail	1.959963985	

Table 22 z-Test: Two sample for means: risk-taking ability

	Variable 1	Variable 2
Mean	4.36	4.44
Known variance	0.275918	0.251429
Observations	50	50
Hypothesized mean difference	0	
z	−0.778980792	
P(Z < = z) two-tail	0.435991029	
z critical two-tail	1.959963985	

Table 23 z-Test: two sample for means: autonomy

	Variable 1	Variable 2
Mean	4.32	4.38
Known variance	0.222041	0.240408
Observations	50	50
Hypothesized mean difference	0	
z	−0.623884693	
P(Z < = z) two-tail	0.532703314	
z critical two-tail	1.959963985	

Table 24 z-Test: two sample for means: entrepreneurial intentions

	Variable 1	Variable 2
Mean	4.12	4.08
Known variance	0.352653	0.075102
Observations	50	50
Hypothesized mean difference	0	
Z	0.432461496	
P(Z < = z) two-tail	0.665406031	
z critical two-tail	1.959963985	

Conclusions

The aim of this study was to test for the presence and relative strength of four constructs of entrepreneurial intentions among management students of the Delhi NCR and Dehradun regions in India. The research examined four constructs connected with entrepreneurial intentions, namely, the self-confidence, need for achievement, risk-taking ability, and autonomy.

Results of the correlations largely support significant positive relationships between these four constructs and entrepreneurial intention. Also, the results of the regression output provide support for significant relationships for all the four constructs (self-confidence, need for achievement, risk-taking ability, and autonomy) and entrepreneurial intentions among students of the Dehradun region while there are significant relationships for two constructs (self-confidence, need to achievement) and entrepreneurial intentions among students of Delhi-NCR. There is a non-significant relationship for other two constructs (risk-taking ability and autonomy) and entrepreneurial intentions among students of Delhi-NCR.

Thus, hypothesis 1, which states that self-confidence is positively and significantly related to entrepreneurial intentions, is supported and accepted for both the regions. Hypothesis 2, which states that need for achievement is positively and significantly related to entrepreneurial intentions, is supported and accepted for both the regions. Hypothesis 3 and hypothesis 4 which state about the risk-taking ability and autonomy respectively are supported and accepted for the Dehradun region, while both these hypotheses are not supported for the Delhi NCR region and not accepted.

Students are found to have a high intention profile toward entrepreneurship in all the constructs namely self-confidence, need for achievement, risk-taking ability, and autonomy for both the samples but all are quiet high in the Dehradun region in comparison to Delhi NCR.

The research finding on self-confidence also supports the findings of Andrew Bernstein (2012). This study found that self-confidence is a major driver of entrepreneurial intention. Findings on risk-taking ability support the study of Douglas and Shepherd (2002) which suggested that individuals with more tolerance for risk and stronger positive attitudes toward income and independence are more likely to want to pursue an entrepreneurial endeavor.

As a comparative analysis, we found that there is significant difference between the two samples for all the four constructs and entrepreneurial intentions. The two samples were drawn from a metro and non-metro city. There could be various reasons of this difference, which is a subject matter of future research.

Recommendations for Future Research

It was a research study of four constructs, which affect the entrepreneurial intentions among management students of the Delhi-NCR and Dehradun regions. A study that involves more members of various regions can be undertaken to determine the factors related to entrepreneurial intentions. Various other constructs can also be included in future research.

References

Acs ZJ, Audretsch DB, Evans DS (1994) The determinants of variations in self employment rates across countries and over time. (Mimeo)

Ajzen I (1991) The theory of planned behavior, organizational behavior and human decision processes, pp 179–211

Akeredolu-Ale EO (1975) The underdevelopment of indigenous entrepreneurs in Nigeria. University Press, Ibadan

Ariffin S, Sabaruddin AS (2002) Keusahawanan: Rahsia Ke Puncak Kejayaan. Prentice Hall, Kuala Lumpur

Aziz Y, Zakaria Y (2004) Prinsip Keusahawanan, 2nd edn. Prentice Hall Pearson Malaysia Sdn Bhd, Petaling Jaya

Bernstein AT, Carayannis EG (2012) Exploring the value proposition of the undergraduate entrepreneurship major and elective based on student's self-efficacy and outcome expectations. J Knowl Econ 3(3):265–279

Bolton B, Thompson J (2004) Entrepreneurs: talent, temperament, technique, 2nd edn. Elsevier Butterworth-Heinemann, Amsterdam

Brockhaus RH, Horwitz PS (1986) The psychology of the entrepreneur. In: Sexton DL, Smilor RW (eds) The art and science of entrepreneurship. Ballinger Publishing Company, Cambridge, Mass, pp 25–48
Brown C (1999) Teaching new dogs new tricks: the rise of entrepreneurship education in graduate schools of business, DIGEST pp 1–4
Carland JW, Hoy F, Boulton WR, Carland JA (1984) Differentiating entrepreneurs from small business owners, the academy of management review, April 354–359
Cohen N (1980) The five ages of the entrepreneur, Venture, pp 40–42
Donatus O (1998) Does level of education influence psychological traits? Evidence from used car entrepreneurs. J Manage Mark Res, httpwww.aabri.commanuscripts09277.pdf
Douglas EJ, Shepherd DA (2002) Entrepreneurship as a utility-maximizing response. J Bus Venturing:231–251
Ede FO, Panigrahi B, Calcich SE (1998) African American students' attitudes toward entrepreneurship education. J Educ Bus:291–296
Eisenhauer JG (1996) The entrepreneurial decision: economic theory and empirical evidence. Entrepreneurship Theory and Pract 12:67–79
Gartner WB (1988) Who is an entrepreneur? Is the wrong question. Am J Small Bus 13:11–32
Gartner WB (1989) Some suggestions for research on entrepreneurial traits and characteristics. Entrepreneurship Theory Pract 14(1):27–38
Gibb AA (1993) The enterprise culture and education: understanding enterprise education and its links with small business, entrepreneurship and wider educational goals. Int Small Bus J 11(3):13–34
Hatten TS, Ruhland SK (1995) Student attitude toward entrepreneurship as affected by participation in an sbi program. J Educ Bus:224–227
Henderson R, Robertson M (1999) Who wants to be an entrepreneur? Young adult attitudes to entrepreneurship as a career. Career Dev Int J:279–287
Henry B (2003) Entrepreneurship education In Kenya: a reality or plodding on? The first international entrepreneurship conference, 23–24 April, Kenya
Hills GE, Barnaby DJ (1977) Future entrepreneurs from the business schools: innovation is not dead, Proceedings of the International Council for Small Business, 27–30. Washington DC, International Council for Small Business
Hills GE, Welsch H (1986) Entrepreneurship behavioral intentions and student independence, characteristics and experiences, frontiers of entrepreneurship research, Proceedings of the Sixth Annual Babson College Entrepreneurship Research Conference, pp 173–186
Hofstede G (2004) Culture's role in entrepreneurship: self-employment out of dissatisfaction, in Innovation, entrepreneurship and culture: the interaction between technology, progress and economic growth, (Edward Elgar, Cheltenham, UK and Brookfield, US, 2004), pp 162–203
Hutt RW, Van Hook BL (1986) Students planning entrepreneurial careers and students not planning entrepreneurial careers: a comparative analysis. Frontiers of entrepreneurship research, Proceedings of the Sixth Annual Babson College Entrepreneurship Research Conference, pp 223–224. Massachusetts, USA: Babson College, Wellesley
Jacobowitz A, Vidler DC (1980) Characteristics of entrepreneurs: implications for vocational guidance, the vocational guidance quarterly, pp 252–257
Karanassios N, Pazarskis M (2006) EU strategies to encourage youth entrepreneurship: evidence from higher education in Greece, Industry & Higher Education, February, pp 43–50
Keat OY, Selvarajah C, Meyer D (2011) Inclination towards entrepreneurship among university students: an empirical study of Malaysian university students. Int J Bus Soc Sci 2(4)
Krueger NF, Brazeal D (1994) Entrepreneurial potential and potential entrepreneurs. Entrepreneurship Theory and Practice:91–104
Kuratko DF, Hodgetts RM (2004) Entrepreneurship: theory, process and practice, Ohio, US, Thomson Learning
Lee SM, Chang D et al (2005) Impact of entrepreneurship education: a comparative study of the U.S. and Korea. Int Entrep Manag J 1:27–43

Maalu J, Stephen M, Peterson OM (2010, 2010) A survey of personal goals and perceptions of entrepreneurial ability among students at the school business, University of Nairobi. Afr J Bus Manage 1

McClelland DC (1961) Intention-based models of entrepreneurship education. The achieving Society, The Free Press, New York. httpcongreso.us.esgpydeDownloada9.pdf

Meredith GG, Nelson RE, Neck PA (1982) The practice of entrepreneurship. International Labour Organization (ILO), Geneva

Mitchell TR (1979) Organizational behavior. Annu Rev Psychol 4:243–281

Mohammed M, Aparna MP (2011) Entrepreneurial intentions of MBA students – a study in Hyderabad. Entrepreneurial Pract Rev 1(4):20–37

Nabi G, Holden R, Walmsley A (2010) Entrepreneurial intentions among students, towards a re-focused research agenda. J Small Bus Enterp Dev:537–551

Narendra (2006) Intention for entrepreneurship among students in India, The Journal of Entrepreneurship, Sage Journals. 15(2): 2006

Norasmah HO, Ishak SB (2009) Attitude towards choosing a career in entrepreneurship amongst graduates. Eur J Social Sci 10(3)

Olakanpo O (1968) A statistical analysis of some determinants of entrepreneurial success: a Nigeria case study. Niger J Econ Social Stud:10–12

Omololu OO (1990) Graduate self-employment: a sociological examination of entrepreneur In Lagos State, Unpublished doctoral dissertation, University of Ibadan

Onah FE (1990) In: Ukpong EA (ed) Employment prospects and training needs for self-employment in Nigeria, Diagnostic studies series. National Manpower Board, Lagos

Ooi YK, Christopher S, Denny M (2011) Inclination towards entrepreneurship among university students: an empirical study of Malaysian University students. Int J Bus Social Sci 2(4)

Othman NH, Ishak SB (2009) Attitude towards choosing a career in entrepreneurship amongst graduates. Eur J Soc Sci 10(3): 419–434 httpwww.eurojournals.comejss_10_3_10.pdf

Pihie ZAL, Bagheri A (2011) Malay students' entrepreneurial attitude and entrepreneurial efficacy in vocational and technical secondary schools of Malaysia. Pertanika J Soc Sci & Hum 19(2):433–447

Rogers CR (1980) A way of being. Houghton-Mifflin

Scarborough NM, Zimmerer TW (2003) Effective Small Business Management: An Entrepreneurial Approach. Prentice Hall, Upper Saddle River

Schaper M, Volery T (2004) Entrepreneurship and small business: a pacific rim perspective. John Wiley and Sons Ltd, Milton

Schumpeter JA (1954) In: Schumpeter EB (ed) History of economic analysis. Oxford University Press, New York

Schwarz TV (2008) Entrepreneurial orientation among undergraduate business students in the U.S. and India. httpusasbe.orgknowledgeproceedingsproceedingsDocs2007datapaperscases056.pdf

Sexton DL, Bowman NB (1983) Determining entrepreneurial potential of students: comparative psychological characteristics analysis, Presented at the academy of management meeting, Dallas, pp 55–56

Shapero A, Sokol L (1982) The social dimensions of entrepreneurship. In: The encyclopedia of entrepreneurship. Prentice Hall, Englewood Cliffs, pp 72–90

Venesaar U, Loomets P (2006) The role of entrepreneurship in economic development and implications for SME Policy in Estonia 1, Tallinn University of Technology, School of Economics and Business Administration, Estonia, Paper presented to the 14th Nordic Conference on Small Business Research, 11–13 May 2006, Stockholm, Sweden

Zaidatol AL, Afsaneh B (2011) Malay students' entrepreneurial attitude and entrepreneurial efficacy in vocational and technical secondary schools of Malaysia, Pertanika J Soc Sci & Humanities, pp 433–447

Index

L. Tadj, A.K. Garg (eds.), *Emerging Challenges in Business, Optimization, Technology, and Industry*, Springer Proceedings in Business and Economics,
DOI 10.1007/978-3-319-58589-5

MIX
Papier aus verantwortungsvollen Quellen
Paper from responsible sources
FSC® C105338

If you have any concerns about our products, you can contact us on
ProductSafety@springernature.com

In case Publisher is established outside the EU, the EU authorized representative is:
Springer Nature Customer Service Center GmbH
Europaplatz 3, 69115 Heidelberg, Germany

Printed by Libri Plureos GmbH
in Hamburg, Germany